Twenty-Eight Years a Slave

or the Story of My Life in Three Continents –
North America, Europe and Africa

An Autobiography

By Thomas L. Johnson

PANTIANOS
CLASSICS

Published by Pantianos Classics

ISBN-13: 978-1-78987-259-0

First published in 1909

The Author

Contents

The Late Mrs. E. E. Stroud Smith

Dedicated

"She hath done what she could."

THESE words recall to my mind an earnest, faithful, and loving disciple of the Master, whose life was steadfastly lived to His glory, and who was content to be "in His will." What that life meant to me is more than I can tell. She it was, who, when abroad, first impressed me with the importance of a consecrated life. She helped me in my Mission work and encouraged me to come to England, where she had previously introduced my name to many friends. Her heart and soul were with me in my purpose to go to Africa, and she finally went herself to the land of my fathers, to carry good tidings to the dwellers in darkness, and comfort and strength to those who were labouring amongst them. And there it was that after a few days sojourn in Africa, she was called home to her eternal rest. To the memory of Mrs. E. E. Stroud Smith, now in glory, I dedicate this little account of my life.

> "The dear Lord's best interpreters
> Are humble human souls;
> The gospel of a life like hers
> Is more than books and scrolls."

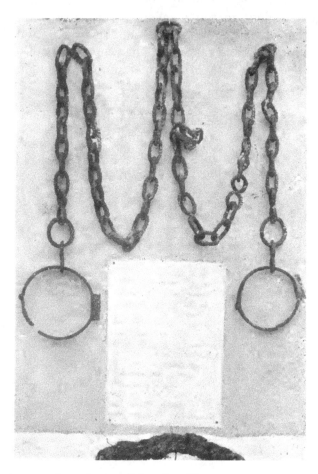

Slave Chains and Lash Used by the Slave Masters on the Slaves in the West Indies

By permission of "The Baptist."

The inscription above is as follows: "In commemoration of the Abolition of Slavery, the Alms Rooms in connection with King s Gate Baptist Church were erected in the year 1838, and these Chains and Lash were buried beneath the foundation. In the year 1904, the buildings were demolished, the Lash and Chains were exhumed, and, through the kindness of Mr. Green, Builder, Eagle Street, they were given to Mr. W. Levitt, Treasurer, to be retained as Church property."

President Abraham Lincoln

Preface to the Seventh Edition

THROUGH the liberality of many kind friends whom God has graciously raised up for me, the Seventh Edition of this Book is called for. This is, indeed, very gratifying. The earlier editions were published more especially in the interest of "the African Mission," of only a hundred pages, and many hundreds of copies were thus distributed. My health completely failed, and in 1894 I was compelled to resign my post as Financial Agent. I have since recovered sufficiently for service evangelistic, and it has been my joy to travel about the Kingdom amongst the different denominations wherever God has led the way, and whenever health permitted, telling of the love of my Blessed Jesus. Thank God I have had many manifestations of His presence with me, and step by step faith has been strengthened. In this new edition of my book I earnestly request the prayers of God's people that I may ever seek the old paths--Jeremiah vi. 16; Like Abraham--have one Look, Hebrews xi. 10; Like Mary--one Choice, Luke x. 42; Like Paul, one motto, Phil, iii. 13--and that, while I live, to earnestly contend for the Faith which was once delivered unto the Saints.

I mention much in my little book which some may consider ought to have been omitted. But how can I refrain from inscribing names and circumstances of people and matters so deeply associated with my very life and work. Let no one do me the injustice of regarding my narrative as egotistic. When I think of what I once was, and of what God has done for me, that from a poor illiterate slave, owned as a mere chattel and treated as such, and that He has blessed me with a knowledge of salvation, brought me into Christian society, and that I have been received as a brother and a man, and privileged to work side by side with many honoured servants of our one Lord. In England, Ireland, Scotland, Wales, Africa and America, I should be ungrateful indeed if I did not mention the names of a few of the very many friends who have helped and encouraged me. I should like to mention them all in this book, but space will not permit; but I have mentioned them all to my Father, and He has their names in the great Book on High.

I shall ever be grateful to the Rev. R. J. Peden, of Christchurch, Hants, who, when summarising the manuscript for me, found there was near enough for 2 Vols.

Thomas L. Johnson.
"Liberia," Boscombe, Bournemouth,
England, 1908.

71. St Pauls Church Yard.
London 188

This book which has been before the Public for some years is one of unusual interest.

It is not only a record of African Missionary work, but also an Autobiography of a Missionary Rev. Thos. L. Johnson who had the misfortune as he has wittily expressed it "to be born away from his native land" Africa.

Our friend "bore the yoke in his youth" in a terribly literal manner as the early chapters of the book describing his sad slavery years so graphically show.

Then his journey in Africa many years later was frequently full of peril in consequence of the hostility of the Native Tribes to the white man.

Commendatory

April 21st, 1882.

I HAVE known and very highly esteemed my dear friend, Mr. T. Lewis Johnson, for nearly six years. It was chiefly through me that the dear man, first came to this country in 1866. He worked with me in connection with the Young Men's Christian Association in Manchester for some time prior to his going to Mr. Spurgeon's College and thence to Africa. I fully believe in our dear brother's zeal for the Lord's work in Africa, and cordially recommend him to all who may be able to further the cause so near his heart.

W. HIND SMITH,
General Secretary Y. M. C. A.
LONDON.

Introductory to the First Edition

By Mr. Edward Stroud Smith

THOSE only who are acquainted with Mr. Johnson know the elasticity of his heart; how, unmindful of self, it throbs for Africa, the land of his forefathers, and that in loving tenderness it encircles every tribe, however degraded in that vast continent. Ever since receiving his first freedom, the liberty of his soul, through simply trusting his blessed Jesus, he longed to be the bearer of the glad tidings of salvation to his benighted countrymen; and no sooner had he gained his second freedom, that of his person, secured by the capture of Richmond and the overthrow of the Confederate Government, than we find him diligently striving to secure the education necessary to the fulfilment of his long cherished hopes, and although his path was strewn with difficulties, and for a time he seemed to make but little progress, yet by prayer and faith he surmounted them all.

We have the most unbounded confidence in Mr. Johnson, full faith in his work, and earnestly pray God to bless and prosper him wherever he may be called to labour. It is now fully ten years since we first met him as Pastor of Providence Baptist Church, Chicago, Illinois, beloved by his own people, and respected by all. He frequently spoke of Africa and his longing to go there, and once, when visiting him in a time of sickness, he said: "Oh, if God would only let me go to Africa and preach one sermon, I would be willing to die." And this in a tone of such intense earnestness that we saw it to be of the Lord, who has proved how He can fulfil the desire of them that fear Him, even exceedingly above all we ask or think; for Mr. Johnson has not only laboured himself in Africa, but succeeded in planting a Mission where Jesus was unknown, which still flourishes.

But he is now an instrument, we believe, in the hand of Omnipotent God, to awaken the interest, and enlist the sympathy of many others, who shall carry the glorious Gospel to the dark hearths and homes of poor Africa, which seems to have borne the cross as well as the curse for so many ages. How shall we answer to the King in the day of His appearing, if we should withhold our sympathy, prayers, and money? Are we not responsible for the discipling of all nations?

May a perusal of the following pages, which prove "All things are possible to him that believeth," lead to deeper consecration, and a coveting of the privilege of a share in "Africa for Jesus," so that sower and reaper may rejoice together; for "all the promises of God are yea and Amen in Christ Jesus."

Edward Stroud Smith.
Douglas, Isle of Man, May 1st, 1882.

Preface to the First Edition

MY object in publishing this little pamphlet is to help to create a fund to send freed men to Africa as missionaries. Since it is obvious that I cannot labour there myself, on account of my health, my life work by the help of the Lord shall be to do all I can to assist others to go. God has, indeed, been gracious to me in permitting me to awaken a deeper interest in African Mission Work among my own people in the Western States of America, so that I feel to-day that I am doing more good for Africa than if I had been permitted to continue my labour there. It is, indeed, my prayer that this little book, giving a simple statement of my slave-life, and how the good Lord has led me, may greatly help in raising money to send Missionaries to Africa--the land of my fathers. Please, dear friends, help us to help ourselves.

Yours truly "for Africa,"

THOS. L. JOHNSON.
LONDON,
May, 1882.

Historical

THE Negroes were imported by the Portuguese from West Africa in 1503. It was not till the beginning of the nineteenth century that any really effective efforts were made to ameliorate the position of the slaves within British possessions and to mitigate their suffering; and finally, after heroic struggles in and out of Parliament, led by Clarkson, Wilberforce, and others, that the abolition of slavery within British territory became a glorious reality. But until the year 1865 slavery existed in the United States, when the original fourteen slaves which the Dutch ship landed and sold at Jamestown on the James River, Virginia, 1619, had increased to over 4,000,000. In 1821 the American Colonization Society formed a free Negro settlement, called "Liberia," near Cape Masuerado, on the West Coast of Africa. The English Government established a colony for a similar purpose at Sierra Leone.

Twenty-Eight Years A Slave

Born a Slave

ACCORDING to information received from my mother, if the reckoning is correct, I was born 7th August, 1836, at Rock-Rayman, in the State of Virginia. I do not know the district, having been "removed" from thence when but a child. From what I have heard my mother say about her father, it would appear that he came from Africa, and was of the Guinea tribe. Both my mother's parents died when she was quite young. Her brothers and sisters were sold when she was thirteen years old. She often spoke of them and of the cruel treatment she received in her youth. My father was an octoroon, that is, he was one-eighth negro blood, and he was a free man. When I was three years old, Mr. Brent, who owned me, removed to Alexandria, Virginia. My father then wanted to purchase my mother and myself, but our master would not sell us. It must be explained that a free man was permitted to marry a slave woman, but the woman's children would be slaves. My father died when I was nine years old, he left money for me to purchase my freedom when I became a man, but the money got into other people's hands and never reached me.

Georgia Traders

I can well remember when others little children and I were very happy, not knowing that we were slaves. We played merrily together, knowing nothing of the world and of the long oppression of our people. But as time passed on, first one and then another of those who were as helpless as myself were missed from the company of little slaves. One day we saw John, who was much older than the rest, with a small bundle in his hand, saying good-bye to his mother, while a white man stood waiting in the hall for him. His mother and mine, with others, were crying, and all seemed very sad. I did not know what to make of it. A vague fear came over me, but I did not know why. We heard that the man who took John away was a "Georgia Trader," or slave dealer. Whenever we saw a white man looking over the fence as we were at play, we would run and hide, sometimes getting near our mothers, ignorantly thinking they could protect us. But another and again another of us would be taken away. All this showed to us the difference-- the great difference--there was between the white and coloured children. White children were free--"free born"--but black children were slaves and could be sold for money. What seemed worse than all was the discovery that our mothers, whom we looked upon as our only protectors, could not help us. Often we were reminded that if we were not good the white people would sell us to Georgia, which place we dreaded above all others on earth.

Mr. Brent, our owner, held some office in the Government, and he removed to Washington when I was about seven or eight years old. I was dressed up and sent into the dining-room at each meal to drive away the flies from the table, and to carry out the dishes and other things. At night I had to bring in my young master's slippers. When I brought them in I was told: "This slipper is for the right foot, and that for the left." Up to this time I did not know what was meant by "right" and "left," and could not understand the difference. The next night when I brought in the slippers I put the left foot one on the right foot. My master was very angry, and gave me a slap on the head. Night after night, with fear and trembling I would carry in the slippers. Sometimes I accidentally got them right, but more often they were wrong; then would I receive a blow on the head either with the hand or with the slippers. When I did get them right, then he would declare that I knew the right way all the time.

My Mother

My poor mother, to whom I looked for protection, could do nothing. I can remember how, after my being ill-treated, mother would say, with tears in her eyes, "My son, be a good boy." Oh, the memory of a loving and patient mother. She taught me what she knew. The whole of her education consisted in a knowledge of the Alphabet, and how to count a hundred. She first taught me the Lord's Prayer. And as soon as I was old enough, she explained to me the difference between the condition of the coloured and white people, and told me that if I would learn how to read and write, some day I might be able to get my freedom; but all that would have to be kept a secret. If a slave were known to teach another slave, he would be liable to be sent to the whipping-post, or he might at once be sold; for the law was very strict with regard to slaves in this matter--they were forbidden education. The Legislature of the State of Louisiana, U. S. A., during the days of slavery passed an Act that-- "Whosoever shall make use language in any public discourse, or shall make use of signs or actions having a tendency to produce discontent amongst the coloured population, shall suffer imprisonment and hard labour, not less than three years nor more than twenty-one years, ordeath at the discretion of the Court." And slaves were not allowed to be taught in Sabbath Schools; whoever taught such a school would "be fined five hundred dollars." In Virginia and South Carolina, any school for teaching reading and writing, either to slaves or free people, was considered an unlawful assembly. If found out, the penalty for each pupil was twenty lashes. It was made the duty of any Justice of the Peace to issue his warrant to enter any house or school-house or meeting where coloured people would be likely to receive instruction. The law in Virginia was not so strict respecting Sunday School lessons, if the master made no objections. In the city of Savannah, Ga., an ordinance was made by which "Any person that teaches a person of colour, slave or free, to read and write, or cause such person to be so taught, is subject to a fine of thirty dollars for each offence; and every person of colour who shall teach reading or writing to be imprisoned ten days and whipped thirty-nine lashes."

My mother's heartfelt desire seems to have been that I should be taught to read and write; and no opportunity was lost in trying to inspire me to look forward to freedom and an education. She told me what she knew about heaven, where there would be no slaves--all would be free. Oh, I used to think how nice it must be in heaven, "no slaves, all free," and God would think as much of the black people as he did of the white. Then mother would talk of Africa; how that they were once all free there, but white people stole us from our country and made slaves of us. This appeared to be all she knew of the matter. I do thank my Blessed Jesus that she knew so much; it was the germ of all I know to-day. My mother's advice and my mother's teaching will ever remain fresh in my memory. I cannot forget her tears as she looked upon me with a mother's love, more than sixty years ago, and told me what little she knew. To her, as to thousands of poor slaves, the Bible was almost a sealed book. I remember her tenderness, and the deep security I felt when, in the evenings of my childhood, nestling in her arms, I listened as she told me how she loved me; not knowing what was passing through that loving mother's breast as her tearful eyes looked upon me. I was the first and only child at that time.

The few following lines, which I put together and often sang, I call "Memories of Childhood," and frequently sing them now in memory of my dear mother:-

> Yes, I remember, remember well,
> When at my mother's knee she often would tell
> Of that sweet prayer the disciples prayed,
> Taught by the Lord who should be obeyed:

Our Father, which art in heaven; hallowed be Thy Name; Thy Kingdom come; Thy will be done in earth as it is done in heaven. Give us this day our daily bread; and forgive us our trespasses, as we forgive them that trespass against us; and lead us not into temptation; but deliver us from evil. For Thine is the Kingdom, and the power and the glory, for ever and ever. Amen.

> And then, in conclusion,
> Mother taught me to say,
> In childlike simplicity,
> At the close of day:
> Now I lay me down to sleep,
> I pray the Lord my soul to keep;

If I should die before I wake, I pray
the Lord my soul to take.

Attempts at Learning

My master was sent on Government business to Buenos Ayres. Some of the slaves were sent to the farm, but others were left in the hands of an agent at Washington. My mother took advantage of this opportunity and paid a freeman fifty cents to teach me for one month. All that I can remember of those lessons is:

ab,   eb,   ib,   ob,   ub,   ac,   ec,   ic,   oc,   uc,

and similar simple combinations.

This was found out by one of the young masters, who was left at home, and in consequence thereof I was sent to Fredricksburg, down in Virginia, to a farm there. After the master's return he settled down on a farm near Alexandria, Virginia, where in two years he died. The estate was divided. It was my lot to fall into the hands of the son who used to cuff me concerning his slippers. He was a doctor, and settled in Fairfax County, Va., and at first boarded with a family of Northern people, who were very kind to me. He found this out, and he desired Mrs. Barrett, the lady of the house, not to permit me to repeat any lesson after the children, nor in any way to give me instruction. He removed to another family to board. When he went from home he left instructions with the gentleman with whom he boarded to do as he liked with me, and he did not fail to use his authority. My own master would often whip me for the most trivial thing, and I was treated in a most cruel manner, far away from my mother, whose sympathy in the past was most precious to me. When only twelve years old I often thought of freedom, and as time passed away I made enquiries respecting Canada. This was the second time I was away from my mother, and I had not much hope of ever seeing her again. 'Freedom" was the subject that occupied my mind greatly at this time.

Queen Victoria

I heard that the Queen of England had given large sums of money to set the coloured people free, and I felt that if I could reach Canada I should be safe. It may be of interest if I mention that we had the idea on the plantation that the Queen was black, because she was so kind. Accustomed to nothing but cruelty at the hands of the white people, we had never imagined that a great ruler so kind to coloured people could be other than black; so the impression was that Queen Victoria was a coloured lady. To me she was the subject of many a dream; she often came before my mind, and filled my imagination with all manner of ideas as to the kind of person she was. I used to picture her as a black lady, amidst numerous coloured attendants, surrounded by a grandeur that exceeded all I had ever seen amongst the wealthy white people. And then I thought what a happy thing it must be to live under the reign of so good a Queen. Many stories were circulated concerning Victoria. Amongst the rest I remember one which had great interest for us. We had the impression that a hogshead (in which tobacco was packed) was the largest measure in existence, and it was reported that the Queen had sent a hogshead of money to purchase the liberty of us poor slaves; but that the money had got into the hands of the white people, who, instead of granting freedom to us, had kept the money for themselves, and still kept us as slaves. The origin of this story I cannot understand, except on the theory that the Queen, who had freed so many slaves in other parts, and whose Government had paid so much to liberate those in slavery, would not willingly leave us in bondage. Alas! there was no way for me to make my escape; the door seemed closed against me.

I would often think of my mother's parting blessing. She put her hand upon my head, and said, "Good-bye, my son; God bless you. Be a good boy, say your prayers, and try to seek religion. The fortune-teller said you were born to good luck." I would look at the sun, and see how beautifully it shone on everything; all was bright but the poor slaves, who were doomed to drag out a miserable existence in bondage, classed as goods and chattels. Their condition was that of dumb creatures; their time, talents, mind and body were all claimed by the slave-owner, whose power over the slaves was absolute. The slave had no legal rights. In no respect whatever was he protected; beyond his master he had no appeal; he was not allowed to give evidence against a white man; his wife and children were by law "things"--chattels--the property of their master, to whom they were compelled to yield implicit obedience. "The New Orleans Bee" newspaper of the 14th October, 18--, says: "The slave who struck some citizens in Canel Street some weeks since has been tried and found guilty, and is sentenced to be hung on the 24th inst." The Quarterly Anti-Slavery Magazine, July, 1837.--U S.A.--"The labour of the slave was compulsory and without any remuneration. The kind of labour, the amount of toil, the time allowed for rest, were all decided by the master or overseer. The clothing, food, and bedding, both as to quality and quantity, depended upon the kind of master the slaves had. Some masters were very cruel, but others were very kind. The treatment of the household slaves-- or, as they are called in England, servants--differed very much from that of field slaves, the latter being for the most part under the control of the overseers, who were often very cruel to them. Yet there were exceptions, some overseers being very kind."

Bargaining for Slaves

Hardly a day passed without some one of my own long oppressed people being led to the whipping post, and there lashed most unmercifully. Every auction day many were sold away to Georgia, or some other of the far-off Southern States, and often could be seen in companies, handcuffed, and on their way to the Southern markets, doomed, doomed to perpetual slavery. So absolutely were the slaves in the power of their masters that they were pledged, leased, exchanged, taken for debt or gambled off at the gambling table; and men women, and children were sold by auction at the public auction block-- husbands and wives separated, never to meet again, and little children torn from their parents' loving arms, and sold into slavery, and into the hands of strangers from distant parts. Here is a pictorial illustration of the slaves being sold at a public auction--

Slaves being sold at Public Auction.

This cut appeared in the book called "Uncle Tom's Cabin," and now used by permission of The Christian Age.

Religious Awakening

In the midst of all their sufferings, the slaves would sing many of the religious songs that were sung by Jubilee Singers. And I often joined in the singing, When I resolved to "seek religion," I was then nearly sixteen years of age. My master was a member of the Episcopalian Church, and would teach me to say my prayers, and the Apostles' Creed, and read to me about Abraham's servants and Isaac's servants, and Jacob's servants, and "servants, obey your masters." He would read these "wise" precepts over to me so carefully, have prayers, and then, when he felt like it (which he often did), gave me a lashing. And whenever he thought I ought to have a flogging, he would say to me: "Report yourself to me to-morrow morning after breakfast." If I did not report to get my flogging, I would have an extra lashing for that. Yet, with all this, my lot was much better than many of those around me. There was a man who owned the next plantation whose name was Jackson. He was so cruel to the slaves that he was known to them as "the devil." I remember well how I used to think of "seeking religion," but whenever I began to think seriously on this matter, a great obstacle confronted me. I was superstitious. Superstition is characteristic of the race in Africa. Having been brought to America, not permitted to be taught to read the Bible, and having every avenue to education closed against us, it was natural we should retain the superstitions of our fathers. My idea was that if I set out to "seek religion," I must meet with that old serpent, the devil. I often heard slaves say that when they set out to "seek religion," the devil set out with them, and this greatly perplexed me. Then I heard them talk of seeing ghosts. But after they were converted they would go six and ten miles at night to a meeting, and God would be with them. I resolved to set out definitely to get religion, with all my strange thoughts and fears. I thought the worst sin a man could be guilty of was murder. I knew I was innocent of that. One day, I was out gathering blackberries, and commenced to pray the Lord's Prayer; I knew not what else to say. As I prayed, a rabbit jumped up from under the bush from which I was gathering the berries. I felt sure this was the devil. I had heard that when he deceived Eve in the garden, he came like a serpent; and, furthermore, he could put himself into any shape. I was never more frightened in all my life. I was afraid to say my prayers at night, not so much because I might disturb the devil, but because he might disturb me. I wept bitterly in my loneliness and in my darkness of mind, having no father or mother to direct me.

Sold To Another Master

About the year 1852 my master took to himself a wife, and then I was sold to his brother, who lived in Richmond, Virginia. Here I again met my dear mother, after having been separated from her for about six years. This brother had always been kind to slaves, and every member of the family followed his example. How much he paid for me I never heard. His son once told me that he had been offered three thousand dollars in gold for me, but that he would not accept the amount. From this time I received better treatment. I was never flogged after coming into his hands. I was told that I was to be the property of his eldest son. He was much younger than myself. Now, during all this time I never lost sight of the lessons my dear mother had taught me, and while I was separated from her I worked hard in order to be able to make the letters of the Alphabet, and had learned to spell a large number of words. But I found out that the white people did not use the large letters of the Alphabet as I did when writing. I was strongly of the impression that an education consisted in knowing how to write, and I also knew that the slave-owners were opposed to their slaves acquiring even the most elementary literary knowledge. There was a slave on our lot named Anthony Burnes, who managed to get to Boston. Under the fugitive slave law he was brought back to Richmond, Virginia, and put into the slave pen for sale. Young Mr. Brent came to me one day when Burnes was in the trader's pen, and told me that Anthony was in gaol. He knew how to write, and had written himself a pass and had gone to the north, and that his master and other gentlemen had brought him back, and now he would be sold to Georgia. All this, said he, Burnes brought upon himself because he knew how to write. "Lor's o'er me," I said, "is dat so?" He answered very gravely, "Yes, that is so."

Literary Struggles

When I got by myself, I said, "If dat is so, I am going to learn how to write, and if I can get to Boston, I know I can get to Canada." With this resolve, I struggled hard to learn how to write. I began by pocketing the nice-looking letters I saw, and go to my room and try to make letters like them. I remember being in a church once, where I saw a lot of letters in a box. The writing looked so plain and nice, it seemed that I could not do better than take a few of the nicest looking ones to help me in my writing lessons. But this did not do, for although some of the letters were very nice, I did not know what to call them. The youngest son of the master had a copy book. When I saw it I decided to have one like it. The first time after this when I had five cents, I went to a book store and asked for a copy book. I had made up my mind what to say if the bookseller should ask me for whom I wanted it. I intended telling him that it was for my master. But fortunately he did not question me in that direction. I told him in answer to his question as to what kind of copy book I wanted, to put them down that I might see them, and I would tell him. I went home and began to learn from this book how to write. The letters were alphabetically arranged. I got on very well, but another difficulty presented itself--I could not spell.

I purchased a spelling-book in the course of time, kept it in my pocket, and at every opportunity I looked into it. But there were so many words I could not understand. At night, when the young master would be getting his lessons, I used to choose some word I wanted to know how to spell, and say, "Master, I'll bet you can't spell 'looking-glass.'" He would at once spell it. I would exclaim, "Lor's o'er me, you can spell nice." Then I would go out and spell the word over and over again. I knew that once it was in my head it would never be got out again. This young man was very kind, and was always willing to answer my questions. But sometimes he would ask why I wanted to know, and I would say, "I want to see how far you are." In the course of time he would often read portions of his lessons to me. If I liked this and wanted to hear it again, I would say, "Lor's o'er me, read that again," which he often did. In this way each week I added a little to my small store of knowledge about the great world in which I lived.

But the door of freedom seemed as fast closed against me as ever. There was a large map of the United States hanging on the wall of the dining room, and each day as I attended to my duties I would stop a few minutes and look at the map. In the course of time I learned to spell the names of nearly all the cities along the railway route from Richmond to Boston, wondering whether I should ever see those cities where all were free. Never shall I be able to express my intense longing for freedom in those long, long days of slavery. During all this my heart was inclined towards "seeking religion." Some of the slaves sang so much about "heaven" and "home," and "rest" and "freedom," and seemed so happy that I often longed to be able to join them. Many of the melodies were sung by the Jubilee Singers. "The home beyond," where there was perfect rest and freedom and peace, and where there would be no slavery, was almost daily before me. But how to get religion was what perplexed me; yet it was essential to my happiness both here and hereafter. See how the heathen grope on in the darkness after God, and how on awakening turn towards Him. When, thirty-eight years afterwards, I went to Africa, I found that on comparison the condition of the plantation negroes in America was but little better than that of the heathen in Africa. But "How shall they hear without a preacher?" Rom. x., 14. Dear Christian reader, will you not do something to send the Gospel to Africa--poor, long neglected Africa, the land of my fathers.

The Great Revival

In the year 1857 there was a great revival in America. The coloured people thought the Judgment Day was coming. Everywhere we heard of great meetings and of thousands of souls being converted. In the Richmond tobacco factories, which employed many thousands of slaves, there were many converts daily. First one and then another of my friends would set out to "seek religion." At last I resolved that, should I live for a thousand years I would not stop seeking religion until I found the peace I needed; but the thought of meeting that old serpent, the devil, was chilling and repulsive to me. The converts used to relate their experience, and some of them said, as before mentioned, that when they set out to seek religion the devil set out with them; that while seeking they would "fast and pray"; and that the devil would do all he could to turn them back. This troubled me above all else. I thought the others had seen the devil with their natural eyes, and in this way I should have to see him. But I dreaded the encounter and feared to go to bed, and sat out in the porch at night, sometimes dozing a little, then awakening with fear, my thoughts being of that dreadful time through which I must go to get religion.

A rat suddenly scuttling across the floor would make me tremble, or a cat creeping along the wall toward me would send me into a paroxysm of fear that the moment had come. All the night I wished for the day, and yet when the day came I regretted the cowardice of the night. Matters came to such a pass that during the day I could scarcely speak to anyone; instead of being lively, and cheerful I was gloomy and nervous, and my master wanted to know what was wrong, and even threatened to send me to Georgia. But I had made up my mind that wherever I went I would not stop seeking religion until I found peace. I knew that God was stronger than the devil and my master, and so I made my request to God, "Please don't let master sell me to Georgia." Then I began to think that I must in some way renovate myself to be acceptable to God; that I must do something to make myself fit. I therefore fasted as long as I could, until I was obliged by hunger to take a hearty meal; but that meant the beginning of the fasting all over again, as I had turned back. Through losing rest night after night, and through abstinence from my necessary food, I was reduced to an indescribable condition; it was just a living death to me. I felt I could stand it no longer.

Found By Jesus

One day I met a coloured man in the street, named Stephney Brown. He was a Christian, and quite an intelligent man. He explained to me the simple Gospel. He told me to go to God, and say: "Lord, have mercy upon me, a hell-deserving sinner, for Jesus' sake; set me out your way and not my way, for Jesus' sake." "But," said he, "you must have faith. Now this is faith: If you came to see me, and asked me for a drink of water, you would expect and believe that I would give it to you. So you must ask God for Jesus' sake to have mercy upon you, a hell-deserving sinner. If you die as you are, you will go to hell, but you must ask pardon for Jesus' sake. He cannot deny you if you ask for Jesus' sake." "For Jesus' sake" seemed to enter into my soul. "Have mercy upon me, a hell-deserving sinner, for Jesus' sake," rang through my heart all the way home, and I began to understand the finished work of my blessed Jesus as I never had before. As soon as my work was done for that night, and all was quiet, I resolved that, if I lived for a thousand years, I would never stop praying "for Jesus' sake." I went into the dining room, fell down upon my knees, and said: "O Lord have mercy upon me, a hell-deserving sinner, for Jesus' sake." Then I became very happy. I got up and went into the porch. Everything appeared to be different to me. The very stars in the heaven seemed brighter, and I was feeling brighter and so very happy. I did not see any great sights, but there was an inward rejoicing. I had not done anything--I could not do anything--to merit this any more than the thief upon the cross, but my blessed Jesus had done it all; there was nothing for me to do. In the matter of salvation, all that God requires of us is to acknowledge with repentance our sins and receive with gratitude His salvation. The blood of Jesus had been accepted as the full atonement for the sin of the sinner. Oh, how many weary hearts and wasted lives there are to-day through failing to recognise this important truth. The Blessed Christ has atoned for my sin, and all I have to do is to accept God's pardon, and eternal life. The Lord Jesus was now not one whom I had merely heard about, but He was my blessed Jesus-- just as much mine as if there was no person besides myself in the world. Precious Gospel-Jesus, the sinner's friend. I used to hear the coloured people say that there were some white people who went to heaven. My idea was that there were not many of them who went to heaven, because their cruelty and life were not at all Christian.

But now I thought that if my master would only come to Jesus he could be saved. I began to pray for the white people, and to tell all around what a dear Salvation I had found.

Spiritual Freedom

"Free indeed," John viii., 36. I had now a free soul. But my poor mother, who had taught me the Lord's Prayer and for years been so anxious that I should "seek religion," had never herself understood the finished work of Christ. She now, however, accepted Him as her own Saviour, and gave herself to the Lord in glad and full surrender. I was anxious, after my conversion, to unite with the Baptist Church. In Richmond there were Churches of coloured people, but they had white Pastors, who never failed to keep us informed about Abraham's servants, and as to the injunction to Hagar. I could not join any Church unless I had a "pass" from my master. I went to him and asked permission to be baptised. He at once said: "No, you shall not unite with the Baptist Church." Mr. Brown, my spiritual adviser, told me to go to the Lord, and say, "Lord, if Thou hast ever done anything for my never-dying soul, please manifest Thyself to me in moving the master to give me a pass to be baptised." I think it was nearly three months before I again ventured to ask him. But when I summoned up enough courage to ask him the second time, he at once gave permission. This was a manifest answer to prayer. When the appointed Sabbath for baptism arrived, my mother and I "went down into the water" hand-in-hand, and were baptised, rejoicing in the privilege of following our Divine Master, and when we "came up out of the water" we "went on our way rejoicing."

Soon after my conversion I felt a deep desire to preach the Gospel. But two difficulties presented themselves: first, I was a slave, for though I had a free soul, yet my body was in slavery; then, second, I could not read the Bible with much understanding, and there was no way for me to succeed but the old way, that, was, by taking advantage of every opportunity to learn all I could. Just about this time a young student (white) came from College on the

Sabbaths to preach to the coloured people. He read the fifth chapter of Matthew. I was much struck with his explanation, and I became anxious to know how to read this chapter. Now there was a box of old books stored away in a lumber room, and amongst these books was a large old Bible. I took this Bible to my room, and day after day, when I had finished my work in the house, and had a little time to spare, I would go to my room, lock myself in, and try to read the Bible, commencing at Genesis and calling over the letters of each word I could not understand as follows:--"In the b-e-g-i-n-n-i-n-g God c-r-e-a-t-e-d the heaven and the earth"; and thus I struggled on from day to day. The young master had been requested by his mother to read a chapter in the New Testament every night. Often when with him in his own room at night I would get him to read the fifth chapter of Matthew for me. To the reading of this I would listen attentively. Thus I got to know the words "multitudes," "mountain," "disciples," "blessed," and in time I had learned to repeat many verses of the chapter from memory. I then began to look about in the Bible, and found in many places the same words in the first and second syllables that I knew. In this way I got to understand a little about the Bible, and at the same time I was learning to spell. After my conversion I would often "Steal away to Jesus" with other slaves, to some quiet place for prayer, over the stable, or in the kitchen when the master and mistress were away, though we knew that if we were discovered we should be locked up for the night, and that the next morning we should receive from five to nine or even thirty lashes for unlawfully assembling together. Over five slaves in such a gathering, though they had passes, constituted an unlawful assembly. At night no slave was allowed to be out without a pass from his master. We used to have such a good time at these meetings. No wonder the Jubilee Singers sang with such deep feeling when those of them who were once slaves remembered the meetings of this kind at which they sang and prayed almost in a whisper for fear of being heard. How appropriate to sing softly and quietly:--

Steal away,
Steal away,
Steal away to Jesus;
Steal away,
Steal away home;
I ain't got long to stay here.

Dear Reader, have you stolen away to Jesus? Has He liberated you from spiritual bondage? His promise and encouragement are found in the words, "Whosoever shall call upon the name of the Lord shall be saved."--Rom. x. 13. Have you ever called in faith? See verse 10. If you have not, then God help you, as you look upon these words, to say, 'I will, God helping me." Let every worldly engagement wait, and every secret plan go, and take God at His word. Doubt not our blessed Lord for a moment when He says, "Come unto Me, all ye that labour and are heavy-laden, and I will give you rest."--

Matthew xi. 28. "Him that cometh to Me I will in no wise cast out."--John vi. 37. Stop and think of what the Lord has done for you. "Steal away to Jesus" now. "Steal away to Jesus" from your surroundings and your friends and your very self. He has proved His love to you by giving Himself a ransom for you--I Tim. ii. 6; Gal. ii. 20. "He came to seek the lost."-- Luke xix. 10. "He bore your sins in His own body on the tree."-- I Peter ii. 24.

After Jesus found me and gave me peace in my soul, I often thought of Africa, the land of my fathers, and a deep desire possessed me to go and tell my own people about my blessed Jesus. During the summer months for several years, my owners hired me out to wait in an hotel at the sea-side. On two occasions I tried to make my escape, but was not successful. It was a very serious thing for a runaway slave to be captured. When a slave was missing from the plantation, then several planters or "overseers" united in what was called a "negro hunt." A pack of bloodhounds were called together. A company of men, mounted on their horses, set out for the woods and jungles as if when purposing to hunt lions and tigers. If the dogs should reach the poor slave before he could climb a tree, or get into some cave, he would be in danger of being torn to pieces. If the slave were not found, great rewards would then be offered for his capture and restoration, and when he was brought back he was subjected to the most cruel punishment. The

A Runaway Slave.

only place of real safety for the poor slave, where he might have refuge, was in the dominions of Her Majesty Queen Victoria. It is worthy of special mention just here that as far back as 1840 we find in the proceedings of the Anti-Slavery Convention, held in London; it is reported that in Upper Canada there were to be found nearly 15,000 coloured people, chiefly fugitive slaves and their children, from the Southern States. They had been assisted in their escape and support for the most part by the Quakers and Abolitionists, who did their work so skilfully and successfully and also secretly that their method of deporting the poor slave to a place of safety was termed "The Underground Railroad." The following are quotations from the records of the U.G.R.R. and Anti-Slavery journals:--

"**$100 Reward.**--Ran away from the Subscriber on the 7th of November, negro slave, Edgar. He was 36 years old, 6 feet high, of a dark brown complexion, very high forehead, is a little bald, and is inclined to stoop in the shoulders. Edgar says he was raised in Norfolk County, has worked about

Norfolk several years. I bought him at the Auction House of Messrs. Pulliam and Davis, the 20th of July, 1856. The bill of sale was signed by W. Y. Miliner for Jas. A. Bilisoly, administrator of G. W. Chambers, deceased. He told one of my negroes he was going to Norfolk to sell some plunder he had there, then go to Richmond, steal his wife, get on board a boat about Norfolk, and go to a free State. He can read and write well, and I have no doubt he has provided himself with papers of some kind. He may have purchased the papers of some free negro. I will give the above reward of One Hundred Dollars to any person who will arrest and confine him, so I can get him.

(Signed) C. H. GAY.

My Post Office is Laurel, N. C. No. 21.

Clinton, "Mississippi Gazette," July 23rd, 1836.

There was committed to the Jail of Covington Co. on the 26th day of June, 1836, by G. D. Gere, Esq.,

"A negro man who says his name is Josiah, that he belongs to Mr. John Martin, living in Louisiana, twenty miles below Nathchez. Josiah is five feet eight inches high, heavy built, copper colour; his back very much scarred with the whip, and branded on the thigh and hips in three or four places thus: 'j.M.' or 'J.M.' The 'M' is very plain, but the 'j' or 'J' is not plain. The rim of his right ear has been bitten or cut off. He is about 31 years of age. Had on, when committed, pantaloons, made of bed-ticking, cotton coat, and an old fur hat very much worn. The owner of the above described negro is requested to comply requisitions of law, in such, cases made and provided for.

J. L. JOLLEY, S.H., F.F., C.C.

"Williamsburgh, June 28, 1836."

Progress and Liberation

It may be interesting and helpful to my younger friends if I go back in history some fifty-five years before the election of Mr. Abraham Lincoln as President of the United States, and see how step by step God has blessed the efforts of the Society of Friends and the Anti-Slavery Society from the day when the question of the "Abolition of the Slave Trade" was introduced in the British Parliament in 1807, to the fall of Richmond, Virginia, in April, 1865. On January 2nd, 1807, Lord Grenville presented a Bill, called an "Act for the Abolition of the Slave Trade"; and on the 5th his Lordship opened the debate by a very luminous speech. Among others who supported him was the Duke of Gloucester, who said: "This trade is contrary to the principles of the British Constitution. It is, besides, a cruel and criminal traffic in the blood of our fellow creatures; it is a foul stain on the national character. It is an offence to the Almighty. On every ground, therefore, on which a decision can be made, on the ground of policy, of Liberty, of Humanity, of Justice, but above all on the ground of Religion, I shall vote for its immediate extinction."

The question being called for at four o'clock in the morning, the Bill passed, one hundred voting for it and only thirty-six against. The Bill was then carried to the House of Commons, where on March 16th it passed without a division. On the 25th, at twelve o'clock, His Majesty King George III. gave his Royal assent; thus making glad the hearts of many who had feared that His Majesty was opposed to the measure. The Bishop of Llandaff said, "This great act of justice would be recorded in heaven." Lord Grenville then congratulated the House "on the completion on its part of the most glorious measure that had ever been adopted by any legislative body in the world." I am persuaded that there is not a friend of humanity who could refrain from saying "Amen" to these remarks. No writer of history down through the dark days of the slave trade to the passing of this humane Act, or since, has been able to delineate the horrible crimes to which millions of poor slaves were subjected. I am sure that no man or woman now living has any true conception of what millions of Africans suffered years ago when they were torn from their native land and sold into wretched bondage. For twenty years the friends of human liberty had been labouring faithfully for the oppressed, and now the end was in sight; and from this time very decisive steps were taken by other Governments, including the United States of America, to put an end to the slave trade.--(Clarkson on the Slave Trade).

Thus the backbone of slavery was broken. These good men, the promoters of this Bill, who gave their time, their talents and their influence to the cause of the oppressed, were God-fearing men, God-honouring men, with undaunted courage, and with absolute faith in their mission; men who knew they were in the right, and that God was with them. The good work did not stop here. moved by refined philanthropy, they considered that if it were wrong to traffic in human beings, it was equally wrong to hold them as slaves. Thus there began the agitation for the emancipation of the slaves in the British Colonies. God raised up many others who united with the pioneers of liberty, and they became as eyes and ears and mouth for the poor slaves, who could not see and hear and speak for themselves. It was manifest to these apostles of liberty that some great plan of Providence was in progress, and, inspired by former victories, they were looking forward to the day when every slave should be free. I do indeed praise God with all my heart for raising up the good men and women who displayed such Christian sympathy toward the slaves as to seek their emancipation with unfaltering effort. As a result of their work we have recorded; the Emancipation of the slaves in the British Colonies. On May 14th, 1833, a motion was made in the House of Commons to liberate the slaves in the West Indies. It was decided to pay £20,000,000 to the slaveholders that the 800,000 slaves might be liberated on the first of August, 1834.

Sympathy of Britain's Royal House

This work was not completed till our late lamented Queen Victoria came to the throne. Her accession to the throne marks the death-blow to slavery throughout the world, for gradually but surely the inhuman traffic has been disappearing, and enlightened nations have abolished it. It was stopped in India in 1845; in Tunis, 1846; in France, or her colonies, 1848; in Russia the serfs got liberty in 1861, when twenty millions had the yoke removed; in the United States of America, four millions and a half slaves were freed in 1865; in West Africa in 1874; and in the Queen's Jubilee year slavery was abolished in the great Niger country and elsewhere; and we pray God that soon there may not be a single trace of human slavery in the world. To this end the Society of Friends and all friends of the oppressed are still labouring. Their noble efforts have met with great success; and in the future, as in the past, may they have the influence and support of the Royal Family with them. "Queen Victoria the Good" was ever the friend of our race. She manifested this in many ways; but perhaps the most striking instance out of many was her treatment of the conquered King Cetewayo. Ancient nations would have submitted the captured rulers of the conquered to all manner of cruelties and insults; dragging them in chains at their chariot wheels, and exposing them to the cruel gaze and the scornful jeers of the populace, torturing them, and only permitting them to live in order to torture them; but our most gracious Queen Victoria received her dark prisoner and treated him with royal courtesy, providing him and his attendants with carriages, and sending her own officers to wait upon him. The public respected him, and London gave him a cordial welcome. By the Queen's kindness he was enabled to hold many any receptions in the beautiful home placed at his disposal, and my wife and I were amongst those who were fortunate enough to have the pleasure of visiting him. It is very characteristic of the English Royal Family to be in touch and in sympathy with all who seek to ameliorate the condition and elevate the life of the African race. In the years 1825 and 1828 the Duke of Gloucester occupied the chair of the Anti-Slavery Society. In 1840 the Duke of Sussex presided at one of the meetings of the Society. The first public meeting in England over which H.R.H. the Prince Consort presided was the great meeting of the Anti-Slavery Society held in Exeter Hall, 1840, when he said: "I have been induced to preside at the meeting of this Society from the condition of its paramount importance to the greatest interest of humanity and justice." The late Joseph Cooper says, in his book on the African Slave Trade: "There is a work, one of the glories of our age, in which humanity must rejoice, and of which England in particular may be proud, viz., the abolition of slavery in the colonies of Christian people. In them the negro has ceased to be game which is hunted, an article of merchandise to be sold, a beast of burden goaded to labour by the lash."

During the nineteenth century England has shown to the world that she is the champion of distressed humanity; her arms have been the cradle of freedom in a very real way, and within her borders the oppressed have found a home.

Speaking of the Royal Family, and of their interest in the welfare of the oppressed, I remember well the visit of the Prince of Wales, our present King, who came to Richmond, the place where the crowning victory of the North was won. Great preparations were made to receive him at the "Exchange Hotel and Ballard House," On the Sabbath afternoon the Prince and his Suite were riding out. They came down Franklin Street. I had a good look at the Prince. I cannot tell when I felt more unhappy in slavery than at that time. I heard that the Prince had given a valuable present to a coloured man. It seemed to me that if I could only see the Prince and tell him how I longed to be free, he would purchase me, and give me my liberty. But how to get into his presence I did not know. I heard that when he was leaving New York some gentleman made him a present of a dog, and that a boy was engaged to look after this dog. For a long time I regretted that I did not make an effort in some way to speak to the Prince, thinking that possibly he might have taken me instead of the boy to look after the dog. "Alas," I thought, "my chance is gone."

Abraham Lincoln - Deliverer

In the year 1860, there was great excitement in Richmond over the election of Mr. Abraham Lincoln as President of the United States. The slaves prayed to God for his success, and they prayed very especially the night before the election. We knew he was in sympathy with the abolition of Slavery. The election was the signal for a great conflict for which the Southern States were ready. The question was: Shall there be Slavery or no Slavery in the United States? The South said: Yes, there shall be Slavery. In 1861 a convention was held in Montgomery, Alabama, to decide the matter. Referring to that convention, the following is from the "Chicago Tribune," 5th February, 1891: "Thirty years ago yesterday the Convention which framed the Confederate Constitution, met at Montgomery, Ala. It was one of the most purely Democratic meetings ever held in the country. None but Democrats attended, and their work was Calhoun-Democratic from beginning to end. Three things distinguished the Rebel Constitution. One was the open unqualified recognition and endorsement of slavery. Another was that no internal improvements should be made at the expense of the General Government. The third was an express provision that no protective duties of any kind should be imposed. This was carrying out the teaching of Calhoun, and the declaration of the Democratic Cincinnati platform, readopted at Baltimore, in favour of "progressive free trade" with the world. Of these three Democratic principles but one survives. The war ended Slavery. The greed for Federal appropriations for the levying of the Mississippi River cured Southern Democrats of their hostility to internal improvements. Free trade is left, however, and is as much a cardinal tenet of the Democratic party as it was in old Montgomery days. That article of its faith was not taken from Jackson, but owes its paternity to Calhoun, the brains of the Democracy."

God-fearing men and women in the North, and in Great Britain and Ireland, whom the Lord had raised up to be our friends, could see in the struggle the Almighty hand stretched out on behalf of a long, long oppressed people, whose cries had ascended up to heaven like the cries of Israel of old under Egyptian bondage.

Richmond--Campaigns of Love and War

Of the campaign around Richmond I can speak from personal knowledge and experience. Richmond was the capital of the Confederate States--the States that wanted to establish a slaveholder's republic. The fortifications built by the compulsory labour of the slaves were massive and strong. This work reminds one of the great arch-rebel himself who compels men and women in spiritual slavery to build up the walls of their own imprisonment against the army of liberty, and who also forces his victim to forge the chains for their own bondage and banishment from God.

The City of Richmond was the stronghold of the Southern States. I can remember the excitement among both white and coloured people in Richmond at the time it was threatened. All the coloured people in Richmond that I spoke to believe that if the North gained the victory they would have their freedom. The white people believed that "Cotton" was King, and that England would in time help them. My master's eldest son volunteered for service, and I was sent into the Army to be with him, and to cook and do other things. I had an opportunity of seeing much of the campaign around York town on the Peninsula, and I have often been in Lord Cornwallis's cave. During the second year of the War, Mr. Brent died, and his slaves and other property fell to his widow, who was, indeed, an exceptionally kind lady to her slaves. After his death I had to be at home most of the time until the close of the war. During some of this time the widow hired me out to a firm to make cigars. She received twenty dollars a week for my services.

In the midst of the warring days I was bent upon a more interesting campaign, and in 1863 was married to Henrietta Thompson, maid to Mrs. Cooper, wife of General S. G. Cooper, Inspecting General of the Confederate Army, and sister of the great General Lee. I had met my wife first at Richmond.

At this time I could read fairly, and could also write a little, and I was able to understand much that was in the newspapers, and I began to teach others what I knew, and had a class of six pupils.

Prophesy and Hope

Many of the coloured people could read the Bible, and they believed that the eleventh Chapter of Daniel referred directly to the war. We often met together, and read this chapter in our own way. The fifth verse would perplex many of our company, and then verses 13-15 would be much dwelt upon, for though the former verses spoke of the apparent victory of the South, these latter verses set forth the ultimate triumph of the North, for did it not say: "For the King of the North shall return and shall set forth a multitude greater than the former...so the King of the North shall come and cast up a mound and take the most fenced cities, and the arms of the South shall not withstand." Thus we eagerly grasped at any statements, which our anxiety, hope, and prayer concerning our liberty led us to search for, and which might indicate the desirable ending of the great War. Whenever we met all our talk would be about what we had heard, and about freedom. Sometimes when we heard of other cities and towns having been taken by the United States Army, we became impatient, and talked of "running the blockade." At night we listened to the booming of the guns, and we were much excited. During the latter part of the Siege of Richmond the poor suffered very much indeed. Toward the end of March much anxiety and restlessness were manifested on the part of the white people. The slaves were joyful and expectant. My master used to ask: "Won't you fight for me, Tom?" And in fear I would reply: "Oh yes, Massa." And then I would feel how wrong it was to say what I did, as it was contrary to my intention, and I would ask the Lord to forgive me. But this was in the early part of the War. On Sunday, April 2nd, 1865, there was great excitement in the city, "General Grant had taken Petersburg and was closing in around us." This was only twenty miles from Richmond.

Fall of the Capital

In the afternoon many of the families began to leave the city, and late in the evening President Davis, General S. S. Cooper, General Lee, and staff all left Richmond. I feel sure that such a noteworthy Sunday night will be remembered by many at this present time, and who were very anxiously waiting for that famous Monday morning, April the 3rd. It will never be forgotten by me. About four o'clock on the Monday morning the great magazine outside the city was blown up by the Confederate troops to prevent the ammunition falling into the hands of the Northern troops. I commenced at once to shout, "Hoozah for Grant and Linktum." My wife said, "Tom, ye'll wake the baby." "Never you mind, Henrietta--Hoozah for Grant and Linktum," I shouted. The large tobacco factories were set fire to, and the fire spread to other large buildings. At the break of day a coloured man was the first to carry the news into General Weitzel's camp that President Davis and General Lee had "skedaddled." At eight o'clock in the morning about forty of the United States

Cavalry of General Weitzel's division, who were already holding the north side of the James River, rode into Richmond, and proceeded at once to the public square of the capital. As these men came galloping up the street they came to a side entrance to the square, where there was a gate which, as the Irishman would say, "You shut it when you want to open it." The horses could not pass through this gate, but soon the whole thing was knocked away by men prepared for such business. After passing through the gateway there was a steep hill to ascend. As one of the men passed through I got him by the leg. His horse galloped on up the hill, but I hung on. I commenced to tell the man of a free coloured man who had volunteered to fight against the North, and who had been made an officer by the Confederates and forced the slaves to military service. Those thus forced to join the company never had an opportunity of fighting, for which they were thankful. I was very serious, but the soldier rode on laughing.

The United States troops soon took possession of Richmond city, and quickly restored order. The damage to property was very great. Soon the Stars and Stripes were seen floating over the old State Capital.

Freedom

The joy and rejoicing of the coloured people when the United States army marched into Richmond defies description. For days the manifestations of delight were displayed in many ways. The places of worship were kept open, and hundreds met for prayer and praise. Of the many songs of the Jubilee this was the chorus of one of them:

> Slavery's chain is broke at last,
> Broke at last, broke at last;
> Slavery's chain is broke at last,
> I'm going to praise God till I die.

I cannot now describe the joy of my soul at that time. This was indeed the third birthday to me:

> Born August 7th, 1836--a "Thing."
> Born again (John iii. 7), June, 1857--a Child of God.
> Born into human liberty, April 3rd, 1865--a Free Man.

No longer was I a mere chattel, but a man, free in body, free in soul; praise the Lord. It is impossible to give an adequate idea of the abounding joy of the people--the great multitude of liberated slaves--after the long years of toil and suffering. Strong men and women were weeping and praising God at the same time. Those who were not Christians exhibited their joy in other ways. They capered about and beat their banjos; some of them climbed up trees

38

and yelled out expressions of wild delight, and others made speeches to the crowds. That scene of years ago comes up vividly before me at this moment. The long night of affliction in the house of our bondage had passed, and that deeply desired and hoped for and prayed for time had come! The cries and groans and prayers of millions of poor and defenceless slaves, with the prayers of their friends in America, England, Ireland, Scotland, Wales, and everywhere, had reached the throne of God. Innocent blood of murdered men and women and children had cried unto God from the ground, and He in His own time, which is always the right time and best time, and in His own way, which is the very best way, answered that cry.

Progress

From August, 1620, to April, 1865--that is, for 245 years--our people had been in the school of adversity, and hundreds of thousands were but little removed from their native conditions as in Africa. Then the prison door of slavery was flung widely open to four and a half millions of slaves, who marched out with joy and rejoicing into the liberty which had been so unjustly denied them for so long; reminding us of Nahum's statement: "For now wilt I break his yoke from off thee, and will burst thy bonds in sunder." These liberated men and women began their work toward the amelioration of the condition of their race and the evangelization and help of Africa, the land of their fathers.

The Emancipation Proclamation sent forth from the pen of Abraham Lincoln, who eventually fell a martyr for American freedom, was the sublimest and most important State paper that had ever been sent out from the Executive Mansion at Washington to the American people. This legislative act elevated Lincoln above the high level of America's greatest statesman. He was a man eminently fitted for the supreme position which he occupied. He saw the peril of his country and knew that the important moment had come. In taking the strong, wise step which he did, he saved the country from ruin and disgrace, and, thank God, made over four million hearts to rejoice. And not only so, but this proclamation was the first step towards the evangelization of Africa by her own sons and daughters; for can we not trace a great work slowly, so slowly, but very, very surely, being accomplished. The coloured people are being Christianized and educated, and thousands are anxious to go to Africa to teach their own people, in the land of their fathers, the great truths they themselves had learnt; and I claim that none are more fitted for this work than Africa's own sons and daughters who are willing to return to their own country and people--the Ethiopian returning to Ethiopia. All will not return or desire to return to Africa. There are millions who are at "home as much as the white man" in America. Brought to the country against his will, the Negro has helped to make the country what it is. In the Revolution he fought side by side with the white man for the country's liberty, and for his own. When the Civil War broke out, coloured men in the Northern States offered their services. And when Abraham Lincoln issued his Proclamation, 150,000 Negroes were found in the army of the Union. Hence the feeling that they have a claim to be included in the Commonwealth of the nation. But there are many who long to go to Africa, the land of their fathers.

The First Wages of a Free Man

My first money received as a free man was earned in this way. A short time after the fall of Richmond, a Mr. Sterns gave General Weitzel and his officers a dinner, and he sent for me to take charge of this dinner. I felt confident that I could manage it, for not only for my master but for his friends also I had managed great dinners and other great social festivities. As already referred to, I had been hired out to wait in hotels, and thus I gained some experience. On one occasion Mr. Brent was offered three thousand dollars in gold for me by a gentleman who wanted me to take charge of his private house. The day of the feast to the General came on. I went to take up my duties. All necessary help was furnished. At the appointed hour all was ready. Wine flowed freely. I felt it a great honour to be waiting on a General and his staff who had so recently made so many hearts glad. As the evening came on, and I had seen to everything being put in its place and all cleared up, I began to think of what I should charge for my services, for the gentleman would be sure to ask me. I thought of how common labourers before the war were paid. I concluded that on such a scale two and a half dollars would be reasonable-- half a guinea. At last Mr. Sterns came in, praised my efforts, seemed perfectly satisfied, and gave me three "green-back" notes; and I thanked him. He also had a package of nuts and sweets put up for me, such as we had not seen for several years. When afterwards I looked at the notes, there were two twenty dollar notes and one ten dollar note--fifty dollars in all--ten guineas. My poor heart leaped for joy. I was soon home to tell my wife and mother of my good fortune, and they were greatly pleased.

Having a longing to acquire more knowledge and looking forward with the hope of doing something for Africa, my thoughts were now turned toward the North, and especially after the death of our little Albert, July, 1865, at the age of eleven months and nineteen days. Within three days after the death of our little boy my mother followed him. We took the little lifeless body down to show it to her and she simply said, "Waft on, my little grandson, grandma will follow you in a few days."

Through the kindness of Lieutenant George Browning, U. S. A., I was permitted to sail on one of the troopships from Richmond to New York. After two days and nights we landed in New York. A gentleman in Richmond had charged me to be very careful in New York. It was reported to be a very bad place, and that a pickpocket could take off a gentleman's vest in the street with watch and chain and all, and he would be unconscious of the robbery until he got home. I believed every word of the report at the time, and to fix the belief in my mind, the first thing that specially took my attention when we landed in New York was, "BEWARE OF PICKPOCKETS." This was a large sign across the Pier, and the same words were on several boards close to the gangway. I lost sight of everything else in my alarm, and I was wholly occupied in passing along in watching for a man robbing another man. After some officers and their friends were safely landed, the news came that the troops were ordered to Hart's Island to camp. I was permitted to go with them. I was much relieved indeed. Here I made up my mind to go to work. I would cook and wash for the soldiers, and do anything I could to make a little money. After gaining about forty dollars I resolved upon making an attempt to get to New York. Lieutenant Browning kindly gave me a letter of introduction to the Proprietor of the Leland Hotel, Broadway, N.Y. expressing a hope that he would give me a situation as waiter. But to me that introduction meant a very different thing from what it was really intended to be. I thought it was a warrant that I should stay at the hotel like a gentleman until I found work. I was quite happy under this delusion when I left Hart's Island. I shall never forget the feeling when going up to the ticket office to ask for a ticket for New York--a free man, no pass required.

New York

When I reached New York quite a number of cabmen-- "hackmen," we called them--got around me, which greatly surprised me. Then they began to cater for my patronage. "Mister, will you have a carriage, sir?" "Yes; do you know where Leland's Hotel is in the Broadway?" "Yes, sir," said several of the men. "Take me there," I said to one of them. All my belongings were in a small haversack across my shoulder. After driving some little while down a narrow street, with fine shops or stores, I commenced to think I had heard my owners talk very, much about "Broadway." "Broadway, New York." I had an idea that it was a broad way, about three or four times broader than Broad Street, Richmond. I called to the driver, "I thought I told you to take me to Broadway?" "Yer in Broadway," said he. "Can you read?" he added. "Yes, I can," I said. "Look on the gas lamp, thin." I did look, and I was greatly relieved to find that we were indeed in Broadway, There were two men on the "box" when I reached the hotel. I asked the first man the cost of the drive. I forget, now, whether it was three or four dollars. I was glad to pay him and ask no questions. I went into Leland's Hotel, and sent my letter into the Proprietor, and asked for a room; then, wishing to display my only accomplishment, I turned to the hotel book to enter my name. I noticed that the clerks, bell boys, and porters were all amused. Then a porter was called and was told to "take this gentleman to some respectable place where he can get lodgings." Oh, the feeling of disappointment. I cannot express it. It was most bitter. The porter soon made me feel comfortable when he told me of a Mr. Bruce, a

Christian gentleman, in Broom Street, who kept a boarding house. On going down Broom Street I asked the way to Mr. Bruce's boarding house, when I was very politely invited into a house and requested to take a rest and to tell all about the army. But I was doubtful about this proffered kindness, and I was anxious to find this "Boarding House." I could see at once that the people were New York sharpers. When I got to Bruce's boarding house I received a real hearty welcome and good advice. The idea prominent in my mind at this time was, to secure a situation in some store, and then to work all day and study hard each night, and thus get a start in the new life; keeping my eyes on the main thing, and that was to prepare myself for Africa. But failing to obtain a situation in any of the stores, even as an errand boy, I saw there was only one course open for me, and that was to become a waiter in an hotel or in a private family. I soon found there was as much prejudice against my race in New York as there was in the South. Eventually I returned to the great hotel as waiter, where I commenced work.

Truth Always the Best Policy

Some of the waiters came around and advised me as to the best way to get on. I was to be careful about concealing the fact that I came from the South. Some of the others were ashamed to say that they had ever been in slavery, and afraid of being called "contraband of war," so told me not to make known that I came from Virginia, but, on the contrary, to state that I had always been free. This was a great temptation. But God helped me to speak the truth, because it was the truth. And this I found to be the best thing to do under all circumstances. Shortly after the entrance upon duty at the hotel a gentleman arrived. He was directed to my table. He ordered what he wanted, and then while slowly eating his dinner, he asked for my name. I said, "My name is Thomas, sir." "Well, Thomas," said he, "where are you from?" "From Richmond, sir." "And who was your master?" "Mr. Brent, sir." "And what are you doing here?" "I am trying to make some money to get an education, sir." "And what do you want to be educated for?" "I want to be educated and to go to Africa to preach to my people, sir." "Well, Thomas," said he, "I am from the South too; I am from New Orleans." He then gave me his name and told me what he liked for dinner, breakfast, and for other times, an told me to have such things ready at the right time, and then he gave me a five dollar note. When the gentleman left then some of the advisers came up, eagerly asking: "What did he give you?" "A five dollar note." I said, "And what did you tell him?" "I told him I had been a slave in Richmond, Virginia, and that my intention was to get some education in order to go and preach to my people in Africa." It was thus in a wonderful way God raised up friends for me, who took a deep interest in me. Others gave me books, and in many ways showed me kindness. Some of the young men who advised me to hide my true history as a slave, when they saw that, in my case at least, the honest truth was the

42

best policy, began to parade their past with great freedom of detail, saying that they came from "Old Virginia," and had been slaves. But some of these men had been born freemen, and how they could tell a lie with the hope of gain I could not understand. He that builds upon falsehood will utterly and awfully fail and fall.

Another gentleman on whom I waited at my table wished me to leave the Hotel and take charge of his private house. I agreed, and he gave me money to send for my wife that she also might come to New York. That day was indeed a happy day for me. It brought great joy to my heart. I longed to have my wife with me, for she was a true helpmeet to me in every way. I at once sent for her to come to New York. The gentleman who engaged me, and also his wife and children, were very kind to us, and allowed my wife to come and stop with me. The lady of the house took a fancy to her, and this resulted in immediate arrangements being made for my wife to remain in the home.

Peculiar Circumstances

Keeping my strong purpose to the front, I sought to increase my knowledge and educate myself. But I was often perplexed over a number of formidable words which I had learned to repeat, without the remotest idea as to their meaning. While in slavery I would catch at every word that I heard the slave master use, and would repeat it over and over again until I had fixed it on my memory. It seemed to me that an education consisted in knowing how to write and say a lot of these big words such as "consequently," "jurisdiction;" "systematically," "diabolical," and others. As soon as I got hold of such words I would use them in talking to my friends without any regard to the meaning. My wife, who knew much more than I did, told me that there was a meaning to each word, and that I should not use them unless I knew what they meant. It was quite a difficult matter for me to give up the practice of using them on many occasions. One special term I used most indifferently was, "Flying Artillery." It got fixed in my mind, as my master's son belonged to that particular division in the army. On my way to New York I heard two gentlemen quietly talking in the railway carriage. One said, "And you see, I left under peculiar circumstances." This seemed to me such a beautiful phrase that I repeated it over and over, and making it even stronger, saying, "I left under very peculiar circumstances." Then came the question as to when I might use the words. At last the happy thought came: "I left," that's it. "I left Richmond under very peculiar circumstances." I wanted someone to ask me where I was from, so that I might have the opportunity of using these fine words. I had not long to wait, for a new acquaintance soon asked me the question: "Where are you from?" And I, with dignity of manner and with much dignity of diction, as I thought, answered: "I am from Richmond, Virginia; I left under peculiar circumstances." My questioner was curious enough to ask what the circumstances were, and I enlightened him, as I imag-

43

ined, by emphasising "very peculiar circumstances." When my wife joined me and heard me make such wild use of fine phrases, and in particular that I publicly declared that I had left Richmond under peculiar circumstances, she admonished me, saying, "Tom, you are continually telling people that you left Richmond "under peculiar circumstances." "Quite right," I said, "I heard two gentlemen on the train, and one said to the other that he had left under 'very peculiar circumstances,' and 'peculiar circumstances' is a very nice way of saying that you 'left.'" "But," said she, "what were the circumstances? People will naturally think that you have escaped from justice." "Is that what it means, Henrietta. Well, people may think so! I cannot explain how perplexed I was. I just felt that I should like to tell the people to whom I had used the expression that I had not left under peculiar circumstances. That was only one out of the many phrases that caused me regret. "Diabolical" was always a favourite word until I got to know the meaning of it.

First Public Speech

After some stay in New York I heard that there was to be a public meeting in what was known as the "Coloured Presbyterian Church," to select a delegate to go to Washington to appeal to congress for the "Freedman's right of suffrage." I decided to go, and as the appeal was made for money, I took a dollar with me for the collection. I felt deeply concerned about the condition of my people, and was most anxious to know of all that was being done for them or against them. When I entered the Church I beheld a sight which made my heart glad. There was quite a large company present, and there were white and coloured reporters at the large table, all busy at work. To see coloured men at this table taking down coloured men's speeches in short-hand, just like white men, and white men taking down the speeches of coloured men in a deliberative assembly, was indeed a very gratifying sight to me. I had never seen the like before. The Chairman of the meeting said that any gentleman was at liberty to speak who so desired; this subject concerned every coloured man. I thought, now is my time. Each one who spoke commenced with, "Ladies and Gentlemen." I listened attentively, but much was said that I could not understand. When some gentleman said something about the suffrage or the ballot-box, and the people clapped their hands, I clapped as lively and as heartily as anyone; yet what the ballot-box was I could not make out; as to the "suffrage" of the coloured man I was quite satisfied that I knew something of that subject, for I had "suffered" a good deal. I began to think of how I should commence my speech, and what I should say. It was every man's privilege to speak. When there came a lull in the meeting, my heart beat very fast, for I thought that now was my opportunity. But I must avoid repeating the formalities of the previous speakers. I sprang to my feet, but as I stood there before that company of people, many of whom were well educated, I trembled very much. I commenced: "M-i-s-t-e-r C-h-a-i-r-m-

44

a-n, G-e-n--G-e-n-t-l-e-m-e-n a-and L-a--L-a-d-i-e-s." Many clapped their hands and others laughed. All my good speech and fine words were gone. Then I gathered up all my strength for another effort, being not a little agitated on account of the laughing. When order was called and restored, then I proceeded: "I know what it is to suffer; I am one who suffered in Virginia" (Applause). This greatly helped me. My idea was that the delegate to congress was to tell how we suffered in slavery, and that the word "suffrage" meant that. "I quite agreed," I continued, "with all that was said about the ballot-box," feeling quite sure that they knew what was intended, and what that box was for, said: "I am willing to help to send Mr. Frederick Douglas to Washington--(applause)--and here is a dollar to help." This provoked great approval, and there was much clapping of hands and shaking of heads, which meant to me that the audience was pleased. My name was called for and taken to the reporter's table.

After the meeting, the late Mr. Charles Reason introduced himself to me. This gentleman was well known in New York, and was a great friend of the young men; also several other leading coloured men came and heartily shook me by the hand--no one-or-two-finger grip, but a real hand-shake that made me feel that, though ignorant and illiterate, I was among friends who respected me. All this was of the providence of God, who had promised to be with me.

In time this very meeting resulted in an invitation to meet the Committee and to help in making arrangements to receive Mr. Frederick Douglas. When I was in the Army I heard the young master say of an officer in the South that he had "immortalised" himself. I was anxious to know what that big word meant. I never heard it before, so my young master explained that the officer had gained a great victory during a campaign. Well, when I returned home from that meeting I made use of the big word to my wife, and declared with solemn dignity: "I have 'mortalised myself to-night." She said: "Tom don't tell anybody else that." I said that I really 'mortalised myself, for I had made a speech, and then explained all about it, but I never again mentioned the matter in the same terms to anyone else. The next morning the New York Times, in speaking of the meeting, noted a "speech by an ex-slave from Richmond-- T. L. Johnson." This meeting was a great help to me, indicating more forcibly than ever the necessity for stricter attention to study.

After this meeting, some young men, whom I met there and who seemed to be well-known, were very attentive to me, and finally invited me to a meeting to organise an "Industrial Association." I attended; speeches were made, and great attention was paid to what I had to say. Finally, the question came up as to how much a share should be, and as to how many shares there ought to be; and it was suggested that twenty-five or thirty dollars would at once help the work, a room could be rented, etc., and could any gentleman advance the money? I was appealed to. All eyes were turned to me. I could not quite understand the business, so concluded to wait awhile. The meeting then adjourned, after arranging the time and place of another such meeting, in order to hear from me. Meantime I saw a Christian gentleman, who advised me to have nothing to do with the young men and their plans. I saw the hand of God in this, guiding me safely.

It was in 1866 that this happened, and I have not called the meeting or notified the committee since that time. The gentleman and his wife and children where I was engaged were most kind to me, but I found it impossible to pursue my studies while with them, and I wanted a situation where I could have opportunity at stated times to study the Bible and follow other matters so as to make progress in my preparation for the great work which was laid upon my heart.

This gentleman was very wealthy. He did not approve of my studying with any such purpose as I had in view, and offered as a counter inducement that if I would remain with him five years he would send to Cuba for tobacco and set me up in business for myself in New York to manufacture cigars. This was generous indeed; but when I began to reckon that it would require a long period of years to get established in business, the matter did not commend itself to me; so I did not remain with him more than six months, Good openings to make money were not what I was seeking. I confess to lack of discretion, but my one controlling thought was about preaching the Gospel to my own people, and not in making money.

The Freedmen after the War

At the close of the War the question to be met was-- The destiny of the millions of coloured freedmen. "How did the freedmen manage to get on after the War?" is a frequent question. Just at that time our friends were perplexed to know what to do with us, liberated, as we were, without a penny to begin the new life. Thousands were homeless, and deprived of intellectual light and spiritual instruction, they were helplessly ignorant. But in the Northern States there were thousands of true-hearted Christians who, at the commencement of the War, had given their sons and millions of money, and true to freedom and the oppressed, these good people came to the front with their money, their time, their influence. Every branch of the Christian Church helped the poor freedmen. The Government established the Freedman's Bureau, of which General O. O. Howard was appointed superintendent. It furnished bread for the destitute, and found homes for the homeless, and established schools to instruct the ignorant. As doors of opportunity opened they went to work--thousands of them for their former masters, thousands for themselves; and many went into the Northern and Western States. Notwithstanding the prejudice which existed against them, and which still exists, to a great extent, at the present time, the coloured people have progressed in a measure unparalleled in the history of any race in similar circumstances. We find them to-day in every branch of industry, farmers, mechanics engineers, tradesmen, merchants, teachers, professors, doctors, lawyers; and some are occupying high positions in the Government institutions as clerks, mail agents, legislators, Members of Congress. But, above all, many who were once slaves have passed through colleges of the country and are now able ministers of the Gospel. The following will greatly help to show to sympathizers and friends of the Negro that he was worthy of all they did for him:--

"After the memorable Emancipation Proclamation by President Lincoln, and when recruiting officers were sent into every town and city wherever the United States troops had gained a footing, thousands of liberated slaves responded to the call and soon entered the Army; but they were not satisfied with being liberated, and engaged to fight for freedom, they desired to have mental training, and commenced at once to establish schools in camp in order to gain an education. Aside from the military duties required from the men forming the phalanx regiments, the school teacher was drilling and preparing them in the formation and use of letters and figures. In nearly every regiment a school was established during the encampments; and in some instances, female teachers from the North, impelled by the philanthropy which induced an army of teachers South to teach the freedmen, also brought them to the barracks and the camp ground to instruct the soldiers of the phalanx. Their ambition to learn to read and write was as strong as-their love for freedom, and no opportunity was lost by them to acquire a knowledge of letters. So ardent were they that they formed squads and hired teachers, paying them out of their pittance of seven dollars per month, or out of bounty paid to them by the State to which they were accredited. In a number of instances the officers themselves gave instructions to their commands, and made education a feature and a part of their duty, thereby bringing the soldier up to full comprehension of the responsibility of his trust. 'Taps' was an unpleasant sound to many a soldier, who, after the fatigue and drill of the day was over, sat himself down upon an empty cracker box with a short candle in one hand and a spelling book in the other, to study the 'ab, eb, ib, ob, ub'; when the truce was sounded after a day's or night's hard fighting many of these men renewed their courage by studying and reading in the New England Spelling Book. And where they had fought, and died where they fell, and their bodies left to the enemy's mercy, they often found in the dead soldier's knapsack a spelling book and a Testament."

Generally, there was one of three things the negro soldier could be found doing when at leisure—

"Discussing religion,"

"Cleaning his musket and accoutrements," or

"Trying to read."

See "History of the Black Phalanx," p. 504.

And in the London Daily Express of January 13th, 1903, we read:--

"Uncle Sam's is an awkward problem, no doubt; but there is no getting away from the fact that he has accomplished a great deal for fitting himself for intellectual equality. Within the space of a generation the negro has reduced his illiteracy 45 per cent., and he has to-day over a million and a half children in daily attendance at the elementary schools, and 40,000 students at the higher institutions. Thirty thousand negro teachers help the expansion of the young blacks' minds; while equipping themselves in classical, scientific, and business courses are 3,400 students. Besides these are 17,000 graduates. Their libraries possess over a quarter of a million volumes. They have 500 physicians of their own, and 250 lawyers. Three banks, and as many magazines, and no fewer than 400 newspapers are under 'black man' management. Since the war of emancipation these people have raised over two million pounds sterling for their education, and among their hundred and fifty institutions for higher education are academies whose curriculum challenges comparison with that of the very best of the white colleges."

Again, the London Daily Express of July 21st, 1903, suggests the equality of the negro with the white in matters of progress:--

"In the advance guard of the negro race stand men who are distinguishing themselves in every field of human activity; in business and commerce, in politics, in the learned professions, in literature and art; they prove themselves the equal of white men in almost every direction. Partial records of the United States Patent Office show that hundreds of patents have been granted to negroes covering all departments of mechanics. The Bell Telephone Company owe their transmitter to the invention of a black engineer, Granville T. Woods, whose electric controller system is that used on the Manhattan Elevated Railway. He has patented thirty-five important devices, including four kinds of telegraphing apparatus, four electric railway improvements, two electric brakes, a telephone system, a battery, and a tunnel construction for electric roads."

Thirty years ago a Virginian negro organized a Mutual Benefit Insurance Society in Richmond, with the modest capital of £30, and no more than a hundred members; to-day that same organization has 50,000 members and £50,000 in real estate. It has paid £400,000 in insurance claims, and has established a Bank, a Real Estate Company, a weekly newspaper, five grocery and general merchandise stores, an hotel, and an Old Folks Home. No signs of negro progress have been of such marked significance as the rise of the negro physician in the last ten years. A short time ago a black man was the best student of his class at the Harvard Medical School. During the meetings of the World's Baptist Congress held in Exeter Hall in July, 1905, a Daily Newsrepresentative interviewed Dr. B. Johnson to some length on the subject of black and white in America, as follows:--

Is The Negro Degenerate?

"What about the tales we hear of Negro degeneracy?" I asked Dr. Johnson, when I had enticed him from the platform to a more or less quiet nook downstairs. "Is it true that he is deteriorating, morally and industrially, that the race is depraved, losing all vitality, and gradually dying out?"

"All these charges which are so continually heard," said Dr. Johnson, "are without foundation. They can easily be disposed of by the official figures of the United States Government. There are ten million negroes in the United States, and of these four million, according to the last Census, are engaged in 'gainful' occupations. 'Gainful' is a technical word of the Census officials, denoting an occupation, such as that of a mechanic or an agriculturist, which directly contributes to the material wealth of the nation. The four products most important in the Southern States, where the negro population is greatest, are tobacco, cotton, rice, and sugar. All these are raised by negro labour exclusively, whether the negro works for himself or for a white man. The negro is the greatest agriculturist of the South; the whites neither could nor would do the labour of the fields. Thirty-nine per cent. of the whole cotton crop is raised by the negroes on their own land, and the other sixty-one per cent. is also raised by him on other people's farms. The fact that in little more than a single generation the negro has been able, beginning with nothing, to acquire two-fifths of the cotton land does not look like degeneracy. These figures show that he is industrious, and not lazy and shiftless. Three-fourths of the negro population live in the rural districts, and not in the towns."

In an interview of the London Daily Express reporter in July, 1905, with Dr. C. H. Parrish, a delegate to the World's Baptist Congress, we have set forth forty-years:--

"Uncle Tom As He Is Now."

"Think of what the coloured race have done in forty years," he said to me when I saw him yesterday. "Out of our penury we, who did not know the meaning of money, have contributed £2,800,000 for the education of our people. We have fully equipped 36,000 coloured teachers in the public schools, we have had 45,000 negro students in the high schools, 300,000 learning trades in the technical colleges, and 3,000 in the classical and scientific colleges. From my own school we have students who have taken high honours at the great American Universities of Harvard and Yale.

"We who had no property at all at the close of the War own to-day 160,000 farms, valued at £8,000,000. Our personal property is valued at £40,000,000, and we have bought up the mansions of the slave owners for our schools and colleges."

The Doctor paused in his forty years' statement of the triumphant progress of the coloured people. "We cannot forget," he said, "that there are 10,000,000 of us--nearly twice the population of London--and though our advance is remarkable, perhaps unequalled in the history of races, we have but laid the foundation work of our people."

The Afro-American students at the College at Cane Spring, of which the Doctor is President, have exactly the same curriculum as that in operation in the other public schools, and what is, perhaps, even more significant, the col-

49

oured girl is given the same educational facilities as the coloured boy. The Institute has its own printing office, its own blacksmith's shop, and its own laundry. The girls as well as the boys take Mathematics, Greek, Latin and French, Moral Science and the History of Philosophy. In the industrial department, the subjects include shorthand, typewriting, printing and proofreading, shoemaking, painting and paperhanging, carpentry, barbering, farming, and dairy work. Every girl student learns dressmaking, and she is also required to attend the household ethics classes, where the proper care of the home is taught.

Negro Achievements

Over 2.500,000 coloured children attend the public schools in America, but in most of the States, Kentucky among them, the coloured child is educated by coloured teachers in separate schools, as in the Eckstein Norton Institute. "The coloured man's cry is to know," said Dr. Parrish. "No race that has always known freedom can understand the negro passion for knowledge. I can recall many instances where mothers of the coloured race, who are only earning £1 15s. as cooks, have gone to untold sacrifices and given almost every penny of their wages so that they might send their daughters to my College." "To-day we see the first results of the negro craze for higher education. Negro doctors, lawyers, clergymen, and men of science are rising up among us, and the women are taking their part in this forward movement. In my own town there are two lady doctors. Miss Nannie Burrows, a coloured graduate from one of the highest schools of Washington, and a well-known public speaker, is in London now. In art and literature it is the same. Mrs. J. E. Givens, a coloured artist, has painted pictures for some of the best people in America. We have our poets and historians. A Greek dictionary that is being used in the white schools and colleges of the South land has been compiled by one of us. Three history books are used in the white schools of Alabama; two are written by whites and the third by a negro."

Perhaps Dr. Parrish, though he is regarded as a conservative by the coloured progressives, is optimistic, but he reads in this forty years' work signs that the day is drawing near when the barrier of colour will be broken down and the white and black races in America will have social and civil equality. Dr. Parrish, whom I have known for many years, may be regarded as the foremost authority in matters affecting the negro race.

A Negro Poet

The London Daily Express of February 12th, 1906, records the death of a negro poet, a slave's son who was famous in literature, as follows:--

50

"New York, Sunday, February 11th--Paul Lawrence Dunbar, the negro poet, died yesterday at Dayton, Ohio, from consumption, at the age of thirty-four years. Paul Lawrence Dunbar had great gifts of writing, both in literary English and in the negro dialect, though he excelled in the latter form. He was the son of slave parents of pure African blood, and his mother, who ardently loved literature, did much to encourage his poetic tendencies. His first literary efforts appeared in the magazines of the public schools before he was twelve years old. Then he obtained work as an elevator boy at Dayton, and made such good use of his spare time that he graduated at the local high school at the age of nineteen. He subsequently did work on newspapers, and produced many poems and several novels. His second book, 'Majors and Minors,' produced in 1895, and warmly appreciated by Mr. W. D. Howells, brought him prominently before the public. One of the best known of his poems is 'When Malindy Sings':--

"Let me listen, I can hyeah it,
Th'oo de bresh of angels' wings,
Sof' an'sweet--'Swing low, sweet chariot'--
As Malindy sings.

Y' ought to hyeah dat gal a-wa'bling--
Robins, la'ks, an' all dem tings,
Hush dey mouths an' hides dey faces,
As Malindy sings."

It will be seen by the foregoing statement that the thirst for knowledge amongst the coloured people was strong, and their capacity to receive instruction and the ability to take their place with the most advanced in all technical trades have now been abundantly proved, and admitted. And it is hoped that soon mere colour will constitute no barrier to equality in any domain of the civic and national life of the country, when no other barrier exists."

"The Tribune," Thursday, October 17th, 1907.

"Lord Rosebery presided last night during an address with which Mr. Andrew Carnegie inaugurated the winter lecture season of the Philosophical Institution in Edinburgh. The audience was so large that accommodation had to be sought in the United Free Assembly Hall. Among those present were the Lord Provost, Lord Ardwell, Sir William Turner, Principal of Edinburgh University, the Lord Advocate, Mr. George McCrae, M. P., Mr. Rufus Fleming (United States Consul), and Mr. Charles Price, M. P.

"Mr. Carnegie chose as the subject of his address, 'The Negro Problem.' Dealing, as he said, with ten millions of people, he traced the slow development of their fathers from slaves into citizens, their rapid growth in numbers, their gradual decrease in illiteracy, and their general inclusion in

51

Church organizations. He cited evidence of the enormous sums spent by the negroes in the Southern States in the building of churches, colleges, and schools.

"Figures were also given showing that the negro was a saving man, that the land hunger had seized him, and that he was entering freely into the landlord class. There was no better test, Mr. Carnegie observed, of a respectable member of society than the production of a bank-book with a good balance or the title-deeds of a house or farm free from debt. He controverted the notion that the negro was lazy, and he showed that, on the contrary, the race was engaged in every field of human activity, even that of the newspaper press.

"The question, he said, used to be: What can be done with the negroes? The question now was: How can more of them and of other workers be obtained? The negro had become of immense economic value, and was indispensable where he was. (Cheers.) He was sanguine that at last there would be a respectable, educated, intelligent race of coloured citizens."

Passing on now to my personal story. In the summer of 1866, I was offered a situation at "Rocky Point," R.I., a summer resort. Here I met Mr. H. M. Kinsley, of Chicago. He engaged the chief steward to go to Chicago to take charge of his restaurant in Crosby's Opera House. The steward desired me to go with him as the second steward.

Not having succeeded, as I had hoped, in New York, my mind was now turned towards "the Great West," and at the close of the season at Rocky Point, I returned to New York, and at once commenced to prepare for the journey West. My wife was anxious to find out something about her people. We had published our enquiries about them in the papers but received no intelligence of them. When my wife was about nine years old, and living with her owners in Georgetown, Maryland, a "Georgia Trader" drove up to the door one morning and called her. That morning her master had gone from the breakfast table and sold her. In a few minutes she was off to the "Slave-Traders' Pen." At the time she left there were seventeen children, and her father and mother.

Just before I left for the West my wife went to Washington, where she found that her father and mother had left long before for the Better Land, the Land of Eternal Freedom. Ten sisters and brothers were still living; Mrs. Richardson, wife of the late Rev. C. H. Richardson, who went with us to Africa, was the youngest sister.

It was in September, 1866, I left for Chicago in company with the chief steward and three young men who had been booked for the Far West. On arriving in Chicago I found that there had been a misunderstanding between the proprietor and the chief steward he then had as to the time for leaving off, and other matters, details of which may not be entered upon. Suffice it to say that I was again disappointed, as I had been in New York in my own plans and expectations. It had cost me quite a sum of money to travel from New York to Chicago, and now to be disappointed and amongst strangers, and with but little money, I was greatly discouraged. And yet when I now look back upon that time I am brought to think of Mrs. Soole, of Reading, who wrote those beautiful lines on disappointment, taking off the "Dis," and substituting "His," thus making it "His appointment." Let us ever praise God for His Appointments. The Hand of God was with me.

Soon after arriving in Chicago I enquired about the places of worship. I found there were meetings held in a hall in Clark Street, and attending there, I met the Rev. R. de Baptiste, Pastor of Olivet Baptist Church, which was known as a "coloured Church." Nearly all the members were freedmen from some part of the South, including one man from my old home at Richmond. Here amongst strangers, and hundreds of miles away from old Virginia, in a country new to me, with new faces all around me, and new customs and modes of living, I was led to consecrate myself more fully to the Lord and His work, and to study hard in order to qualify myself for the future.

After a short time the way opened up in the matter of employment, and I engaged in the restaurant, not as second steward, but downstairs in the pantry full charge of that department. There were four or five girls kept in this pantry to wash the dishes, and I had to see that each girl was in her place during meal time, and that she kept the dishes clean, and to keep a strict account of all dishes broken and other things in connection with that particular branch. I was not very popular amongst the girls. In very busy times I was obliged to help. I did not object to take charge of the pantry, though I had travelled so far--some eight hundred miles--for the better place. Time was money to me, and while I would be waiting for something better to turn up, my board bill would be going up also, with less chance of keeping it down. I gladly accepted the position, and said nothing about what I could do or had done, but just settled to work and did the best I could in the situation I had taken, and never losing sight of Him who gave me freedom of both soul and body, and who was still guiding me.

Between times I had to do odd jobs and one day I had to sweep the side walk, when a grand carriage drove up. A lady got out and entered the restaurant to give an order, for "Kinsley's" was the leading caterer of Chicago. As I kept on sweeping, and came close to the coachman, a coloured man, I asked him if he were a Christian. He could not give a satisfactory answer, and as I continued sweeping, never looking up, I pressed home the message of Truth upon the man. Thirteen years after this, and after I had been to Africa and returned again to America, I met this same man in Baltimore at a friend's house. He had been to the missionary meeting, where I had been speaking, and came on to the house to see me, when he told me of the good effect of that little talk while I was busy sweeping and he stood waiting. This was a lesson for me that I should lose no opportunity of speaking for my Blessed Jesus.

I continued to attend to the pantry work, when one day I was called upon, in the rush of business, to come up into the large dining room to help. I had an opportunity now of using what knowledge I possessed of "waiting," and I

53

availed myself of it. I had taught myself how to fold napkins to almost every letter of the alphabet, and could fold them in sixty different ways. Here was an opportunity of going forward by being right and doing right. Above all I desired to honour God. Now Mr. Kinsley would sometimes scold the men sharply, and they would take offence and leave. I could not do that. He had the money and prestige, and I had neither. I was his servant while he paid me, and to be suddenly offended and leave would be like "cutting off my nose to spite my face." No, I would not do that. And when he scolded I would just say: "All right, Mr. Kinsley, I will attend to that, sir." When the bell rang for one watch to go off, and the other to come on, I noticed that men hurried off at once, but I was in no hurry, and always saw that all was right at my table, and if a lady or gentleman were at my table I remained with them. Before going off duty I would enquire if I were wanted longer. I knew how I had pleased the slave-master. I endeavoured to show that I had an interest in all I had to do. The master and his family became friendly with me. I lodged in the same house where the chief steward and several of the waiters lodged. They used to play cards, bet, and drink, and go to the theatre. I would talk to them continually. The time came when they showed respect for me, if not for my Lord, by abstaining from swearing in my presence. In a short time the way opened for me to still further improve my position by attending to gentlemen's offices, going in the early morning and cleaning them up, and lighting the fires, and doing other little things. For this kind of work I received more money and had much less to do, and had more time for study, for I had every evening to myself, and each day from ten or eleven in the morning till four or five in the afternoon, and the whole of Sunday. But after a while I found it very trying. The weather was very cold in the winter in Chicago, and I had to be up on winter mornings at six o'clock. One morning, when the snow was about a foot deep, as I went down the street, when it was yet dark, I became very cold and sleepy. I felt that I must give up. I could not endure it, and so I went into a doorway and there prayed, and I made an effort, and the Lord helped me to get to one of the offices. What a privilege to carry everything to God in prayer. About this time I lived at the cost of one meal a day in trying to save money to send for my wife. My methods of economy in this way would be to buy a pound of "Oyster Crackers"; the cracker was as broad as a shilling, and was sold at five cents a pound. I would take a half-pound for my breakfast, and the other half-pound I reserved for my supper with a drink of water. At noon I went to Mr. Wright's restaurant in Clark Street, where I was allowed to wait from twelve till half-past one o'clock and thus earn my dinner. So my food cost me two-pence half-penny a day through the week; but on Sunday I had three meals in the house where I lodged. This I did throughout the winter, and when I had saved enough money I sent for my wife.

Mr. Kinsley, of the Crosby's Opera House, referred to, had the lunch room at the C. B. and Q. Railway Station. One day the man who was in charge of this department left, and Mr. Kinsinn sent for me to take over the duties at once. I agreed to go, and he gave me full control. Here I took in from £1 to £10 and

£15 a day, and made my report each evening. For this work I received twelve dollars a week and board, and had every Sunday free. When Mr. Kinsley built a new place he requested me to take the place of chief steward. This offer I accepted,

At this time the responsibilities of chief steward were very great. I had not only to see after the work in the restaurant, but to the setting of the tables at gentlemen's houses, at weddings and great suppers. When the Union Pacific Railroad was being laid, the company frequently had excursions, parties of the officials, and others, when Mr. Kinsley catered for them, and I had to attend. I remember that on one occasion a large company of editors left Chicago on an excursion over the Union Pacific Railroad, and when this company dined I had the oversight of the business, and to look after twenty-seven helpers besides the two cooks.

At this time the Lord was so manifestly gracious to me, and gave me many friends. On these occasions, as a rule, Mr. Pullman would furnish his fine palace cars. It was during these trips that I became acquainted with Mr. Pullman, and his brother Mr. Albert Pullman, both of whom were very kind friends to me; and the friendship of these gentlemen, and of Mr. Perry Smith, Mr. George Dunlop, Mr. Norman Williams, and the Hon. Robert Lincoln, will never be forgotten, and the practical sympathy of Mr. and Mrs. E. S. Ishan, of Chicago, will always be remembered with gratitude. These friends, with many others, can never know how they made the heart of a poor ex-slave rejoice. What they did for me seemed small to them no doubt, but to me it was very, very great, and for it I still praise God.

During all this time I continued my studies, the chief of which were in the Bible, in which I learned to spell. This was a great help to me when I began to do a little home mission work under the late Rev. R. de Baptiste, D. D., who, from the time of my meeting with him, when I first went to Chicago until I left the country, was a genuine friend to me. After I was called upon to speak at some meeting I would commence to prepare for another so as to be ready for when I had spoken at a meeting I always felt that I had told all I knew. my first attempt to speak was in Rev. R. de Baptiste's Church. It was from him I received my "License to Preach"--credentials showing what church one is a member of, and is in good standing with, and has satisfied the church that he is sound in the faith.

Resigning To Enter Mission Work

The thought of giving up work and of preparing for the ministry led to much prayerful consideration. The continual hard work day and night was telling on me, and it left me no time for study, and to prepare myself for my life work. At length I decided to leave the matter entirely in the Lord's hands, and I resigned my position as chief steward. Mr. Kinsley was not at all favourable to this, but I was fully persuaded in my own mind now that my life work was to preach the Gospel. Mr. Kinsley promised that he would always be a friend to me, and should I find that I could not get on, well, I could come back again, and there would be a situation for me.

Before fully entering upon mission work among my own people, three great temptations presented themselves. First: Before I resigned, a gentleman who had been a real practical friend to me in illness and in health, had a very special talk with me for an hour or so with the distinct idea of dissuading me from the purpose of giving up my employment and entering the ministry. He said that "God thought most of the man who looked after himself." On looking at this gentleman's prosperous business, and his great success, had I indulged the thought I might have yielded, but my Blessed Jesus helped me, and kept my mind stayed on Him, and the call I felt in my soul was a call from God. This gentleman added that religion was a thing for women only.

After leaving Mr. Kinsley's I commenced to look about for odd jobs to save, by earning something, what little I had collected, and to prepare as best I could for the work before me. Mr. Kinsley and others would pay me from two to five dollars a night, either to take charge of or to assist at parties and great suppers; to set and decorate the tables, which I took great pride in doing, and as I found that Mr. Kinsley and many of the guests were pleased with.

The second temptation was: Mr. Kinsley's pastry cook, a German, who was well up in all cooking, made me the following offer:--That if I would select a place where we could have a first-class restaurant or lunch-room for gentlemen, with first-class catering, he would furnish the money. We could have a private agreement and I should be full till partner for the use of my name, which would be printed over the establishment as "THOMAS'S RESTAURANT." I could then take full charge and management, and he would see to all the cooking, both in kitchen and pastry room. Here was an offer of full management, and equal partnership without having a shilling to advance. But this I also declined.

The third temptation was: That when out taking charge of a large party one night, and the table was set and all was ready for the guests, I observed in the hearing of a gentleman that I wished I had the value of all that was on the table. The table was heavily laden with valuable silver. This well-known gentleman said: "Well, what would you do with it?" I replied that I would open a first class lunch stand. He said: "I will set you up in business if you like, and let you have five hundred or a thousand dollars to commence with, for you deserve it." This matter had been talked over between a friend of mine and myself. This offer was very tempting indeed. The idea I had was to open a lunch stand in a locality where I could reach the wealthy merchants who knew me as "Thomas," and work on for three or four years, during which time I could meet all expenses, and have something when I commenced my studies in earnest; and then my friend who would be partner with me would take over my share and pay me for it. This was about settled upon. We both knew influential gentlemen who would patronize us and influence their friends to do so. My Pastor, the Rev. R. de Baptiste, D. D., thought well of it. I

56

went and succeeded in finding a suitable place, which was offered at a reasonable price. Here I would have every afternoon and evening, and every Sunday--all day--for myself, and yet be making more money than ever before in my life; and with none of the great responsibilities of large suppers and parties and be continually on the move, as would have been the case had I accepted the other offer referred to. Before sealing the bargain I went to see the gentleman to enquire if he would confirm what he said at the great party. He repeated his offer and said that I deserved it. Before signing papers for a lease, Rev. de Baptiste called to see me with a letter from the members of a little Church in Denver, Colorado Territory. Three or four of the members of his church had settled at Denver. There were about eight thousand people in Denver at the time, only seventy-five being "coloured" people. They wrote the Rev. de Baptiste to do what he could to help them, to get some one to come out West and take charge of this little mission. As soon as he received the letter he thought of me; and a conversation followed. The cost to go to Denver in those days was seventy-five dollars. Mr. de Baptiste said that the cost would be met for me, and he was sure that another seventy-five dollars could be raised for Mrs. Johnson.

Entering the Pastorate

He considered that it would be a good start for me; and I could go into that new country, take charge of that little church, and have an opportunity for study and self-improvement, and to find out by experience my personal needs for equipment, and for a course of study. He said that I might have a rough time of it, but that in the end the experience would prove invaluable. But he put the alternative to me, and said that if I preferred to enter business for myself, and after four or five years found that I had enough on which to comfortably pursue my studies, then he would advise me to do so. This was a testing time. What should I do? While he left me to my own choice, I could see that Mr. de Baptiste would rather I went to Denver. This helped me. My heart was in the work. At that time, however, I averaged in earnings seventy-five dollars a month. All these, with the offer to set up in the cigar business in New York as referred to, were very strong, and would certainly have prevailed, had not the stronger claim of the Lord's work, with my deep love for it asserted itself. The mission in Denver sent word that it could only raise twenty-five dollars a month for me; but the financial consideration was a minor one; here was an opportunity to speak to my people of the love of Jesus. Finally, I decided to go to Denver, and let every other idea or prospect pass, trusting God for the future. I told Mr. de Baptiste of my decision, and he at once communicated with the brethren of the little Mission Church at Denver, of only nine members, to let the people know. At first they wanted a single young man, but acting on the advice of Mr. de Baptiste that point was set aside. In due time a reply came enclosing money for my expenses. Soon another difficulty presented itself, and which seemed altogether against me. At the monthly business meeting of the church a brother proposed, that, before sending me to Denver to take charge of this Mission Church, a Council be called respecting my ordination. I was present at the meeting. This came as a great shock to me; being unfortunately without an education. How could I pass a Council? Moreover, my friend the Pastor, made no objection to this course, and the motion was put and carried. I cannot now describe the feelings I had at the time; and I confess that I was greatly vexed with the brother who made the proposition calling a Council, and I was under the impression that he did not want me to go to Denver. But I afterwards found out that it was the very best thing for me that such a course was pursued.

God's Hand

The reasons for calling this Council were fourfold; first, to satisfy the church that I was sound in the faith, and held the fundamental truths of the Bible; second, that when I took charge of the mission that I might then baptize converts; third, that I might feel called to administer the Lord's supper; and, fourth, to be able to officiate at, marriage ceremonies. Only ordained ministers were permitted these official duties of the church. On the motion being carried the Pastor was authorized to call a Council of all the "white" Baptist Churches in Chicago to examine me for ordination. It was understood that the examination was on Biblical and not on secular lines. In those days there were thousands of our people who preferred an illiterate man of their own race, who was known to be true to the Evangelical faith, to a white man. The Council was fixed for the 15th April, 1869. After a talk with the Rev. de Baptiste, who gave me an idea of the nature of the examination, I gave up all work of a manual character, and for fifteen days gave myself to prayer and the study of the Word of God. I would leave home and go to Lake Michigan, and walk up and down by the lake unobserved, praying and reading. Oh, it was then that I had some wonderful times with my Blessed Jesus. The day arrived when I was to be examined. Quite a company of people gathered at the church, and there were seven or eight "white" ministers, and two "coloured" ministers present. I was first asked where I came from; but while I told them that I came from Richmond I took care not to add this time that "I left under peculiar circumstances." I told the Council of my conversion, and then had to answer questions about the truths of the Bible. Many of the questions had to be simplified by the Chairman before I could understand them. I was on my feet before that Council for over an hour. In the end I was asked what course I intended to pursue if the Council did not see fit to ordain me. I replied that I would just go on studying with a view of preparing for another examination, and that if I should fail again I would make another effort, and so continue until I succeeded; for I was thoroughly convinced that God wanted me to preach the Gospel. I was then requested to retire into the vestry. As

I sat there alone it was an anxious ten or fifteen minutes for me. I was re-called and was then informed by the Chairman, the Rev. Dr. Taylor, of the Union Park Baptist Church, that he was glad to tell me that the Council was satisfied that I was called of God to preach the Gospel, and that in the evening I should be ordained. When the evening came there was a very great compa-ny, and many white friends were present. The sermon was preached by Dr. Taylor from Proverbs xi. 30,-- "He that winneth souls is wise." I was after-wards solemnly set apart for the ministry.

Soon preparations were made for my journey to Denver. Through the in-fluence of Dr. Blackall, of the Bible Publication Society, of Chicago (now in Philadelphia), many valuable books were sent me, which proved a great help to me indeed. Several farewell meetings were held, when God raised up many friends, and soon all the necessary money to meet the expenses of my wife's journey was raised. The railroad officials were considerate in allowing reduced rates. In those days--forty years ago--there were no fast trains, such as we have to-day. We departed for Denver in the month of May. Our first stop was at Omaha, the next at Cheyenne, Wyoming Territory. Here we met some friends. After a short stay we took the overland stagecoach for Denver City, Colorado Territory, at eight o'clock on Saturday morning. It was a beau-tiful May morning. Soon we were out of sight of everything indicating human habitation, and there was neither house nor similar object to be seen, noth-ing but great stretches of prairie, giving one the idea of being on the high seas in a sailing vessel. There was not a bush or house for miles, nothing but prai-rie grass, and not much of that in places. Once in a while we would come to what was called "Dog Town," where there were hundreds of little prairie dogs, a little larger than a guinea pig, with their little heads peeping out over a little mound which concealed the body. They barked something like a dog. The little mounds which formed their fortress were like the mole-hills we see in England, only just a little larger. Occasionally a drove of antelopes would be seen. The antelope was very plentiful in those days. Late in the evening you would see a herd of buffaloes. There were hotels on the way, where the passengers could get their meals, and where the horses were changed. After this long journey, continuing all through Saturday and Saturday night, we arrived at Denver on Sunday morning at eight o'clock, having travelled one hundred and ten miles. On our arrival in Denver City we were made very happy by the hearty welcome we received. The stage coach ran on to the post office, deposited the mail, for which many were anxiously waiting, then went on to the house of one of the officers of the church, who was to be our host. Here we met some very old friends, who had been kind to me when I first arrived in Chicago as a stranger. Soon we felt quite at home. But at that time my most serious thought was concerning the beginning of my pastorate, and the conducting of the services as a pastor. This was all new to me. Rev. de Baptiste, my pastor, had kindly given me some valuable hints with regard to my special duties, and after a short service in the afternoon at the Sunday School, and a service in the evening, I felt greatly relieved.

Work In Denver

On having a sight of Denver City I was greatly impressed with the place. From it there was a commanding view of the Rocky Mountains, with their peaks white with snow, which remained on them during the hottest time of the year. To-day, Denver, Capital of Colorado, has a population of largely over one hundred and forty thousand. The view from Denver for many miles around was simply magnificent. The great mountain range seemed only a few miles away, but this was deceptive, as the distance was twenty miles. Had I taken note of all that I heard and saw during that first week in Denver, I could fill many pages which might interest one about the town. A gentleman travelling in the country went out one morning from Denver for a walk. He purposed going to the Rocky Mountains and back before breakfast. After several hours' walk the mountains seemed as far off as ever, and at length he decided to give up the business and return to his hotel like a wise man. But many thousands of young people are just like that gentleman, deluded regarding distant though apparently near and delightful things, but some have not the same sense to return until it is too late.

In the days to which we are now referring, lynch-law was recognised. I was taken to a bridge across a small stream--I think the stream was called "Clear Creek"--I was shown a spot where a man had been hanged for stealing. The affair only happened a short time before our arrival at Denver. I was quite shocked at the information, but I was told that this kind of thing was in the hands of a Committee, and that life and property were quite safe.

The second Sunday after our arrival at Denver I gave notice that I would preach an introductory sermon. My text was Acts x. 29. I will not attempt to tell what I said and how I said it when preaching that sermon, nor can I estimate what illumination my hearers enjoyed, but I do remember that years after that particular deliverance, when Mr. Hind Smith sent for me to come to England, I set fire to a large bundle of old sermons and notes; and I do know this, for I was a witness, that at least the blaze of that conflagration gave considerable light that day. One thing, however, I endeavoured to impress upon the people in that sermon was that I wanted to know nothing, and I was going to teach and preach nothing, but Jesus Christ.

As time went on I was greatly encouraged when I found that the members of the church were pleased and helped by my services in the Gospel. My constant study was the Bible; I was anxious to keep close to God's Word, and to so preach that all I said could be sustained by the Scriptures. For a month or more the old subjects I preached from before I went to Denver were a great help to me, and no one there had heard them before except myself, and my wife. The time came, however, when fresh subjects had to be found. Then a struggle began. I shall never forget the help I received at that time from the study of the conversion of Paul, taking as a text, "Behold he prayeth," Acts ix., II. Step by step I was led to see more and more the necessity of prayer, as I read and re-read the life of the great Apostle and the record of his sufferings and service.

Another great help to me was a little pamphlet which came in the collection of books referred to, and which was sent to me from the Bible Publication Society; it was called the "Preachers' Prayer." It was an address given by the late Rev. C. H. Spurgeon to his students. This just suited me. It told me that if I wished to reap in the pulpit I must plough in the closet. The preacher must go from prayer to the pulpit. I remember that no book that I possessed at the time, apart from the Bible, gave me such assistance. Although I had prayed over my addresses before this, yet I had not seen the matter in the same light as this little book put it. I had the great pleasure of showing this little book to Mr. Spurgeon afterwards. Oh, how often since then have I felt the presence of my blessed Jesus with me when I have gone from prayer to the pulpit. To my great regret I lost this little book in Africa. I had read the book many times, and often used many of the expressions found in it. And our Father God alone knows how the book helped and inspired me. It was an American edition. A gentleman gave me a book of Mr. Spurgeon's sermons in which I found so many and valuable and helpful truths set forth so beautifully. I remember that the Rev. de Baptiste told me that I should be careful not to plagiarise. After getting an explanation of this wonderful word I began to be careful. But what I read so got hold of me that it was always the very thing I wanted my people to hear, and know, and do. So the only way to avoid the doom of the big word "Plagiarism" was to repeat continually, "and Mr. Spurgeon says" --and "again Mr. Spurgeon says.' I would lay the book aside, but would again ask it a question under some text, when "again Mr. Spurgeon said." At length I gave this book to a young preacher who was called on to go and preach for some church. He told me afterwards that he took the book of sermons with him, and after he had read the lessons, and conducted the other preliminary portions of the service, he took this book, opened it, laid it on the Bible, and preached Mr. Spurgeon's sermon from the text, Romans viii. 7. The people, of course, were greatly delighted with the sermon. The reason for my parting with this volume was chiefly that I could not think of anything else when it was near me, and when I read it the statements there would not part with me, and I could not part with them, and I just went on quoting Mr. Spurgeon.

On some occasions nearly all the coloured people in Denver would be at the service. There were at that time only seventy-five coloured people in Denver. There were very few who were well-to-do. The little company of nine members had made a great effort to get me out there by raising seventy-five dollars to meet my expenses, and they were anxious to do all they could to help me. The collections were generally small. One of the members allowed me to live in one of his houses rent free for six months or more. This house rented at twenty-five dollars a month. That was the amount the Mission promised to pay me per month. The work commenced and steadily went on both in the Mission and in the Sabbath School. The first person I baptized and received into the Church was my wife, who was indeed a great help to me in my work; in perfect sympathy with me she would daily read her Bible, then we would talk over the subject or chapter together. In addition to this we continued reading the Bible through in consecutive order. In those days I had a retentive memory and could keep a subject in my mind much better then than I can to-day. I would ask those in the Church who had been more favoured with educational advantages than myself to take note of all my mistakes in references or pronunciation. Some one gave me a book on Analogy. I tried to read it, though much of it was too deep for me. But I got to know the meaning of the word, or what I thought to be the meaning of the word, and then on one occasion I used the word in this way: "Now don't you see the an-a-log-y," making a syllable do for a word. I saw my friend the remembrancer putting down something. I felt that I had once more blundered. On the Monday morning he called to explain the matter and to give the pronunciation. At a Sunday evening service a "white" gentleman and two ladies--also "white"--came in. They were strangers to me, and it was an unusual thing for "white" friends to attend our Mission services. I felt a little nervous. I read for a lesson Acts xxvi. the "Agrippa" chapter, making a few remarks on verse 24, and Paul's reply in verse 25. Coming to verse 28 I spoke of the effect the Gospel had on the two men. In reading the verse I said: "Almost thou per-su-a-dest me to be a Christian." I could see my faithful friend jotting down something. This quite upset me; yet I persisted in repeating the mistake: "Yes, yes, Paul, almost thou per-su-a-dest me to be a Christian." I was greatly perplexed when my friend told me of my mistake, which I kept on repeating. The white gentleman present at the service was a minister from the mountain side, and at the close of the service he invited me to his church to preach for him, and to tell the story of my life. I received a very hearty welcome when I visited his people.

Ministerial Experiences

Soon I began to see that I could not live on twenty-five dollars a month; and I commenced to look for work. I soon found odd jobs to do, for I could turn my hand to many things; besides gardening and house-cleaning I assisted in bill-posting in the night when many people would be asleep. An influential gentleman who took a deep interest in me and became a personal friend, had a talk with me respecting my becoming a teacher in the coloured school. The question of allowing the coloured children to attend the public schools with the white children was being discussed at the time. This gentleman thought it would be a great help to me. I could meet all my expenses by this additional means of income and have more time for study. The School Board would pay me seventy-five dollars a month, which with the twenty-five dollars I received from the church, would be 100 dollars per month; and then the School Board would rent the Church Buildings for the coloured School and pay my officers fifty dollars a month. This was very tempting. But I reminded him that I was not educated, and could not pass the examination. He got me to read before him. He told me that I read nicely; and that I could undertake the duties for a while. They would see to it that I passed all right. He felt sure that my own people would be perfectly satisfied; and then in a few words he assured me that if I would accept the position I should pass all right. I was doing work for this gentleman at the time. After I had thought over the matter for a while, I refused to accept the position on principle, first, because this money which would be paid me would be paid by the State for the education of children of the State, and in selecting teachers for the schools of the white children they had to pass a rigid examination. This was the law for the coloured as well as for the white teachers; and it stands the same to-day. Second, my idea was that the coloured children should have as good teachers as the white children; third, I did not consider myself sufficiently advanced to understand even the first grade, as I had never taken a course myself. His argument was, teach them what you know for a while. I knew a young coloured man who had all the advantages of education and was a scholar, whom I recommended. He came before the Board and passed satisfactorily, and was appointed.

I had not been long in Denver before I saw, as Rev. de Baptiste told me I would, that which I needed most was a thorough course of study. I commenced to gather all the information I could about Colorado Territory, its possibilities, its gold and silver mines, and other mineral stores. I read up its history as best I could from books lent me by the ex-Governor Gilpin who was kind in imparting to me much useful information; he having been, if not the first, at least one of the earliest governors of the territory. My intention was to get up a lecture, and to go back into the States to deliver it, and to raise money to pay my way into college, and take a regular course. I had not set my time, neither did I know how to get the money to meet expenses at home while I should be away. During this time a company of Eastern gentlemen came to Denver. Mr. Pullman furnished them with his fine palace cars. When I met him he gave me a hearty hand-shake, and asked after my health and the Church. I told him I should like to go back with him; and he invited me to return with the company. I took him at his word and arrangements were soon made, and I journeyed all the way from Denver to New York. The railroad had been laid to Denver by this time. My passage and food for the whole journey were free. I went to Washington and there made enquiries respecting the prospects of entering some College--Howard University or some other college. After gathering all the information I could I commenced to lecture on "Colorado Territory," At this time I made slow progress.

I well remember going to see the late Mr. D. L. Moody in Chicago, seeking his aid in helping me to get Farwell Hall, which stood in those days to Chicago what Exeter Hall long did to London, with its Y. M. C. A.and kindred associations. He sent me to Mr. Revell, who let me have the lower hall very reasonably. Here I gave my lecture, which was extensively published. The few I had to hear me appeared to greatly appreciate the lecture, but I was greatly, very greatly disappointed. A subject such as 'On Colorado Territory," and given in Farwell Hall--that was enough--never mind the man. But then, too, I had been well-known in Chicago; but the night was cold, and the wind blew, and the snow seemed to come from every point of the compass.

It became clear to me that merely meeting expenses and losing time were not the roads to an education such as I required. I resolved to return to Denver. I was taken very ill on the way; and after my arrival at home I went to bed and for quite a while it was thought that I would not be able to get up again. For many weeks I was unable to attend the Mission work. But God was pleased to raise me up, and I commenced afresh to prepare for the future. My one thought was that one day I must go to Africa, the land of my fathers, to preach the Gospel to my long-benighted people. Many of my friends became greatly interested in all I could tell them of Africa.

The congregations in the little mission increased as the town increased in size and grew in population, but there seemed no way for me to accomplish my one immediate purpose of taking a course of studies. It was about this time my health began to decline.

Colorado was a territory and Denver city the capital. Enterprising capitalists were making Denver a great city. Already plans were formed for the erection of huge buildings. A well-known gentleman who had showed kindness to me made an offer to me of one hundred dollars a month to take charge of his buildings when completed. With this I could do mission work, pay for a home, and hold the eighty acres secured through pre-emption granted by the Government, and on which stands to-day a portion of Denver city. This was very tempting and I confess I had nearly made up my mind to accept the offer; but when I consulted my good wife, she wisely said: "No, Tom, I would not; what does the Bible say? 'No man having put his hand to the plough and looking back is fit for the kingdom of God.' Luke ix. 62." That was the turning-point. We sold the eighty acres which, with that which is built upon it, would be worth millions of dollars; but I have never regretted taking my good wife's advice on that occasion. The Hand of God was with me.

The Lord raised up friends to help us back to the States. After spending three years in Denver we returned to Chicago in May, 1872, preparatory to our going to Africa. My intention was to go into some institute for a little training; but the Rev. de Baptiste, my friend and former Pastor, with other friends advised me not to think of going to Africa for the present. I had set my mind on going to Washington to study. Soon I had two calls, one was to take a small church in Elgin, composed of freedmen, the other to supply for a few months in Springfield, Illinois, once the home of President Lincoln. We made the matter a special subject for prayer.

The Rev. de Baptiste, who was generally looked upon as a leader and adviser among the Mission Churches, advised me to go to Springfield for a short period. There was a conviction within my heart when I came out of slavery, and this conviction deepened as years passed on, and more especially after my wife's thoughtful advice at Denver, that I could not go to school or college until some provision were made for her to whom I owed so much for her real help in my life and work. I could not think of her taking a situation to work for her living while I was at school or college, knowing her state of health, though she was quite willing to undertake that. I concluded to go to Springfield. Here I remained nearly a year paeaching in the old Theatre, when, in 1873, through the introduction of Rev. R. de Baptiste, I had the unanimous call to the Pastorate of Providence Baptist Church, Chicago. Here I came in contact with quite a different class of people, most of the members of the congregation being freed slaves or the descendants of freed slaves; and as the young folk were attending the schools daily, many of them knew more than I did; at the same time they thought I knew more than they. This disquieted me much. I endeavoured to persuade my friends to be very candid with me, and inform me of my mistakes. They would do this once in a while, but I fancy they felt unable to keep pace with my blunders. Again and again I was advised to study the English grammar. A friend gave me a copy, but I could make nothing of it. I did not see how it could possibly help me in preaching the Gospel; I was mainly anxious to know the Bible. When I took the oversight of the Church I found a nice Sunday School. The Superintendent was a white gentleman, a member of the Western Avenue Baptist Church. With him there were three white teachers, who kindly came each Sunday afternoon, which was indeed a great help. I felt myself as much in need of help as the scholars in the Sunday School. This stimulated me to further study. The International lessons were of great assistance to me as I was expected not only to be at the teachers' meetings each Thursday evening, but also to take a class in the Sunday School; and to give an address occasionally. To meet these appointments required much prayer and diligence.

English Friends

God was ever raising up friends to help me. Mr. and Mrs. E. Stroud Smith and their two daughters came to live in the neighbourhood. They belonged to England, but had been in America for many years. They came to our Sunday School and kindly offered their services, which we gladly accepted. We soon discovered in them the high characteristics of the truly English Christian people; showing sympathy with the oppressed coloured race, they not only came on the Sabbath to teach, but attended two nights in the week with their two daughters to give instruction at a night school to the freedmen. The scholars at the night school were mainly of the older people who had spent their early years in slavery. All they wished to hear was how to read the New Testament.

Everyone in the mission and school soon learned to love Mr. and Mrs. Smith and their two daughters. Mr. Smith was indeed a great help to me in every way. I could go to him in confidence and ask for information upon any subject, or seek advice on any matter when he was ever ready to give me a hearing. In time it was arranged that he should come to my rooms at the mission once a week and give me lessons for one hour. The late Rev. J. J. Irving, who came from the Pastor's College was at that time Pastor of the Western Avenue Baptist Church (white). Mr. and Mrs. Stroud Smith were members of Mr. Irving's church, and through them Mr. Irving became a dear friend to me, and a helper. As a general thing there was a Sunday School Teachers' meeting one night in the week, when the Pastor would be present with the Superintendent, to explain the lessons to the teachers, and each teacher would become more equipped for the class on the Sunday. Mr. Irving kindly offered to help me in these lessons. He would give his teachers an address on the Wednesday evening; and then on the Thursday afternoon he would give me an hour and explain the International Lessons which would prepare me for my Sunday School teachers on the Friday night. My memory was retentive in those days, and this proved a great help; and Mr. Irving would never allow anything to interfere with his arrangement.

During all this time I could not lose sight of Africa. Many of those to whom I would make known my desires sought to dissuade me from my purpose, telling me of what they had read and heard of Africa and its venomous reptiles, cruel fevers and cannibal tribes. But these things did not move me. There were times when I would seriously consider the question of health and other matters; but there was something which kept Africa continually before me with its great need of the Gospel; and I was concerned about my preparation to go and tell the people the good news of the Gospel of Jesus Christ. I was told that I must be educated before I could be sent as a missionary. I earnestly prayed over the matter; and I begged the Lord that if it were His will, He would send me to Africa to open up the way.

On enquiry I found that the American Baptist Missionary Union had no stations in Africa, and that there was no missionary organization among the coloured people for sending their own people to the land of their fathers. I felt quite convinced that if I could reach the heathen, not for the purpose of telling them of the arts and sciences, of which I was ignorant, but of my Blessed Jesus who had given me eternal life, by commencing with John iii., 16, someone else, better educated and better fitted for the work, might follow and teach the rest.

It was sad news for me when Mr. Smith informed us that he, with his wife and daughters, intended leaving shortly for England. I well remember the afternoon that they left Chicago. All who could leave their work went to the station to see them off. I remember saying to them, "Remember me when you get to England." But little did I dream at that time of ever seeing England, or of seeing Mr. and Mrs. Smith again. Africa alone was my objective. And now that these dear friends were gone, Africa became more than ever the subject of prayer on the part of both my wife and myself. For a long time my health had been failing, and I had a severe attack of illness after Mr. Smith returned to England, and my friends thought I could not recover.

Missionary Matters Again

Through advice I wrote to Dr. Murdock, of the American Baptist Union, Boston, respecting my desire to go to Africa. When he was on a visit to Chicago, he called to see me. I was not well at the time. There were three matters he enquired into: first, as to my age, I would be forty the next birthday; second, as to my health, and that was so bad that I was unable to go and see him, and so he had to come and see me before he returned to Boston; third, as to what educational advantages I had enjoyed, but I deplored my educational disadvantages. The answers were all against me, and I could only speak the truth; but I told him my mind was made up to go to Africa. He then promised to pay the passage of my wife and myself from New York to Monrovia, Liberia, but he could offer no other assistance. Then came the real testing time. I was thoroughly convinced that the Lord had said to me, "Go," and so I believed that all the money required would come in due time. I remember reading in a book or a tract, of someone who saw on looking into a certain Bible that it was marked in different places--"T and P"; and on asking what it meant, the owner replied that the letters stood for "Tried and Proved." I was greatly struck with this. One day when I was reading I came to Psalm xxxvii. 3, "Trust in the Lord and do good, and so shalt thou dwelt in the land, and verily thou shalt be fed"; verse 4, "Delight thyself also in the Lord and He shall give thee the desires of thine heart"; and my heart's desire was to go to Africa; verse 5, "Commit thy way unto the Lord, trust also in Him, and He shall bring it to pass." Now there had been too much anxiety about Africa and the means of getting there, and not enough trust in God and His faithful promises. Here in Psalm xxxvii. we have trust, and then rest; fretting works evil. I prayed over the matter, and then said to my wife, "Henrietta, we will trust in the Lord"; and so we marked "T" at each of these verses. There was in those days, in Chicago, a dear Christian (white) lady, called "Aunt Lizzie," who walked and talked as one who lived always at the feet of my blessed Jesus, and was filled with His spirit. It seemed that my case was much like that of the Ethiopian eunuch, and "Aunt Lizzie" was as Philip to me. I was at the point of surrender, but I required help. It may have been on the very day when my wife and myself had decided to fully trust God in the matter, that "Aunt Lizzie" called to see us, a most unusual thing for her to do. We told her of our decision. She cheered us greatly by her loving advice, and then followed up her good counsel by an earnest appeal to God in the name of Jesus. It was clear to us that God sent her to encourage us in our resolution, and we were willing to wait God's leading. God's Hand again with me.

Soon after this visit I received two letters from England. This was about February, 1876. One was from Mr. Stroud Smith, telling me of a conversation with Mr. W. Hind Smith, of the Y. M. C. A., Peter Street, Manchester, about my wish to prepare for mission work in Africa; and one from Mr. Hind Smith himself to say that if I could come to England he would see that an opportunity was given me of taking a course of study before going to Africa. When these letters came I was in a weak state, and still suffering from a long illness (many of my friends had no hopes of my recovery). I at once replied that (D.V.) I would come to England. I then wrote to thank Dr. Murdock for his kind offer to help me to get to Liberia. The members of the mission were much surprised at the news that I was going to England. When I recovered sufficiently to get out, a friend came to drive me about for a change. He said, "Brother Tom, these people say you must have money; now I know you won't mind telling me how you stand." I said, "No, I have only fifteen dollars (three guineas), but I have faith in God." I felt sure God would take me to Africa, but I never thought He would take me to England, Ireland, Scotland, and Wales also. According to arrangement I gave notice at the mission that my engagement would terminate in six months. At this critical period the Lord raised up more friends. In due time Mr. Stroud Smith sent me the required information about the journey, and gave me the name of the ship as the S. S. Spain, of the National Line, sailing from New York. The friends and members of the mission had a farewell meeting, at which they gave me a purse containing ninety-six dollars, which was a great help to me. After a short stay at Washington, where Mrs. Johnson spent a short time with her people, we sailed for Liverpool on the 19th August, 1876, in the S. S. Spain. Never having travelled abroad before, I felt a little anxious about the journey, but not as to my reception by the English people, as my experience of them already was most encouraging, having met a large number of them in Chicago, where they had settled. The captain and other officers on board showed me every kindness and did everything for the comfort of my wife and myself. And I would record with gratitude the kindness of Mr. and Mrs. Marshall, of Northampton, and Rev. Thomas and Mrs. Arnold during the voyage.

On British Soil

We reached Liverpool safely on September 1st. When collecting our packages together I was told that a gentleman was on board who wished to see me, and on going on deck I there met a young man whom Mr. W. Hind Smith had sent over from Manchester the night before to meet us. He handed me a letter of welcome from Mr. and Mrs. Hind Smith. After passing through the Custom House, he took charge of our luggage, purchased our tickets, and we were soon off to Manchester. Mr. E. Stroud Smith, and Mr. W. Hind Smith met us at the Manchester Station, and we were at once driven to Mr. W. Hind Smith's house, 5, Addison Terrace, Victoria Park, where we received a very cordial welcome by Mrs. Hind Smith and the two dear children, Willie and Martin. I cannot describe the joy of my soul of meeting once more Mr. and Mrs. E. Stroud Smith and their daughters, who had been so kind to us abroad, as, referred to. My first Sunday in England made a lasting impression on me. In the morning I went to hear Dr. Maclaren, of Manchester. Here I was introduced to quite a number of friends, and invited to visit the Jackson Street Ragged School in the afternoon, where I gave my first address in England. On this occasion there were two subjects which fixed themselves upon my memory, FIRST the picture of Queen Victoria presenting a BIBLE to an AFRI-CAN Prince who was on his knees with open hands receiving it. I was told he had come to England to find out what was the secret of England's Greatness; when the Queen gave him the Bible, and said, "This is the secret of England's greatness." From that day in September, 1876, this statement has been again and again confirmed, in my mind, that the secret of England's greatness is the BIBLE, God's message to this sin-cursed world.

The SECOND was, when the children commenced to sing, a book was put into my hand, the words were:--

> I was not born a little slave to labour in the sun,
> Wishing I were but in my grave, and all my labour done;
> I was not born as thousands are where God was never known,
> And taught to pray a useless prayer to BLOCKS OF WOOD AND STONE.

I could not join in with this great company of happy little English children, for I was born a little slave, and had laboured in the sun. In the evening I was invited to speak at the Y. M. C. A., Peter Street, when I gave my second address from 2nd Thess. iii. I, "Brethren, pray for us, that the Word of the Lord may have free course and be glorified, even as it is with you." I felt then, as I do now, the need of God's help all the time. I was daily with Mr. Hind Smith at the Y. M. C. A., assisting, as best I could, not only in the work there, but in mission work in Manchester. Mr. Hind Smith kindly introduced me to many of the Christian workers and merchants in Manchester, who became kind friends to me, among them Mr. James Boyd and his brother, whose kindness and that of their wives and children will never be forgotten. Mr. Hind Smith also took me to see the Bishop of Manchester, who received me very kindly, and said if he could help me in any way he would be pleased to do so. As time passed I could see more than ever the necessity for improvement in myself. Mr. Hind Smith kindly engaged a young student of Owen's College, Manches-ter, to come and give me private lessons (I regret so much I cannot remem-ber his name); this was a great help to me. But one of the first books he pro-duced for me to study was my old puzzler the English grammar, which up to this time, forty years of age, I had not been able to grasp or understand the contents of one page. I could not see how it would ever help me in Mission Work in AFRICA. The one thought of my mind was AFRICA FOR CHRIST. But this young man told me that by all means I must study this grammar; howev-er, I had settled it in my mind that I could manage without it.

Little Willie and his dear brother Martin soon became my great friends. Before we came to Manchester, Mr. and Mrs. Hind Smith had given hospitali-ty to the Jubilee Singers, to whom they became very much attached; hence they were always eager to hear all I could tell them about the Emancipated

Slaves, and their little children, and about my own life as a slave boy, and not permitted to be taught how to read the Bible, that tells how Jesus loves little children. They were both very fond of singing, and were never tired of hearing me sing some of the Slave Melodies. They knew a great number of the "Sacred Songs and Solos." I can never forget when I heard them sing, "When he cometh, when He cometh to make up His Jewels." They knew many of the Jubilee Songs; their favourites were "Steal Away to Jesus," "He arose from the dead," "I've been redeemed," "Brothers, don't stay away," "Mary and Martha just gone along." I cannot forget the joy it gave me to be with them in the nursery down on the floor building houses with their blocks, or taking walks with them in Alexandria Park; wherever we were their little minds never tired of asking questions about the little slaves and their treatment. In October, 1877, the Lord took little Martin home to be among His jewels. Everywhere I went, whether among the rich, or poor, learned or illiterate (for I met with all classes in connection with the work of the Y. M. C. A.), I was received as a man, a Brother, and a Christian, and made to feel perfectly happy. In America they speak of England as "the Old World," but it was a new world to me. Since those days of my first introduction to English friends I have been welcomed and entertained by ladies and gentlemen throughout the British Isles.

Here is an interesting picture. This is a facsimile of a blackboard lesson given by my friend, Mr. E Stroud Smith, one Sunday morning at the Children's Service in Dr. Maclaren's Chapel, Manchester. He first drew the heart, saying, as he did so, "Children, I want to show you Mr. Johnson's heart, which is so elastic that it is large enough to contain the whole of Africa." Then, drawing a map of the "dark continent" and the Bible, he said, "Jesus is the Light."

Mr. Smith introduced me to Dr. Maclaren, who treated me very kindly, and he also introduced my name to the Committee of the Baptist Missionary Society in London. The late Rev. C. Bailhache, Secretary of the Society, sent for me to visit London. The kindness of Mr. Bailhache and Mr. Baynes remains a sweet memory with me. I availed myself of the visit to London to see something of the great city, knowing that within a few days I must return to Manchester; I made an effort to comprehend a few of the wonders of the great city. My first visit was one to the Zoological Gardens, and from that day in November, 1876, to the present time, whenever I can manage it, I make a visit to the Zoo.

Lost On Clapham Common

On my way back from this visit I enquired of the 'bus-driver about Mr. Spurgeon and the Tabernacle, and as to where the great preacher lived. He told me what 'bus to take in order to reach his house in Nightingale Lane. It was getting late by the time I reached Clapham Common, and I had yet a good distance to go. Alas, when I did reach Mr. Spurgeon's house, I found that he was not at home. I thought nothing of the distance when going but it was weary and alarming work returning. When I turned from Mr. Spurgeon's door to cross Clapham Common, my heart began to be heavy. It was now quite dark, and this my first night in London. Cab after cab passed me, but each one had an occupant. I found myself wandering about on the Common enquiring my way back. At last a hansom cab came up, and I asked to be driven to Bloomsbury Square. I do not remember what the driver charged, but I was quite willing to pay all he might ask for. He drove across London quickly. The impression made upon my mind that night can never be removed. After returning to Manchester, and when suffering from damp and cold, Mr. Hind Smith thought further south would suit me better during the winter months. He wrote Mr. Spurgeon to ask if he would admit me into the College to hear the lectures. The reply was characteristic of Mr. Spurgeon. A postcard came with the words: "Dear Mr. Hind Smith,--Yes, let the dear man come.-- C. H. Spurgeon." Thus the way was opened up for me to enter the Pastor's College, where I began my first regular course of studies at forty years of age, for this step resulted in my being admitted as a student of the College in the course of time. I cannot describe the gratitude I felt towards my blessed Jesus for the privilege of coming to England, and for the kind friends. This had already moved me to deeper consecration, but the College course was beyond my highest anticipations. When, as a slave in Virginia before the War, I heard my owners talk of Mr. Spurgeon, I was regarded, even according to law, a "thing," a "chattel"; there was no idea on my part of ever seeing Mr. Spurgeon, though I had often thought and felt how much I should like to hear him preach. Well, the Lord knew this, and granted me more than my desire, And this is the way the Lord treats His children, doing greater things for them than they ask or think. Again the Hand of God was with me.

In The Pastors' College

I do not think that my anxiety on leaving America for England was any greater than on leaving Manchester for London. This was one of the great events of my life. Many of the young men and other friends whom God had inclined to help us sought the Lord's blessing to accompany us. Mr. Hind Smith gave me ten guineas for expenses. We arrived in London December 1st, 1876. Our first home in London was with Mr. and Mrs. Wigney, in Lorrimore Square. Mr. Wigney is now the Secretary of the Metropolitan Colportage Association, and one of the Elders of the Church. This was a real home for my wife and myself. Mr. Wigney conducted a very large, Bible Class of young men in the College Building. I became a member of this class. Mr. and Mrs. Wigney have been friends to me ever since.

On the 3rd of December I went to the College to report myself. The first student to give me a welcome was Mr. Winter. This good brother early went home to be with the Lord. The next student with whom I became closely associated was Dr. Dean. Indeed, all the students gave me a very cordial welcome on that memorable morning, and I felt quite happy. When I told Dr. Dean that I had come to listen to the lectures he gave me a list of the subjects, and named the days and hours when they were dealt with. I then went to Professor Fergusson's room. He invited me into the class-room, and then questioned me about my past life, and as to what educational advantages I had enjoyed. Brother Dean, who came into the room just then, asked Mr. Fergusson something about books, to which the reply was, "Yes." This good brother went out and soon returned with several books which he handed to me. The bell then rang, and all the students took their places. The hearty manner and welcome of the students soon banished all misgivings. Professor Fergusson opened the class work with prayer--such a prayer as I shall never forget; and he prayed very earnestly for me. Then came the lessons, when, to my astonishment and embarrassment, the first book opened for me was my old enemy--the English Grammar--the very study I had made up my mind to do without. I shall never forget the kindness of Mr. Dean--now Dr. Dean--who afterwards became a medical missionary, in helping me with my grammar, and he would come to my lodgings to assist me with my lessons. A short time in college revealed to me the fact that I had not been fully aware of my own ignorance. But this was not very surprising, seeing that "a man must be very learned, must have acquired a vast amount of knowledge, before he is able to comprehend the amazing amount of his own ignorance." Each day there were subjects, questions, and words of which I knew nothing. If the College had been what I had anticipated, I could not have made progress, but thank God every student was a friend and a brother. The kindness and patience of the Professors with all my darkness was Wonderful. Professor Fergusson took such pains to instruct me. He honoured me by inviting me to his home in Ealing, where he helped me. His dear wife and daughters all took a deep interest in me. All help thus received was very welcome to me. Often have I been up late at night getting my lesson. I remember being on my knees about one o'clock in the morning in prayer, for often I could not succeed until I had sought special help from my blessed Jesus. I was not in College very long before I met Mr. Spurgeon. I had been very anxious to speak to him. His first words set me at ease, but his sympathetic kindness was beyond my highest hope. He took me by the hand, asked me a few questions, and wished me success. The fear all vanished, and I felt I had been talking to a dear loving friend. I at once fell in love with dear Mr. Spurgeon. I know not how to express my feelings about this first meeting, and can only say that I felt so happy in his presence, and so at home with him, that I could not help saying, "Well, thank God he is my friend." It was so like Mr. Spurgeon to make everyone happy with whom he came in contact, be they "home born or a stranger within the gates." The "Preacher's Prayer," the book to which reference has been made, influenced me very much, but little did I ever think of seeing the author of it. I believe it often happens that one reads a sermon or an address, or a book, and there comes a desire to meet the author. But in some cases after meeting the author the sermons and books are not so highly prized, for there is such a difference between the author and the production. It was otherwise in the case of Mr. Spurgeon, for had you met him anywhere or under any circumstances, in the street, in his home, in his study, or in the vestry of the Metropolitan Tabernacle, you would have recognised the agreement between the man and his works.

There are many classes of professing Christians with whom one meets when travelling through the world. First, there is a class that claims to be the children of God, who look upon their fellow creatures with piety; and second, those who look upon them with icy indifference; and yet a third class, who seem, somehow, to be able to look with cruel satisfaction upon the sufferings, wants, and claims of their fellow men at home and abroad. Of those at home they say: "Let them do as I did, or as someone else did"; or "Let them go to Mr. A. or Mr. B., he is the man to look after them without going abroad." But thank God there is a large class of Christians who really have had "two Birthdays" or, as a writer has put it, "Who have the degree of B.A., or Born Again," and who look upon their fellows with tender and self-sacrificing sympathy, and who seem to have before them the thoughts, "What did Jesus say? what did Jesus do? what would Jesus do?" Mr. Spurgeon was of this class; a man of refined philanthropic life. He discerned with Peter, who said, "Of a truth I perceive that God is no respecter of persons," and with Paul he knew that "God hath made of one blood all nations of men to dwell on all the face of the earth." He was ever like the driver on the fast railway train with his eye on the track. He never took his eye off the Word of God, and he always spoke the language of the Word, and paid little regard to what others said, or to what it was the Age demanded. "What hath God said?" was the only concern for him. There are some, when preaching, only preach three-quarters of the truth, or less, when serving up dishes of soul-food to suit the palates of those they must please. I was at one of Mr. Moody's meetings, when he gave one of those faithful discourses of his. Three ministers were speaking of the message, one of them saying, "We could not afford to preach to our people like that; it would drive them away." I went nearer, and almost in a whisper, asked, "Is God dead?" They were all startled, and one answered, "No." I shalt never forget the looks they gave each other. In the late Mr. Spurgeon we had one in whom faith and courage and faithfulness in preaching God's Word were predominant features of his ministry. In the first week of January, 1877, I had Mr. Spurgeon to myself for quite half an hour, when I laid before him my history in brief, telling him of my journey to England through providential arrangement; of my health, which at that time alarmed my friends in London, and of my desire to go to Africa, and of the unfavourable outlook. He told me to make myself perfectly happy, for if other channels failed I could depend on him to do his part. I returned from that visit with thankfulness to God in my heart, and with gratitude for that honoured servant of His who was so kind to me.

When I entered the College the first week in December, 1876, it was only to attend the lectures, but God put it into the heart of Professor Fergusson to become a friend to me. His kindness and patience greatly impressed me, and eventually I enquired of my friend Mr. Wigney the best way to Ealing, where my tutor held a Pastorate, that I might go and hear him preach. I was up early one Sunday morning, and found my way to Paddington Station, and arriving at Ealing, and at the Chapel a long time before the service I walked up and down till the caretaker came and let me in from the cold weather without. Professor Fergusson was surprised to see me. At the close of the service he introduced me to his wife and daughters, his church officials and friends, and then invited me to dine with him. From that Sabbath Day God raised up many friends for me at Ealing, especially in connection with the Sunday School.

West Ealing Baptist Church

The favourable report that Professor Fergusson gave our President, Mr. Spurgeon, on the progress I had made at College resulted in my being admitted a student. I can truthfully and gladly say that I had never been treated more kindly or made to feel more at home and more happy than when at the Pastors' College. The President, Rev. C. H. Spurgeon; the Vice-President, Rev. J. A. Spurgeon; the Professors, Revs. George Rogers, David Gracey, and Archibald Fergusson, and all the students, with whom I came in contact, were most brotherly, and ever ready to help me in my educational struggles, and answer any questions too hard for me. Some of my enquiries seemed to amuse both the tutors and the students, and to upset their gravity, but they were serious enough on my part. Our dear friend, Professor Fergusson, was talking about the "Antipodes" in the course of the lesson one morning. I used the privilege accorded to every student, and made enquiry as to the meaning of the word. The Professor treated of the etymology of the word in order to show its construction and full meaning, explaining that it meant the people on the other side of the globe. My "intelligence" felt quite offended, and I enquired in a rather peremptory way if the Professor intended to suggest that people on the other side of the globe hung on like flies. But my enquiry did not seem of grave importance to the students, and general laughter followed. When Professor Fergusson remonstrated with the class, I said: "It's all right, sir; the brethren can't help it; it's common knowledge to them, being taught it from childhood, and when I get it into my head it will be mine, and then I will be able to laugh at someone else afterwards.

But in all my life of forty years I never had such a chance of acquiring knowledge, and I was determined to make the best use of it. I had heard of the theory before of the rotundity of the earth, and had tried to grasp it, but up till that time I did not believe in the truth of it, and paid no attention to the subject. But this was only one of the many subjects which puzzled me, and I fancy the readers of these lines would have been equally amused had they heard my strange questions. After being in College about a month I heard a young man confessing to the Professor that he had not been aware he was such a fool as he had found himself to be until he entered the Pastors' College. This confession was an indirect encouragement to me, for here was a young man who was considered clever, and who had enjoyed educational advantages from childhood, and yet I was in advance of him in knowledge; for I did know that I was a fool before I entered College, and I felt in myself that out of one hundred and ten students in the College, there was not one who did not know more than I did.

One day I heard that Mr.---- had received a "Blue Letter." "Blue Letter? Blue Letter?" I wondered what it could mean at all. I enquired of Brother Davis if he could enlighten me about the matter. "Well," said he, "You know Mr.----? He has made no progress, no proficiency. Men coming to the College are looked upon as men, not as children, and are supposed to take advantage of the opportunities offered them. If they fail to do this they are advised to leave, and the advice is generally given to them in the form of a letter." "That's it," thought I. That "Blue Letter" haunted me. Mr.---- had left quietly, and no one seemed to know where he had gone. After this, in the tram, in the 'bus, in the railway carriage, at home, or at meeting appointments, not a moment would be lost in my effort to grasp my lessons. In fact this "Blue Letter" information was quite a help by stirring me up to more earnest endeavours. I regard my connection with the Pastors' College as the turning point in an important passage of my life's history, for which I feel continually grateful. I am sure that I never could have so well succeeded in the African Mission, or in Evangelistic work at home, had it not been for the training and fraternal helpfulness of the Pastors' College, with its many advantages, and I shall remember in all my work how that I gathered strength and wisdom from the faithful tuition so kindly given me; and it has been my endeavour to show that this kindness has not been vainly bestowed. My prayer is that God will continue to prosper the College which has been privileged to educate and send out a thousand men to preach the Gospel, and that it may in the future as in the past, send forth a large company of faithful men for the Lord's service, who, in their faithfulness to God's truth, and in devotion to His cause, will contend earnestly for the faith which was once for all delivered to the saints;" and I pray that many of them will turn towards Africa, to labour among a long-oppressed and neglected race.

My First Sermon

My anxiety as to my first sermon in College was very great, as any student may imagine, for I had heard other sermons criticised. I preached from Acts xvi. 31. I studied up the subject night and day. Before coming from America I had been presented with three volumes of Andrew Fuller's works. I read these works diligently, and was struck with his remarks--that to be born again was to be "re-created"--and I found some passages that just suited my subject. Notwithstanding that I was told not to "plagiarise," I felt that I could not say the thing better myself, and so made use of some expressions which I found answered the subject. I thought that the book, being old, no-one would detect it; the students would be sure to be taken up with the new books. But the students went for me when I had finished my sermon. However, when they had done with me, Professor Rogers, who presided, said: "I don't think our brother is deserving of such severe criticism. (Hear, Hear). If Mr. Johnson, who is forty years old, and having no advantages, can study the English Grammar--(Hear, Hear)--it shows what he is capable of. Look at him, brethren, I see in him an 'Andrew Fuller!'" The students cheered and clapped and thumped the desks, and one brother shouted, "Cheer up, Johnson." Thus ended the first sermon. But I felt that I had been detected by the ever vigilant Professor Rogers, and I sat looking into the fire in the grate and studied "fireology" for the remainder of the sermon class. My sin found me out. This was indeed a great help to me.

Professor Fergusson

An interesting biography of any one of the tutors might easily be written, but the students of a certain period will quite understand how very much dear Mr. Fergusson's personality impressed itself. He received the men in the "rough", and out of such strange material as came to hand he shaped, by the vigorous use of "English" tools the forms that were to be sent forward to the other classes for the more advanced studies. But the man who could successfully endure the drilling in Mr. Fergusson's class had little to fear. I often met this beloved tutor after he had had retired from both the College and the Church work through failing health and sight. It was such a privilege to meet him and have his always cheery word and welcome. The last letter he wrote me was as follows: "My dear old friend,--I am very sorry to hear you are so poorly and laid aside from that work in which you found so much pleasure; but time to rest and time to retire lie in the hand of God as completely as the time for going to bed of the child who lies in the hand of the parent. But be of good cheer; if the work is done, and God has been glorified, rest assured the time of triumph is not far off when you shall spread your wings and rise in the presence of Christ, no longer a slave nor a sufferer, but a glorified spirit. . . . My longer daughter Grace and all of us have found great comfort on many occasions through your sweet hymn, 'God never makes a mistake.' You will find that He has made no mistake in your present affliction. Trust and not be afraid. With love from us all to Mrs. Johnson and yourself.--Very sincerely, your old Tutor, A. Fergusson."

I cannot describe my feeling when on the morning of December 29th, 1900, I read the following: "30, Drayton Road, West Ealing, December 28th, 1900.--Dear Mr. Johnson,--Our dear father passed peacefully away yesterday afternoon.--Yours sincerely, Grace Fergusson."

When I entered College in December, 1876, I was taken by the hand and given a hearty welcome by the First President, Rev. C. H. Spurgeon; the Vice-President, Rev. James A. Spurgeon; Professor Rogers, Professor Gracy, and by my dear kind friend, Professor Archibald Fergusson. Both Presidents and all the tutors of my time are now with my blessed Jesus.

The following is a paragraph from The Baptist of January 4th, 1901:--

"GONE HOME.
"PROFESSOR A. FERGUSSON (formerly of the Pastors' College.)

"Rev. Archibald Fergusson, formerly one of the tutors of the Pastors' College, has just passed away at Ealing in his eightieth year. He was tutor for thirty years; in addition to English subjects he conducted classes in mental and moral science, Angus's Bible Handbook, and Butler's Analogy. A chord of sympathy will be struck in the heart of many a man now doing service in the Home or Foreign field who received his first help in Professor Fergusson's classes. In his earlier days he was engaged with others in Mission work in some of the slum districts by the river Thames, and two small volumes which he wrote long ago describe the conversion of some remarkable characters. Nearly forty years ago, whilst a tutor of the College, and living at Battersea, he commenced work at Ealing, where he preached in a room or barn connected with the 'Green Man.' The roof was leaky, and the audience had sometimes to stand with their umbrellas open. Once the Rev. C. H. Spurgeon preached to an immense audience in a field adjoining the meeting place. The weekly congregation increased, the present Chapel was built, and Mr. Fergusson, who had in the meantime removed to Ealing, continued as Pastor for many years. Nine years ago, after an attack of influenza, he felt compelled to retire from College, and about twelve months afterwards increasing infirmity, with an affection of the eyes, resulting in blindness, necessitated his resignation of the Pastorate. By his people he was greatly loved and respected, and his ministry highly valued. He bore his affliction with fortitude, took a keen interest in current events, and in the affairs of the Tabernacle and College and retained his mental clearness and vigour almost to the end. The last illness was an attack of bronchitis, and he peacefully fell asleep on the Thursday after Christmas. The funeral took place at Ealing last Wednesday. Mrs. Fergusson and three daughters, two of whom were married, survive him.--H. K."

Tribute by Principal M'caig

"The announcement of the death of Professor Fergusson will bring a pang of sorrow to many a heart. All over the world there are men engaged in the service of the Saviour, who received not a little of the fitness and inspiration for their life-work from the teaching and example of this stalwart hero of the Cross; and they will be saddened to think that they will see his kindly face no more this side the River; but at the same time they will thank God for what they have known of him and rejoice that he has entered into his rest.

"Mr. Fergusson's life-work has been wrought in connection with the Pastor's College, and perhaps it is fitting that an old student, admirer, and friend of his, now a tutor in the same institution, should be asked to write a few lines concerning him.

"For many years, formerly, even as now, the three principal divisions of the United Kingdom were represented on the tutorial staff of the Pastors' College, Mr. Fergusson worthily representing the land of 'brown heath and shaggy wood.'

"Readers of M'Cheyne's life will remember that while that worthy man was visiting a Palestine in 1839, W. C. Burns, subsequently renowned as a Missionary in China, occupied his pulpit in Dundee for three months, during which time a great revival took place. Archibald Fergusson was among the number of those who were then awakened to higher life and service, all through his career he carried with him something of the spiritual fervour and savour of Burns and M'Cheyne.

"His connection with the Pastors' College dates back to 1862, when he undertook the work of the evening classes. From the first his work was a great success. Large numbers of young men entered the classes and found in Mr. Fergusson the very helper they needed, many being furnished for Christian service, but also better equipped for their business calling. Frequently do we meet with men who confess their deep indebtedness to him in those early days, several attributing their success in business as well as their usefulness in Christian work, to what they learned from him. Six months later he entered upon regular tutorial work in the College, while still continuing his work in the evening classes. Having charge mainly of the English department, to him necessarily fell the rougher work of the College. The rugged blocks of marble, out of which were to be hewn 'angels of the churches,' were first entrusted to his care, and much hard cutting and chipping they received before being passed on the other tutors for the perfecting and polishing. The process was not always pleasant to the subject of it; but while many might feel that they were somewhat roughly handled, they could not but see that their tutor was full of love for them, and inspired by an earnest desire for their highest good, and they came to know that all the discipline had been necessary. It was soon found, indeed, that under a somewhat bluff and rugged exterior there was a very tender heart. The saying was fulfilled that 'Deep and true is the North.' Every man could count upon Mr. Fergusson's deep interest in the work in which he was engaged, and all found in him a sympathetic friend. His love for the Gospel was intense, and often when in the class the love of Christ was spoken of--and whatever might be the subject, he could easily find a by-way that led to Christ--the spectacle might be seen of the tutor in tears. No wonder that the student's heart was knit to such a man, and that in his presence they learned to love more dearly the Gospel which he prized so highly. His was indeed a strong nature, and he was conspicuous for these two things--strong faith and ardent love. He believed in the Lord with all his soul; he held the Word of God with a tenacious and unwavering grip; he believed the Gospel without the shadow of a doubt; believed it for his own salvation, believed in it as the one remedy for the ills of humanity, the power of God unto salvation. And out of that faith grew the love of which we have spoken. Some time ago we read in an old church book under date, 1765, a description of a "great minister," and first and chief among his natural qualifications was this, that he had 'a flaming ardour of temper'-- 'temper' being equivalent to temperament. This was true of our departed friend. By nature he had the 'flaming' ardour,' fitting him to be a Boanerges; brought under the influence of Christ that 'flaming ardour' was consecrated to Him. He burned with love to Christ and souls, he was 'fervent in spirit, his zeal for the Lord seemed ever at the boiling point.' His strong loving nature impressed itself upon his students. His love evoked love. The affectionate nature of the regard in which he was held is perhaps not inaptly, if somewhat quaintly, indicated by the title so frequently given him by the students--'Dear old Fergy.' Mr. Fergusson was a Pastor as well as a Professor. For many years he carried on a successful ministry at Ealing, where he built up a strong Church, and exerted a widespread influence. About ten years ago, after a very serious illness, which left him with greatly reduced strength, Mr. Fergusson felt that he could not continue to do both tutorial and pastoral work, and so was led to resign the post of tutor which he had occupied so long and faithfully; and after two more years he was obliged to relinquish the chief work of the Pastorate, finding a worthy successor in one of his own students, Rev. W. L. Gibbs.

During the last few years he was afflicted with loss of eyesight, but one could not be long in his company without finding that if dark without he was full of light within. It was an impressive sight to see the dear old man with his comely crown of grey hair, and his face all aglow with heaven's own light. He liked to speak of himself in these last years as a 'prisoner of the Lord,' but he would quaintly add, 'I am in love with my gaoler.' 'The prisoner has now gained his liberty. From the darkness he has passed into the shadowless day.'"

After I became acquainted with the members of Mr. Fergusson's Church, and with the officers of the Sunday School, I was often invited to take part in the services, and preach Anniversary sermons. And after Mr. Fergusson's resignation, and when the Rev. W. L. Gibbs became pastor I was still invited to occupy the pulpit, and asked to preach the Sunday School Anniversary Sermons, and also to conduct a Mission. When I met with an accident in 1900, which many will remember, and was ill so long, I got a message from Mr. Gibbs to say that as soon as I was able to come he and the friends with him would like me to preach at Ealing. When I did visit them I was requested to  repeat the story of my life, and which I had given several times before at Ealing. It had been quietly arranged about the collections, and the result of the Sunday and Monday collections--sixteen pounds--was handed over to me. As I write, the great kindness I have enjoyed at Ealing passes before my vision. Here is a picture of Ealing Baptist Chapel:

The African Mission

In August, 1877, the Rev. C. H. Richardson and his wife came to England to go with us to Africa. Mr. Spurgeon admitted him into the college, where, like myself, he received considerable help. During our stay in college Rev. C. Bailhache and Mr. A. H. Baynes showed us no little kindness. Being often called upon to do deputation work in the provinces for the Baptist Missionary Society, I frequently met these gentlemen, especially Mr. Baynes, from whom I received support while in college. Before leaving for Africa our hearts were made glad by several farewell meetings in London and the provinces, the greatest being the one held at the Metropolitan Tabernacle.

The following is an extract taken from The Baptist of October 4th, 1878:--

"Special farewell services to the Revs. T. L. Johnson and C. H. Richardson, who are going to Africa as missionaries, the former having been accepted by the Baptist Missionary Society and trained by them for the past two years in the Pastor's College, were held on Wednesday last week in the Metropolitan Tabernacle. There was a very large attendance, and Mr. Spurgeon occupied the chair, introducing Mr. Johnson, who delivered an interesting address upon slave life, mission work in Africa, and his expectations and purposes respecting the future.

"Rev. T. L. Johnson, who was warmly received, acknowledged the universal kindness with which he had been treated, both at the Pastor's College and throughout the country, on his way to the land of his fathers. There was something solemn about saying farewell to the friends who had everywhere received him as a man, a brother, and a Christian, and had made him feel happy and at home. He had enjoyed two years of real freedom. If he took one minute for each year of his slavery his speech would occupy twenty-eight minutes and forty-five seconds representing twenty-eight years and nine months. He then went on to speak of the horrors of slavery. If the negro wanted to know anything about the Bible, he must know it from his master, or some appointed one; and any white man who imagined that the negro has as much religious liberty as himself would soon find the climate unhealthy for him. The preacher was the negro's high priest, and such an assumption of authority he, the speaker, could not digest. He had little faith in what he said, and less faith in what he was. He could remember when his poor loving mother taught him the Lord's Prayer, and later on taught him the Alphabet, and then to count a hundred, which was about the extent of her own knowledge. When her anxiety about his learning came to be observed he was removed to another slave field. He used to hear talk about Spurgeon during the war, but he did not stand very high in the estimation of his masters. Alluding to the statement that negroes were slaves by their own will, he said he could not remember ten minutes time when he wanted to be a slave. He wanted freedom, but like the caged creature, could not get out. He tried several times to run away, but failed. He looked upon white people as a bad lot. In July, 1857, he felt he must go and preach the Gospel, but first wanted to be baptized, but the master did not want that. He had to obtain a pass from him for that, and that he would not grant, as he wanted him to join the Episcopal Church, for which they were erecting an edifice. He went into the array with his master during the war, and well he remembered how at its close, on the morning of 3rd April, 1865, at eight o'clock he got his freedom. He should never forget that. Not long after this he lost a little boy whom he had hoped to train as a preacher. Subsequently he accepted a call to some mission work in Colorado, hoping it might lead to his being able to obtain an education, the necessity for which he continually saw. He there read some tracts of Mr. Spurgeon's which increased his feeling of responsibility in the matter. In spite of what modern thought men might teach, he was sure that Negroes had the same feelings as white men. He described his visit to Manchester and his admission thence to the Pastors' College to take his first course of study. He could not tell them the good it had done him, in enabling him to go to Africa and preach the everlasting Gospel. Mr. Richardson had come on from America to join him. He had had seven years experience in school teaching. They were going to be together; although the Missionary Society would only support him, the speaker, they should have all things in common like the Saviour when on earth. He knew the Lord was with them, and that they would be successful, because, if only for the conversion of one soul, it was worth going to Africa; but he wanted ten thousand. The farewell word should be, 'pray for us.' They needed the people's prayers, the prayers of friends at home, who were as a light in the land of the Lord to light up the world. In conclusion he pleaded with them for the sake of two hundred million of people in Africa, the land of his fathers, for the sake of the Christians there, for the sake of the missionaries who had left their home comforts and families, for the sake of England's future brightness, for the sake of humanity, for Jesus' sake, to do all they could to stop the slave trade in the land of his fathers, and to take possession of the great Congo with that end in view.

"Mr. Spurgeon, speaking of the capability of the Negro race to rise, said they only needed the evil of slavery to pass away, and they would find them produce some fine competitors. They must stand up for the Negro in spite of his colour.

"Several hymns were interspersed in the proceedings suitable to the occasion, upon 'Ethiopia's pride,' 'Africa for Christ,' and others. Some of these the missionaries and their wives sang alone--one or two in the African language, --with a singularly impressive effect.

"In pointing out the pecuniary needs of these friends, Mr. Spurgeon said he hoped the sympathy of the audience was more practical than that of the man who pitied the poor fiddler who had lost his fiddle, remarking that it was a sad case; whereupon the fiddler replied that he did not mind the case if only he could recover the fiddle. He--Mr. Spurgeon--felt like ten pounds, and several other friends felt to the same extent, and contributions amounting, within a few minutes, to forty-seven pounds were given, and this sum was afterwards supplemented by a collection. The Sunday School at the Tabernacle presented Mr. Johnson with a purse of money contributed by them, and it was handed to him on the platform by one of the little girl scholars, Miss Rosa Wigney, being acknowledged with considerable emotion.

"Mr. Richardson gave a short account of his life and call to the ministry, and of the determination of himself and his wife to go to Africa to preach the Gospel. He expressed his thanks for all the sympathy and instruction he had received, and said he hoped friends at home would not be long without some interesting information respecting their work in Africa, and especially that many of the heathen were born again. He mentioned that they had been learning the African language under the tuition of Mr. Saker, who had had so much experience in the country as a missionary and a translator."

Mr. and Mrs. Spurgeon's Interest

One of our farewell meetings is mentioned by Mrs. Spurgeon in her book, "Ten Years of my Life," and one of the hymns is referred to in her most charming style:--

"February.--A quaint message comes to me to-day across the sea from Africa. It stirs pleasant memories and well fulfils the loving commission given to encourage and strengthen my heart. Thus it runs: 'Tell dear Mrs. Spurgeon to "Keep inching along, Jesus Christ'll come by-and-by."'

"I must explain the nature of this uncommon communication, and why it so interests and touches me. When our two coloured brethren, Messrs. Johnson and Richardson, were on the eve of departure for Missionary work in Africa, they came with their wives to our dear home to bid us farewell. A very pleasant and memorable time we spent together, their Pastor encouraging them in the work to which they had devoted themselves, and their love and sympathy overflowing to him and to me--then very sick--in return. At the request of my dear husband they sang to me some of the strange sweet songs of their captivity, for three of them had once been slaves; and all who had heard these plaintive melodies sung in the Tabernacle at their farewell meetings will agree with me that sweeter, yet sadder, melodies could scarcely be imagined. My heart was especially attracted by a peculiar song, to which they sung as a refrain these most curious words:--

"Keep inching along, keep inching along,
Like a poor inch worm--
Jesus Christ'll come by-and-by,"

"It is impossible to describe the weird pathos with which they invested these few sentences, and my interest was so aroused that I asked if some special history attached to this strange song. Then they told me how in the sorrowful days of their bondage, they would stealthily gather together night after night in one of the low miserable huts they called their home, in darkness and terror, they would pray with one another, and in muffled, tones would whisper, 'Keep inching along.' Sing it aloud they dared not, for fear of their master, who would have exacted full penalty by stripes for such an assertion of nature's rights; but rocking too and fro in time to the wailing melody, they found a 'fearful pleasure' in the disobedience which brought spiritual comfort to their oppressed souls. The glorious hope of future deliverance excited and enraptured their hearts. 'Sometimes,' they said, 'one of the number would forget the caution and silence so essential to our safety, and a voice would ring out in the darkness, jubilant, and clear, 'Jesus Christ'll come by-and-by.' Then all would sit trembling after such an outburst, lest they should be discovered by the shout of anticipated triumph, and angels might have wept for the poor, down-trodden souls and have longed to bring the sweet chariot 'coming for to carry them home.' (On many of the plantations the slaves were allowed to sing all they wanted to.)

"'Will you sing to me in whispers as you sang then?' I asked, and they very sweetly complied with my wish, though, blessed be God, their surroundings were now so happy that they could give but a faint copy of the terrible reality. I shall never forget that painful hushing of their voices. There was not a dry eye in that little company when the song was ended; but we wiped our tears away, soon remembering that the cause for sorrow no longer existed. The 'poor inch-worms' are now free, noble educated men and women; they can sing and pray and preach as loudly and as long as they please, and are bound for the land of their fathers, with the intention of exercising these privileges to the full, and making known the Gospel of the Grace of God to their kindred according to the flesh. The Lord go forth with them and prosper them. The echoes of that singular song have lingered with me ever since, and many a time have they comforted my heart. Day by day the work of the Book Fund has kept 'inching along,' and though prevented by my weakness from taking giant strides, how gracious is the Lord to allow His unworthy child to creep even inch by inch along the pleasant road of service for Him. I should like to send forth fifty parcels weekly. I should like each parcel to be a complete library of theological lore, so that very soon not a true minister in the land should faint and fail for lack of knowledge; but as my highest aims cannot be fulfilled, I will thankfully do what I can, and with the Lord's blessing resting on the books sent out in his name, my ten to twenty packages a week will not fail to accomplish His good purpose. Thus, cheerfully, gladly, I 'kept inching along,' and for me, as surely as for the greatest saint on earth-- 'Jesus Christ'll come by-and-by.'"

Sailing for Africa - The Land in Sight

November 6th, 1878, we bade farewell to London. On the afternoon of the 9th we sailed from Liverpool on the S. S.Kinsembo, and in the evening of the 22nd we came in sight of Cape Verd, on the West Coast of Africa. As soon as I caught sight of the peak, nearly thirty miles off, I went into the state room for the telescope presented to me by the Downs Chapel Young Mens' Bible Class, and turned it towards the first visible portion of African soil. For years my prayers had been that I might see Africa, the land of my fathers, and now my prayers were answered. "Delight thyself also in the Lord, and He will give thee the desires of thine heart. Commit thy way unto the Lord; trust also in Him, and He shall bring it to pass." This text was "tried and proved." My feelings of joy were indescribable. I could not leave the state room without falling upon my knees and thanking my Heavenly Father for permitting me to see the poor suffering land of Africa. So delighted was I to be near the coast of the country for which I had prayed, and of which I had dreamed, that I could sleep but little. On the morning of the 23rd I was up at four o'clock to get another look at "the land." Then we entered the month of the Gambia River, As we proceeded up the river I heard that a pilot was expected to meet us. Having been fourteen days on the steamer, we were all anxious to be once more on land. At last we saw a small boat. "There's the pilot; there's the pilot," cried out first one and then another. The little boat was quickly by the side of the steamer, and the pilot came on board. He was a native, and as soon as possible I had an interview with him. His name was William Holfner, and I found him to be an intelligent Christian. It was not long before we found ourselves anchored at the beautiful little town of Bathurst, on the Gambia River. It is about ten miles from the mouth of the river, and contains quite a number of fine dwellings. Here we first put foot on...

African Soil

The chief stores of European merchants front the river. I was surprised to find such fine buildings, a Government House, and barracks and hospital, on a line fronting the river.

Mr. Walcott, a coloured lawyer, who had been educated in England, invited us to his house, as also did Mr. Brown, the American Consul.

We had quite a pleasant time inspecting the town, meeting with different native gentlemen holding office under the British Government. The harbour master, postmaster, city clerk, Queen's Counsel, and the Customs House officers were all native black men. We also met native merchants, shipbuilders, and men in almost every capacity of business, educated in England or in Sierra Leone.

There were two fine churches and a thriving day-school, which made my heart glad. Here also we had the first opportunity of seeing the tall Mandingoes, Joloffs, and natives of other tribes in their native dress. In the back part of the town we saw many huts formed of bamboo, and thatched with long grass.

The Gambia River is a magnificent one, is said to be navigable for a distance of nearly four hundred miles. But what was better still, the streams of Gospel blessing were flowing, and messengers of life were doing great business, and merchants of the commerce of heaven were trading largely for the King of kings.

It was on the morning of November 27th, we entered the harbour of Free Town.

Life in Sierra Leone

The first British settlement formed on the West Coast of Africa for the suppression of the slave trade and the encouragement of legitimate commerce was Sierra Leone. Free Town is the capital, and is indeed a beautiful place, situated on the south side of the river; and the first view of it impressed us with its grandeur. The land in the neighbourhood inclines gradually upwards, and is covered everywhere with vegetation, presenting a most picturesque view. Most of the buildings in the district are substantial, and almost every house has its large garden in which banana, orange, cocoanut, pineapple and many other kinds of delicious fruits grow. High up on the hill, in the rear of the town are to be seen the Government House, barracks, hospital, and the signal station.

At ten o'clock we went ashore and visited the market house, quite a large building, where fruits, vegetables, and articles of tin and hardware were displayed for sale. Many of the natives speak the English language well. I was greatly pleased to meet with some who talked to me about our blessed Jesus.

A wedding in Africa is an interesting sight. A large gathering of people stood around the gates of the Episcopal Church, a fine building, close by the market house. We had been told that a grand wedding would take place in this church at eleven o'clock; the daughter of a Free Town merchant was to be married to a merchant from Switzerland. We passed through the gate into the church and found that a large company of all shades from black to white had assembled. Nearly all of them were fashionably dressed. After a few minutes of waiting the bride and the bridegroom made their appearance, with their relatives and many friends. Mr. Broadhurst, the bride's father, was a wealthy merchant, and very popular among all classes in Free Town. On this occasion all the principal business houses in the town were closed. After the ceremony we took a long walk along the street leading from the church to the residence of the bride. Along the entire way flags were hanging out of almost every window. In many places ropes were stretched across the street with flags and mottoes suspended. We were invited by the bride's father to the house. The bride had many valuable presents, including a handsome silver tea set which was sent to her from England.

The most pleasing feature in Free Town, and from what I heard, throughout the colony, is the progress of peace. Nothing can or has civilized and elevated like the Word of God. Christian schools have long since been established, and for years made most wonderful progress.

Liberia

Our next stopping-place was Grand Bassa, in the Republic of Liberia. Liberia at that time included the grain coast of Northern Guinea, West Africa, 600

86

miles along the coast, and over 200 miles into the interior. Liberia was originally founded by the American Colonization Society in 1821; and in 1847 it became an Independent State, acknowledged by all the European powers. It was formed entirely by coloured men and women and their descendants, and the Government was modelled after that of the United States; and the first article in the code of laws is that "Christianity is the foundation of all true law"; the next is that "Education is a necessity admitting of no neglect." There were 30,000 freed slaves and their descendants, and 2,000,000 natives subject to their control, and all under this elevating code of laws. The natural beauty along the coast of Liberia, from Grand Cape Mount to the Gulf of Guinea is wonderful, and the scenery is very fine. A few miles from the coast the country rises to hills, with gigantic trees, presenting a panorama that could only be described by the skilful artist.

Monrovia is the capital of the Republic. It is surrounded by trees, and rests on a beautiful hill overlooking the sea. There are many fine buildings in the city, which are a credit to the Monrovian people. The President's house is built of brick, as are also many of the other buildings; some are built of stone. The wharves face the sea and there are firms belonging to natives and doing large business with Europe and America. While in Monrovia I called, in company with the Hon. John H. Smith, U.S. Consul, at that time, to see the late General Sherman, who did large business both with England and America.

The soil of Liberia is extremely fertile and will produce all kinds of tropical fruits, sugar canes, indigo, Indian corn, rice, cotton, cocoa, peanuts, and coffee--the finest in the world. Vegetables are cultivated with great success. There are to be found the best dye-woods, the ebony, the gum plant, and the gigantic palm trees which produce the palm oil. On the way to England from Africa 1,500 casks were shipped on the same steamer to Liverpool, a good share of it being from the coast of Liberia. Goats, swine, sheep, cattle, and fowls all thrive in Liberia. This responsible Republic has a glorious work to accomplish in the future.

November 30th at six o'clock in the morning we arrived at Nifou, on the coast of Liberia. I counted forty-nine canoes, with two or three natives in each, going out fishing. At twenty-five minutes to ten we stopped at Grand Cess, Liberia, and here fifteen canoes came out, with from three to twenty natives in each. These belonged to the Kroo tribe, the aborigines of a part of Liberia. They are a fine-looking people and very industrious. But for this class of people I do not know what the European traders or the African Steamship Companies would do. all the steamers reaching Sierre Leone and the coast of Liberia take on board a gang of "Kroomen" to do the work of the ship in the hot climate. One hundred and thirty were taken on board to go down the coast to work. Many of them speak broken English. It is quite a sight to see these people coming out to meet these steamers. Their canoes are very light, carved out of one piece of wood, and formed like a cigar. They are propelled by several of the men, rowing or paddling, who sit down upon their heels in the bottom of the boat. Their yells as they approached the steamer, and when they came on board to do their work were simply distracting. Each man selects a name to suit himself: "Salt-water," "Coffee," "Shilling," "Glass-bottle," "Pea-soup," "Bottle of Beer," and the like, are common names among them. "Coffee" seemed to be the favourite.

There are many interesting things one would like to mention about the Grebo people, the Bassa people, the Golas, who years ago when the Liberians were in danger of being defeated, under their chief boatswain, took part with the young colony; also of the Deys, who were once a powerful tribe, and the Veys, who years ago invented an alphabet for writing their own language, and this they can boast of as being done entirely by their own ingenuity and enterprise. Accounts of this were published in the "Missionary Herald" for July, 1834; but we have not the space for the their insertion here. The coloured Foreign Missionary Convention of the Southern States of America has done a great work among the Veys. It is estimated that there are ten thousand of this tribe. It is also believed that at least 100,000 people of the adjacent tribes speak the Vey language. We thank God that now hundreds of boys and girls and young men and women from Africa are in the schools and colleges of Europe and of America, being prepared to return as teachers and missionaries. But there are also some good schools in Liberia; and in Monrovia there is at least one college, built at great cost, and having a faculty of several coloured professors. Newspapers are published and there is a regular postal system.

Elmina on the West Coast had a population of about 20,000 in 1881. Cape Coast Castle is a beautiful place, with its ports, lighthouses, signal, and large castle. Around on the heights are to be seen beautiful houses of the wealthy natives and Europeans. Accra is another lovely place, and important also. These are all on the Gold Coast.

Lagos was said to be the most populous town on the West Coast. It has wide streets, nice stores, and many fine dwellings. The people have their markets, soldiers, police force, churches, schools, court-house, Government house, custom house, and barracks. It had an estimated population of 80,000 people.

Bonny, one of the stopping places, was in past years a favourite rendezvous for slave ships. Only about fifteen years prior to this time they were nearly all cannibals. This place is so unhealthy that European merchants live in hulks out on the river.

Archdeacon Crowther, who had charge of the Mission work at the time, invited me to dine with him.

Here I had the pleasure of dining also with an African Princess--The Princess Florence Cecilia Pebble Pepper. She and her brother, King George, were both educated in England. Mr. Crowther took me to the school, where I was delighted to hear the children repeat passages of Scripture, give their opinion about them, then go through history, arithmetic, and geography, in all of which they seemed proficient.

I took a walk round the native huts. I saw that several huts had skulls hung up in them. I was told by Mr. Crowther that these were the skulls of captives taken in battle, and that these very people, years ago were cannibals, and had eaten the flesh of their enemies to make them brave. But now, thank God, through the influence of the Gospel among these people, this custom had passed away, and they were ashamed to be reminded of the past. Not only has the preaching of the Gospel done great good in Bonny, but far in the interior they are giving up their idols, and bowing to the one true God.

Ashantee

In travelling on the West Coast of Africa years ago one often heard of Ashantee as a powerful kingdom. The Ashantees are very numerous, warlike, and strong. This kingdom lies inland from the English settlements between the rivers Assini and Volta, and is estimated to have a population of four million people, who are noted for their skill in manufacturing and colouring cotton, and making earthen-ware goods and swords. They tan leather and do work in all kinds of metals. They are a well-made and cleanly people, and have proved to be courageous warriors, and have given the English expeditions much trouble. Abundance of gold was found in the country. According to the statements of Bowditch Dupuis and others, many years ago the display of gold was surprising. They found the attendants of the King laden with ornaments of gold. The common articles for daily use were made of gold.

But it is repulsive reading about the human sacrifices which were offered in those days. These gentlemen saw at the King's palace the royal executioner, with his hatchet on his breast, and the fatal blood-stained stool before him, ready at the sound of the death drum to do his fearful work. They heard that the King had recently murdered--over his mother's grave, three hundred victims. On the death of a royal person, many hundred people were massacred. In late years, through the influence of missionaries and the authorities at Cape Coast Castle, there has not been so much of this wholesale slaughtering of human beings; yet often there are many murdered.

Dahomey

This is another powerful Kingdom in West Africa, separated from Ashantee by the River Volta. Wholesale murder in years past was one of the chief features in their religious and state ceremonies. Abomey, the capital of Dahomey, has been referred to as a human slaughterhouse, where the king's chiefs and people found their greatest pleasure and excitement in sacrificing as many as 2,000 victims at one great festival. They not only murdered a large number of people on the death of a great man, but believed that in the other world a king is still a king, and a slave is still a slave; hence they annually kill the complement of slaves to send to the departed king. Also, whenever the king wanted to send a message to his deceased relatives, he delivered it to one of his slaves, whose head was instantly cut off, that he might carry the message to the other world, that the deceased might know that he was not forgotten. Some years ago, when the King of Dahomey died, 280 of his wives were murdered.

The King's palace at Abomey was surrounded by a clay wall twenty feet high, the top of which was said to be covered with human skulls. Thank God, through the work and influence of Christian Missions and civilization, this is vastly changed.

Our Destination and Sphere

After stopping a short time at the island of Fernando Po, where we were entertained by the wife of the British Consul, we arrived at Victoria, Cameroons, on the afternoon of Saturday, December 14th, 1878. This was our destination.

Victoria was a beautiful little place with a population of 500 inhabitants, fronting Ambas Bay, with a commanding view of bay and sea. On the North, South, and East are high hills. In the distance can be seen the Cameroon Mountains, 13,000 feet above the level of the sea. The place was beautifully laid out with broad streets. Each house had a large garden, in many of which were to be seen the palm, lime, cocoa-nuts, bread fruit, custard fruit, orange, banana, and plantain trees. The cottages were neat and clean, and built after the style of European cottages. These were occupied by the English-speaking people who were native Christians, and many of them had for long years been earnest workers for our blessed Jesus.

The day after our arrival being the Sabbath, the late Rev. Q. W. Thomson, Missionary-in-charge, invited me to take the morning service. A few minutes before seven o'clock in the morning the bell rang, and we were soon at the church, a fine stone building capable of seating 350 to 400 people. In a short time quite a number of well-dressed intelligent looking people had assembled. I gave out a hymn, and they sang as well as many congregations I have preached to in America and England. When I began to read, nearly all of them opened their Bibles to follow me in the lesson. Here I had the opportunity for the...

First Time to Preach in Africa about Jesus

I took for my text, "Believe on the Lord Jesus Christ, and thou shalt be saved" (Acts xvi. 31). I cannot remember ever preaching to a more attentive audience.

At ten o'clock we all went to the sabbath school. Rev. C. H. Richardson and myself were invited to take classes; my class was of young men. All of them could read the Bible. At the close of the school I requested the children to sing, "Come to the Saviour." They sang it beautifully. The school was well attended and perfect order was observed during the service.

For years Victoria was a city of refuge. The late Reverend Alfred Saker, who laboured in Africa about thirty years, established this station in the year 1858. He purchased from the natives for the Baptist Missionary Society of Great Britain a tract of land extending ten miles along the coast and five miles inland--Victoria about centre. Here no one was allowed to hold slaves or to sell his daughters for wives, and no one was to be punished for witchcraft. It was the custom for each man to have as many wives as he was able to purchase among the natives. On returning to the coast from the interior I stopped with a chief who had forty wives. At Victoria no man was permitted to have more than one. It often happened among the natives that when a child died one wife accused another of having bewitched it. The accused was then arrested and made to drink the juice of a wood called cass-wood, which often killed at once. Men also were accused of witchcraft, and were made to drink this juice. If they died they were considered guilty; but if they recovered, as some did, a payment was enforced. If the people who were accused made their escape to Victoria they were safe.

The Missionaries and Christians have for years rescued many of these people who were on the very verge of death. In one month the late Rev. Q. W. Thomson rescued eight who had been condemned to death. In 1880 there were over 400 of these refugees in Victoria, where they were under the influence of the Gospel, and their children were taught in the day school. Many of them became Christians.

This barbarous superstition stilt exists in many places. The following appeared in the Daily Chronicle, August 18th, 1897:--

"West Coast of Africa.--A strange superstition.--The British and African Company's royal mail steamer Roquelle arrived at Liverpool yesterday morning from the west coast of Africa. The Roquelle left Bereby on the Kroo coast, on the 21st ult., when a remarkable circumstance was reported. Some time ago a steamer was lost and a number of Kroo boys from Bereby were drowned. Several other Kroo boys from the same place were saved, and returned home. The relatives of the deceased boys became imbued with the idea that the surviving Kroomen had caused the accident to the ship which resulted in the death of their relatives. They thereupon resorted to the native superstitious method of making them drink cass water. This cass water is a poisonous liquid, but if the native drinks and survives it is taken as a proof that he is innocent. Should he, however, die he is regarded as guilty. It is seldom that any who drink the real cass water recover. In the present case it was reported that the natives were not content with dealing with the survivors they could lay their hands upon, but also made some of their relatives pass through the terrible ordeal. It was said that in all about twenty natives perished in this way."

MISSION HOUSE AT VICTORIA.

Incidents in the Interior

We had been in Victoria three days only when I was taken with the fever. On January 20th, Rev. C. H. Richardson and Rev Q. W. Thomson left for the interior, to select a new station; I, being ill, could not go. On the 4th of February, Mr. Thomson returned. Mr. Richardson having suffered with fever, had been left at Bakundu, eighty miles in the interior, with two native Christians. Bakundu had been selected as the new mission station, and he would remain there until joined by his wife and by Mrs. Johnson and myself. The only road through this country were narrow footpaths from town to town, sometimes in the tracks of the elephant. All provisions or luggage had to be carried on men's heads. The account we had of the route was anything but attractive to Mrs. Johnson and Mrs. Richardson-- high rugged hills to climb and strong swift flowing streams to cross. Although we knew that the traders along the river objected to interior mission work we concluded that we should go by water on account of my wife and her sister. The late Rev. George Grenfell, at that time a merchant at Victoria, kindly offered to go with us.

On Thursday, the 6th of February, before daybreak, and after a season of prayer with the Rev. Mr. Thomson and the native brethren, we left Victoria in an open boat rowed by Kroomen, followed by a large canoe with our provisions and eight men, and before night we came to Mungo Creek. Here our one interpreter and guide lost his way. We had intended to get by Mungo and Mbungo, the two principal towns, in the night. We passed Mungo, but at daybreak we found ourselves between the two towns. At about eight o'clock we got under the bank of the river, took out our things, and prepared breakfast under the palm trees. Being discovered by the natives we left in the afternoon. As we passed Mbungo there were a few people on the bank, to whom we spoke, and passed unmolested. On Friday night, a man passed us in a canoe, and commenced to beat his drum as he went up the river.

Talking By Drum Telegraphy

These people can talk to each other on their drums almost as well as we can send a message in this country by telegraph. They have schools in which to teach their children this drum-beating telegraphy. On this occasion this man said on his drum, "White man come into our country." The natives with us, twelve in number, did not tell me of this till the next day.

On Saturday morning at nine o'clock, as we were taking our breakfast on the river bank, several canoes passed us, with fifteen to twenty men in each. Seeing they were well armed with guns and cutlasses, we began to feel suspicious. About ten o'clock we came up with them. They had all stopped on the bank, put on their war caps, and stood in a line along the river.

We were ordered to come ashore. We told them we would not; if they had anything to say to us they must come out in their canoes. They tried to make us leave our boat and go on the beach, but we resolved to stay in our boat. I do not know of any time in my life when I realised the precious promise of my blessed Jesus more than in this hour, "Lo, I am with you alway." I said to my wife and her sister, Mrs. Richardson, "We lean upon the Lord."

At one time we were surrounded by nearly one hundred men, armed with cutlasses, ready to cut into us as soon as the young prince gave the word of command. We soon found that it was impossible for us to proceed.

Prisoners

We had to return as prisoners to Mungo. We were within six hours of Bakundu beach. Late in the night we arrived at Mungo. Here they wanted us to leave our boat, and go into the town and see the King. We knew how superstitious they were about our English boat, so we resolved, if we had to die, to die in the boat.

There were many of the traders in Mungo who could talk broken English, and who knew how the English protected the Missionaries. Mr. Grenfell, who had been several years in Africa, and knew something of the people, threatened them with English authority. After the King and his men had held a consultation, the King said to me, "You must pay for passing through my country." To this we agreed. I gave him a large overcoat, a bag of rice, a box of sugar, a blanket, and a barrel of hard biscuits. While he was admiring the coat which he soon put on, we pushed off. I have never seen that King since.

Great was the anxiety of that night; the continual looking back to see if we were being pursued, and a constant outlook also on either side of the narrow river against wild beasts; but God, who had said, "Go," was with us.

Our disappointment at having to return so far was very great indeed, but not so great as our anxiety about Mr. Richardson, alone, ill, eighty miles up country, with hostile tribes between him and us. A report, circulated by the natives, reached us that Mr. Richardson had died. Something had to be done. A consultation was held, and the late Rev. James R. Newby, who was present, volunteered to go at once to Bon Junga, seven miles up the mountain, and at that time the only station on that line to the interior, in the direction of Bakundu. This journey had to be made at night, for it was after dark when the brethren met. It had also to be made on foot, on a narrow path, through the thick wood and bush, where there were many wild beasts and great serpents. A young man offered to go with Mr. Newby. They put their trust in God, and set out with guns and lanterns in their hands, and were soon out of sight. Thank God they reached the Mission Station in safety. Rev. Mr. Wilson, a native missionary, and one of the native Christians, joined them for Bakunda the next morning. The following Saturday night they returned with the good tidings that Mr. Richardson was much better and at work, preparing to receive us.

Nine days after our return to Victoria we commenced our journey, this time going overland. Mrs. Johnson and Mrs. Richardson were carried in hammocks when they did not prefer walking. Our provisions and luggage were carried on men's heads.

I have already mentioned that the best roads in this part of Africa are mere footpaths through the forest, from town to town, on which the natives walk in single file, a few yards from each other, each man with his load on his head, and his cutlass in his hand or at his side, to defend himself against any beast or serpent that might be in the path. This was the way we started out of Victoria for our long journey through the wilderness.

MISSION HOUSE AT BAKANDU,
WEST AFRICA.

Trials of Travel

The first days' journey we made seven miles only, as we were advised by our chief, Mr. Thomson, to stop the first night at the mission station, Bon Junga. On Tuesday we travelled about seventeen miles, as far as we could judge, and we spent the night at the house of a chief, who made us welcome, and who begged to have a missionary left with him. On the Wednesday we made an early start, but did not make much progress. I became very ill. Then began our experiences of the native carriers in the overland travel in Africa. Several of the men refused to go any further. Some were away ahead in the path, and some a long way behind. After a short "palaver" or talk with the men, we persuaded them to go on, Mrs. Johnson and Mrs. Richardson helping to carry some of the loads. We had hoped to get more native help at the next town, but the tribe was at war, so we could not get any men to come with us. Our

95

next difficulty was the crossing of a deep river; the natives plunged in and swam across. We had to cut down trees and make a raft; on this we put a large tub, into which first Mrs. Johnson got and the raft was then pushed out into the current. Some of the natives swam by the sides of the raft, keeping it up and directing its course. Mrs. Johnson was not sorry when the other side was reached. Then the men brought back the raft and tub and her sister crossed in the same way; and last of all I came with the provisions.

As we advanced into the interior we found the people along the route in a better condition than we had expected. They had fixed dwellings, many of them built neatly of bamboo, and well thatched with mats made from the palm fronds. They had their gardens and farms, their laws and customs, so that wherever we stopped at night we and our goods were safe.

There are some eight or ten towns between Victoria and Bakundu. We left Victoria on Monday morning. On the following Saturday afternoon we arrived at Bakundu, where we found Mr. Richardson well. We had a company of thirty men with us when we arrived and our arrival gave rise to much excitement.

The first thing that struck me as singular was the joy of the old King. For years he had desired to have a Missionary in his town, to teach the people, as he had heard that the natives were taught on the coast. Not only the King, but his sons and all his head men seemed delighted to see us. On Sunday we held a meeting in an old unoccupied house. We found the people slaves to superstition and witchcraft, but not so bad as the other tribes around them.

The custom of giving cass-wood juice prevailed here as among the Bakwalli people, of whom I have made mention. The first case we heard of was a young man in the town who was accused of witching his sister's child. He was made very ill from the effects of the juice, but finally recovered. As soon as we heard of it, Mr. Richardson, who was always fearless and ready on all occasions to admonish the people, went at once to the King and told him how wrong it was to allow such a practice. The King promised to put a stop to it. He kept his word, and during the nine months I was in the interior I did not hear of another case.

In The Work in Africa

When we first arrived at Bakunda we could hardly sleep at night for the yells of the people in their dance and the beating of the drums. This was kept up day and night. They knew nothing of a Sabbath; hence they continued their drum-beating all the week round. Mr. Richardson went to the King to have a law passed that no work or drum-beating or dancing be done on the Sabbath. The old King at once consented. The people then wanted to know how they were to distinguish the Sabbath. Mr. Richardson promised to walk up and down the street every Friday night blowing a trumpet, to tell the people that the next day was Saturday, and that they must bring enough provisions from their farms to last them over the Sabbath. This plan is worth adoption in civilised countries where there is an increase of the heathen rioting, though it appears a little more intelligent.

The people had great faith in what the Bible said. On one occasion, while Mr. Richardson was away with men at Victoria, the women came to me to get me to ask the Bible if their husbands were safe, and I read the promises of protection to them that believed.

A Dying King

Not long after we came to Bakunda we all began to pray that God would convert the King, who was about ninety years of age. One day we heard that he was very ill, and soon afterwards he sent for us and we attended him, gave him some medicine which seemed to do him good; but we soon found that his sickness was unto death. One day he sent for me, and I noticed that he was very ill indeed. He had a wooden bowl by his bed, in which was a liquid thick and black, and this he was taking occasionally as I talked with him. I asked him what it was. He said, "Witch make me sick, tell me not to take white man's medicine, and I take this medicine get my stomach full, old witch come in my mouth, go in my stomach, then get blind and come out." I tried to persuade him that all power was in the hands of God; that by believing Him and trusting in Him all these fears would leave him. He had always listened attentively to what we had to tell him about the great plan of salvation.

We continued to visit him, and day after day he would send for medicine. One Sabbath afternoon my wife and I both lay ill in bed. Mr. and Mrs. Richardson went into the town to hold a service; they found the King very ill. The excitement was such that he could not hold a meeting, so he returned home. Then we were sent for; I was hardly able to get out of bed and crawl into the King's house. Women were not allowed to see the King, not even his wives, but the house was full of men, and one man sat at his back to hold him up, and two men were on either side, three of these men being his sons. The old man was very weak, and it seemed he would soon pass from time into eternity. He looked first at Mr. Richardson and then at me. His youngest son, "Ngatee," about ten years old, was called to his side. He took one hand of the lad and put it into Mr. Richardson's hand, the other into mine, and said, "I give this boy to you. Take him and bring him up as your own child; dress him like white man; teach him to talk English and to read and write. His brothers will get a wife for him." He requested that we should also take the girl whom the brothers selected and keep her in the family and educate her. He then said: "Don't fear; I am going now. The town belongs to me and I now give it to you. My son Etau will succeed me. Take care of him, be a father to him and the people." This son Etau was about thirty years old. He then charged Mr. Richardson to take the names of the boys and commence school at once. Some sixty names were taken the next day. Mr. Richardson then told him again the story of God's great love, and that if he would believe and rest in what the Word of God said they would meet each other in heaven. I then said, "Ta Ta Nambulee" (for that was his name), 'you say that you are going now; are you prepared to meet God?" "Ah!" said the old man, "I have been ill these ten days, and He has taken care of me; I can still trust Him." We then wanted to pray with him, but his sons preferred that we should let him rest, as he was so weak; so we went away, leaving our interpreter, who told us that after we had gone the King said to his son who was to succeed him: "Etau, whatever these men tell you, believe it, for I have found them to be true men."

Oh, how we all rejoiced to hear this; so often had we prayed for the conversion of this man. One evening we sent our cook up to the King to tell his experience and to pray with him. He was a native convert. The old King enjoyed it very much, and said, "Tell white man to pray to God and ask Him, if it is His will please spare me a little longer; but if not, please prepare me to meet Him."

For years this King had heard of the work of the Missionaries on the coast, eighty miles away. A year before we settled at Bakundu, Rev. Q. W. Thomson had visited him and promised to send a Missionary to labour among his people. After we had settled among them he was anxious to see how we succeeded. He sent for the women, who do nearly all the work on the farms, and charged them not to work on the Sabbath, as it was God's day; that they must attend Divine Service instead.

This old King, with whom we had to speak through an interpreter, and who usually referred to us as the "white people," was eventually taken to his farm, where he died in two or three days. We arrived in Bakundu in February 22nd, 1879. The King died in the latter part of June in the same year.

Oh what gratitude we ought to feet for that we have been favoured with the Gospel which opens the heart of man and the country he inhabits.

I believe there are to-day in West Africa thousands like Ta Ta Nambulee, who have heard through traders and travellers something about the great mission work and the one true God, and who are anxious to hear more; who are not satisfied with their condition, and who want to know more but who have no way to learn; their souls craving something upon which to rest, something stronger, better and firmer than idols of wood and stone. In this condition they move about from year to year like the beast in the cage, ever walking up and down, trying to escape, but never able to succeed. But how can they hear without a preacher?

> "'Come over and help us,' is their cry,
> 'Come now, oh, do not pass us by;
> We are seeking truth, we are seeking light,
> We seek deliverance from dark night.
> Can you, who have the Gospel, fail
> To hear our cry, our doleful wail?"

God is now preparing the hearts of the people to receive the truth. Let us send it to them.

Conditions of Life

The attention which the people gave to the preaching of the Word every Sabbath was very encouraging. The men and boys always attended in the morning, the women in the afternoon. One Sabbath afternoon it was found that some of the women had gone to their farms to work. The young King at once left the meeting, called his brothers and the head men together and passed a law that "if any man or woman did work on the Sabbath they should pay a cow. If they had no cow, their house should be pulled down over their heads."

In Bakundu, as in all the towns along the route in 1879, all the children were naked. Men and women had a cloth around their waists. The men generally dressed more than the women. As soon as they became better acquainted with us they wanted us to give them clothing. Tobacco and cloth are the currency in trade in the interior. Some of the people on the Mungo river raise corn and sweet potatoes, and when baked, fried or roasted, it is a very good substitute for bread. The yam and cocoa are plentiful; the former is very like potatoes when cooked. These they raise on their farms. They have fowls, goats, sheep, and cattle all through the country. The sheep have hair like goats. The Bakundu people are not a savage people, nor cruel like their neighbours and other tribes. One never hears of any murdering among them as among other tribes. They are very kind-hearted, and in every way differ much from the surrounding and coast tribes. Many of the West African tribes are continually at war.

The Undisputed Territory of the Devil

You hear of their drinking the blood and eating the heart of their enemies; of walls covered with human skulls; of a pavement made of human skulls on which to walk. Truly the dark places of the earth are full of the habitations of cruelty.

Some tribes pay homage to lakes, rivers, and mountains, believing that their gods live there. In some places you hear houses are kept for serpents, and these repulsive reptiles are worshipped. At Dix Cove, on the west coast, it is said they once had a crocodile which they worshipped. At Duke Town, on the Old Calabar River, in 1859, human flesh was sold in the markets; but I saw nothing of this at Bakundu.

These people have queer superstitions, and one must be among them to realise what slaves they are to them. When it rains they beat their drums to make it stop. There is a bird which makes a noise at night something like an owl. This is called a witch bird. When it is heard the children are afraid to go out, and guns are fired to frighten it away. In passing their farms you often see a stick set in the ground, split at the top, with a piece of cloth or wool put crosswise in it. I was told that this was to keep off thieves. One night a man came to get medicine for his child, and soon after he left the house he cried out in the most pitiful manner,--"Witch come to take my child." How sad and helpless are those who are without a knowledge of God.

During the rainy season food generally becomes scarce; the elephants destroy their plantain farms, and the continual heavy rains prevent hunting. One day I heard the natives shouting and singing near our house while it was raining very fast. I looked out and saw a crowd of men at the gate putting up palm branches over it, and burying something under the gateway. I was told that the palm branches were to keep away famine, and that what was buried was to draw game near the town. It was indeed remarkable to see the earnestness and the excitement of these people while they were going through this performance, for they appeared so confident of success.

It was very amusing one day to see their excitement at the lighting of a match, The news soon spread through the country that I could carry fire in my pockets, and take it out and make it burn when I wanted it. One day some ten or twelve men and boys came to see us light a match. When I took the box out of my pocket, they ran as though I had taken a pistol to shoot them. "That's it, that's it," cried the knowing ones, and their consternation seemed to have no bounds.

These people have their Ju Ju houses, or Fetish Temples, like the rest of the tribes; there were three in Bakundu. Here they have their secret meetings. What they do and how they do it I could never find out; but this I do know, that the preaching of the Gospel and the untiring zeal of Mr. Richardson, fighting against error, have been the means of many of the young men losing faith in Ju Ju. Before I left Bakundu, Mr. Richardson had been to hold services in the Ju Ju temples.

They believe that there is a Supreme Being who has great power, but they do not in any way connect Him with themselves. In this they are not much worse than some professed Christians. They do not expect anything from Him; neither do they attribute to Him any qualities good or bad. Their gods are many. The name of their general profession is "Ekodde;" when they are performing any religious ceremony they will tell you that they are "doing Ekodde." Certain medicines have certain names and powers attributed to them. They will take a medicine and use it, and then ask the Ekodde god or other god governing that medicine to give power. Here is instruction for those worshipping the true God. They have a wooden man in their Ju Ju temples called "Mosango," upon which they take oath, believing that a lie told by any person who puts his hand on the head of this image will be exposed.

I was told by a native Christian that men often hold out till they get to the Ju Ju house, but so great is their fear of "Mosango" that they will confess before putting their hand on his head. They used to think that after death they would roam about in some unseen form, often troubling those who had come in for property they had left behind.

Rev. Mr. Wilson told me that the lives of many of the Bakwilli people were miserable all the time; nothing but one continual dread of the witch and what this spirit can do and may do at any time. I believe it to be the same to a great extent among the Bakundu people.

But thank God the everlasting Gospel has made a great change in the people, in a short time.

I was greatly impressed with the intense desire of the people to be taught. Their great wish seemed to be to have their children taught how to read and write, and to talk English. Mr. Richardson had not begun school more than two or three days before he had over a hundred boys. The children learned remarkably quickly, and were very intelligent. Their interest was soon awakened, and they were bright and eager learners.

I was much moved one Sabbath morning. While Mr. Richardson was telling about the love of Jesus, a man asked if the children would be able to tell them the same story out of the Bible after Mr. Richardson had taught them to read and talk English. Here was a joy in store for them.

Mission Joys, Hopes, and Sorrows

The young King and several of his head men requested me to form a class of men and to teach them, while Mr. Richardson taught the children. One Sabbath evening after the service about twenty came to the Mission to be more fully informed about the plan of salvation.

Here is a little report of the work as recorded in The Sword and the Trowel, August, 1879:--

"Messrs. Johnson and Richardson in Africa.--We have news from our coloured friends down to the middle of May. When they wrote they had been for some time settled in their new station, Bakundu, Victoria, Cameroons, where they had commenced work under the auspices of the chief of the village, which contains about 1,000 people. This worthy was very ill in April, and thinking he was going to die, made his will. In one of the clauses he commended his youngest son to the care of the Missionaries, and in another commanded his subjects to obey and protect the Missionaries and their wives. He seems to have been still living when our friends wrote, and through his influence all the boys in the village had been sent to the Mission School. On Sundays services are held in the hut which serves as a temporary schoolroom, and by this time Messrs. Johnson and Richardson are probably able to preach to the people in their own language, although at first they need an interpreter. The people appear to be very favourably inclined toward the Missionaries, and ask them many questions about the Gospel they bring.

"The rainy season had commenced when the last letter was written, and Mrs. Johnson and Mrs. Richardson were still suffering from the fever from which their husbands had recovered. They send very kind messages for all Tabernacle and other friends, and ask our prayers that they may be sustained and blessed in their work. If any friends wish to help them they need not send money, as that is of no use where they are, but they require clothes for the naked population, cloth, prints, buttons, cottons, thread, medicines, etc., for barter and use, and books, slates, pencils, etc., for their school of one hundred and six boys."

Habits of Life

In reference to their food we may say they eat everything, from a snake to an elephant. Dogs are quite a delicacy among them. One of the king's sons brought in a serpent one day. I think it must have been sixteen feet long. They had quite a feast over it. Monkey is another favourite meat. The men are great hunters, and have wonderful tales to tell about monkeys and baboons.

The Bakundu people are very clever with their hands. They make their own fishing and hunting nets, and baskets and beautiful bags out of grass. We had not been in Bakundu long before we found they were anxious to have clothes, especially shirts. They willingly brought us meat (our choice, of course), and offered it in exchange for shirts. Soon quite a number of the head men bought themselves garments. One Sabbath morning just before service, a man came in with his shirt folded under his arm, evidently thinking that was the right style, and when the service was about to begin he put it on.

It was indeed extraordinary to see the attention these people paid, and how earnestly they listened to the good news. A woman came to Mr. Richardson one day, and said, "I have never stopped praying since you first told us what the Bible said." This was several months after his talk with her on some Bible truths.

In Memoriam

About the first of March, 1879, my dear wife was stricken down with the African fever. For months she had most faithfully and patiently watched over and nursed me until I recovered from an attack, and then she fell a victim to the fever, and from that time until her death she was never well. About six weeks before her death she seemed so much better that we all thought she would soon be well, but she insisted that she would not live long.

During the months of May and June we were building our new house. I often said to her how much better we should be in the new house, and what we could do. She replied, "Yes, that is if I live to see it." After the rainy season set in, I said, "We must be careful about our provisions"--we had to send to England for most of them--"as it will be a long time before we can get any more." "Yes," said my dear wife, "but I am going to enjoy those only that are here, for I shall not be here long."

The Bible was her daily study. Mr. Spurgeon's sermons, which were sent out monthly by our kind friend, Mr. S. Wigney, from London, she would read and re-read. Day after day, from morning till night, and from week to week, she found the greatest comfort in reading the Bible.

On Sunday morning, June 29th, I lay in bed ill. Mr. and Mrs. Richardson had gone to hold services in the town. My wife sat down near the bed, and began to talk over our married life of fifteen years and seven months. On Friday, July 4th, she had another attack of fever. The 5th she slept nearly all day. At night she said, "All this day has been lost; I have not read my Bible any." I read for her John xiv. On the Monday night she was delirious nearly all the time. In the morning she said: "Although my mind leaves me at times, I have not lost sight of the rest, that rest. Whom the Son makes free is free indeed."

She repeated her favourite text, "I shall be satisfied when I awake with Thy likeness." About noon she lost her speech, and in this state she lay until eight o'clock on Wednesday evening, July 9th, when my blessed Jesus called her home from the land of our fathers to "that rest, and that crown."

The house was soon filled with the natives, manifested great sympathy. Late in the night Mr. Richardson told them that they could go home--King, Queen, and head men were all present. They said "No, this is a bereavement in which we are all concerned. It is our grief as well as yours." Thus they remained all night. Though my wife could speak but a few words of the language, she was already dearly beloved by the men, women, and children of Bakundu. They called her "mamma." I do not think a more devoted wife ever lived. Her heart and soul and service were with me in all my efforts for my blessed Jesus.

The following appears in Mrs. Spurgeon's book, "Ten Years of my Life." News comes from Africa of the death of Mrs. Johnson, one of the dear souls who sang so sweetly to us before leaving for missionary work there, and who joined in sending the message to me, "keep inching along." She is now singing the new song and has full realization of the blessedness of being "for ever with the Lord." Stricken with the fatal fever, she has laid down her life in the land of her fathers, without having had much time to tell "the sweet story of old" to those for whose sake she bravely dared danger and death. We weep not for her; Jesus has come and taken her to Himself, and her bliss is perfect; but the desolate heart of her husband claims our sympathy and fervent prayers. Encompassed by danger, exposed to scorching heat by day, and deadly damps by night, weakened by fever and sorely cast down by the loss of his dearest earthly companion, our poor brother surely needs that we should "speak for him to the King" now in the time of his need and overwhelming distress. One feels that a return message to him could scarcely bear a fitter termination than the words which came over the sea to us: "Keep inching along, keep inching along, Jesus will come by and by."

Mr. Spurgeon wrote in The Sword and the Trowel January, 1880: "Our beloved friend, Mr. Johnson, sends us a very touching account of the illness and death of his dear wife, a few extracts from which will, we feel sure evoke the heartiest sympathy and prayers of those of our readers who made their acquaintance while they were with us. It appears that the journey from Victoria to Bakundu occupied nearly three weeks, in consequence of the opposition raised by the King of Mungo to the passage of the Missionaries through his dominions. They were within six hours march of their destination when they were stopped by a large band of armed natives, who compelled them to return to Mungo, where they were heavily fleeced, and sent back to Victoria. The exposure to the hot sun by day, and the heavy dews by night, together with the threatening attitude of the natives, seriously injured the health of the whole party. After a week's rest they started again, Mrs. Johnson and Mrs. Richardson being carried in hammocks. The men who were carrying Mrs. Johnson stumbled over a stone or stump of a tree, which hurt her back very much; and to crown all, poor Mr. Johnson was seized with fever; so that he also had to ride in a hammock. After they reached Bakundu Mrs. Johnson took the fever; and, although she rallied for awhile she was never really well. Much of the time both husband and wife were ill together, and so unable to help each other. Of the later weeks of Mrs. Johnson's life her sorrowing yet rejoicing partner thus writes: 'The blessed Bible, which gives comfort and consolation such as nothing else can do, was her constant companion. Day after day and night after night she would seek to know more of its contents. The rest which remains for the people of God was a theme she much delighted to dwell upon. The "Morning by Morning; or, Daily Bible Readings," was indeed a source of great comfort to her. The "Sermons," which are sent to me every month by Mr. Wigney's class, were read and re-read by her. About six weeks before her death she was much better, and the fevers all left her. . . . On the following Wednesday afternoon I said: "Henrietta, do you love Jesus?" Her lips moved, but she was too helpless to lift her hands. Just before candle-light I asked her if I should read the Bible. Her lips again moved, so I read part of John xiv. At eight o'clock she commenced to breathe hard, and looked at me as though she wanted to speak. This lasted just a minute or two, and then she went home to live with my blessed Jesus. She is indeed now at rest and free. Since the death of my dear wife I thought at one time I should soon follow her. My heart seemed to be affected in some way, and I suffered also from fever and neuralgia; but God has seen fit to raise me up again. I am much better, but far from being well. I wish sometimes I could come home and stay for five or six months. I sometimes fear that I shall not be able to do the good I had hoped to do in Africa, but my Father knows all about it. If He wants me to serve Him in this way, Amen, God's way is always the best way. . . Please ask the friends at the prayer meeting to pray for the success of our work at Bakundu. I am praying for the conversion of the young King.--Yours truly, for Africa, Thomas L. Johnson.'"

Returning to the Coast--Incidents

From the time of my arrival in Bakundu in February, 1879, to November, I do not think I spent two weeks in succession of good health. I suffered both from an affection of the liver, which becomes very seriously developed in West African climate, and from sciatica and muscular rheumatism, with which I had been troubled more or less ever since.

Soon after my journey into the interior I was delirious three days and nights. After suffering from month to month, unable to attend to my duty, Mr. Richardson doing all the work, the late Rev. Q. W. Thomson, then Missionary-in-charge at Victoria, sent the Rev. Mr. Wilson, a Native Missionary, up from the coast, with sixteen natives, to accompany me to Victoria. I was so ill and weak that I had to be carried eighty miles in a hammock through the thick woods and over rivers, on the backs of natives.

I left Mr. and Mrs. Richardson in charge of the work. On this journey down to the coast there were three memorable events.

When we reached E'catto, one of the group of villages, the Chief, Mocasso, was away from home. I was carried in the hammock to call on his wife. I gave her a knife as a present. After a little rest we resumed our journey. As we left the village we had to cross a small stream, though quite deep. The trunk of a large tree, which had fallen across the water, formed a bridge. A long vine of some kind, something like a large grape vine, was stretched across as a support for one crossing over. I was carried over on the back of a native. Mr. Wilson went ahead. The man who carried me was trusting greatly to this vine to support himself. When we were half way across a son of the Chief appeared at the other end of the bridge and ordered us to go back. This Mr. Wilson refused to do. He then threatened to cut the vine loose if we did not go back. The current of the stream at this spot was very strong, and as I looked at the water, my head began to "swim." Mr. Wilson then said, "Look up, Mr. Johnson." I did so, and at once commenced to pray for deliverance, and benefited doubly by the act.

Mr. Wilson then said to the young men in native language, "Mr. Johnson has been to see your mother and made a present--'dash.'" and he at once allowed us to cross. It was evidently God's leading in my going to see his mother and giving her that knife, which had proved to be keener of edge than I had thought. Again I see in this God's hand.

Another day, as we were passing along the narrow path, we came to where over a dozen of men were working in their gardens. As soon as they saw us they came with a yell, their cutlasses uplifted, and though this occurred over twenty-eight years ago, I seem to see those flashing eyes and fierce and awful expressions on those tattooed faces, as those men attempted to leap upon me. We had hired two men of this tribe to assist the young men from the coast in helping to carry the hammock. As soon as my men saw that these men meant mischief, they ran in between them and the hammock, and the two men with the hammock ran as fast as they could, leaving my guide and men contending with our opponents. When they came to the fence they took me over and gently put me down in the edge of the "bush," and were about to return and leave me alone--one of them was in the act of getting over the fence--when I beckoned to him to come to me. I could not speak in their language. After exchanging a word with each other the men came back. In the meantime I could hear loud talking going on down the road. Soon Mr. Wilson, who well understood his own tribe, came up with our men and several of these natives, to whom he advised me to give presents. I asked what the trouble was. These people said that this was the second time I had passed through their country without their permission, and that they wanted my blood, and intended to have it. On Mr. Wilson remonstrating with them, we were permitted to pass unmolested.

The third event was, that when we had travelled about three-fourths of the way we heard, early one afternoon, men talking in the road along which we were passing, and soon we found ourselves in the midst of quite a company of native soldiers, some standing, some sitting by the wayside. There was every indication that they meant trouble. No doubt a message had been sent on ahead of us to inform the people of our approach. Mr. Wilson had a talk with their chief, who appeared sullen and very reserved. We concluded to give the chief and each man a present. Before doing so, I offered to shake hands with the old chief. I was in the hammock. When I held out my hand he drew himself back, refusing to give me his hand. I insisted, when he slowly put out his hand. As I grasped it I was not a little surprised to find that the man was trembling with fear. After the chief had set the example each man in his turn came up and very cautiously took me by the hand, and then retreating very quickly they laughed heartily. Again we were permitted to pass on. Finally, we reached the coast in safety. During all that journey of eighty miles, my blessed Jesus protected me. He and He alone knows how, as I lay upon my back in the hammock, looking up to heaven, I called upon Him to protect me.

The following extract will illustrate the travelling dangers to which we were exposed. Rev. Joseph E. Burnley, who was trained at the Congo Institute, Colwyn Bay, writes of his experience in 1897:--"As you know, since my arrival in 1895, I had been rendering help voluntarily to the Lord's work at my home, Victoria. At a meeting which was held in July last, I was nominated for Mission work in one of the larger towns in the interior, a distance of forty-five miles from Victoria. After all needful arrangements were made, I took leave of my friends and relatives on the 8th August, and arrived at my future field of labour on the 11th. On my arrival there I had a very hearty reception from the King and his people. I have been staying with His Majesty, and will continue to do so until he has put up a temporary house for me. Sopo is one of the largest towns at the foot of the Cameroon Mountains, which is said to be 13,000 feet high. Previous to the taking of this district by the Government, the people of this town were very wild and blood-thirsty. The King's elder brother, Mokako, told me that, when our brother, Mr. Johnson, and his brother-in-law, Mr. Richardson, were passing through the town on their way to Bakundu, he had orders from the King Woloa, to fire at them, and he said, 'Had it not been for your friend Sako'--that is the present King, who was and always is friendly to foreigners--'I would have killed them.' How true God is to His word. 'Go ye into all the world and preach the Gospel to every creature .... and lo, I am with you alway, even unto the end of the world. Amen.'"

Thank God for such a Friend, who has all power in all places, and who uses His power for the safety and comfort and help of His people. He never changes, nor leaves, nor forsakes, and every soul is called upon to trust in Him at all places. Again I see God's hand.

At Victoria Again

After remaining a few weeks at Victoria, where I received every attention from the late Rev. G. Grenfell and Rev. Q. W. Thomson and their families, and making no improvement, Mr. Thomson advised me to return home by the next steamer. He added that if I remained longer it would be at my own risk, as he would not be responsible.

There was no set time for the steamers to call at Victoria. All was excitement when one of the British and African Steamship Company's vessels hove in sight. Soon I had notice to be ready to join one of the steamers. I was helped very tenderly by Mr. Thomson into the surf-boat, and then into the larger vessel, which stood about half a mile out, and his request to the doctor and officials of the ship respecting me was so kind. I was the only passenger getting on here. Soon the vessel put out to the open sea. I had been carried to my room, where I was glad to lie down, for I was scarcely able to walk. I knew no one on the steamer, but I soon found that I was in the midst of friends, and much kindness was shown me by the officers of the steamer and by Dr. Irving and all the stewards, and by a Mr. Stent, who represented a large business house in London. The voyage greatly benefited me.

In England Once More--Invalid

On landing in Liverpool, January, 1880, I found it very cold, and, indeed, I suffered much from cold. When salutations were over, the passengers set out to look after their luggage. One of my boxes was missing. I left a notification about the box, and then weak and cold I came away. Up to the present I have not heard of that box.

Dr. Irving had thought of sending me to a hospital in Liverpool, but on arriving in England I was so much stronger that he let me go on to London the next day. This was now the trying time. Oh, I can hardly describe it. My wife whom I married in the days of slavery, and with whom I had lived for fifteen years and over, had gone home. I had no relatives of which I knew; in bad health and almost exhausted, and no home to go to. I went to a boarding house in Liverpool, where the late Mr. Lockhart, Pastor of the Toxteth Tabernacle, called on me, offering to help me in any way he could.

God raised up friends to cheer me and help, very memorable amongst them being Mr. Spurgeon, Mr. A. H. Baynes, Mr. J. B. Myers, Mr. and Mrs. Hind Smith, Mr. and Mrs. Wigney, and Mr. and Mrs. Freeman, and Miss Skinner.

After medical examination, I was advised not to return to Africa; that should I return, in two or three weeks I would suffer as I had suffered for nearly twelve months. The matter was brought before the Committee of the Baptist Missionary Society. I remember of nothing more trying in all my life, unless it was the anxiety I felt when I set out "to seek religion." But how sweet to me was the promise, "I will never leave thee nor forsake thee." All I could do was to take the matter to my blessed Jesus in prayer. My prayer now continually was, "Since I cannot labour in Africa, please, Lord, let me do something for Africa."

In my sickness and weakness I found a loving home with Mr. and Mrs. S. Wigney, where I stayed when I first came to London. Mr. A. H. Baynes, Secretary of the Baptist Missionary Society, was most kind and attentive to me in my condition, visiting me often. As soon as I was able to move about, I was invited by Mr. and Mrs. J. R. Smith, of Southampton, to spend a time at their home. Those were very happy days. After a while I returned to London.

Back to America

Medical advice, and that of my friends, was for me to return to America, and the doctor having said that I was well enough to travel, the following letter from Mr. Baynes reached me-- "June, 1880.--I have great pleasure in stating that our esteemed brother, the Rev. T. L. Johnson, has been connected for more than twelve months with the Missions of the Baptist Missionary Society on the Cameroons River, West Africa, where he suffered the loss of his wife, who fell a victim to the African fever, and that he only left that station in consequence of the utter failure and prostration of his health. Medical testimony being strongly in favour of his returning to America, the Committee of the Baptist Missionary Society felt that the best course for Mr. Johnson would be to return to his former field of labour in the United States. He returns to America with the confidence and prayers and good wishes of the Committee of the Baptist Missionary Society, and they desire to commit him to the hearty sympathy and loving regards of the Christian Church in America.-- Alfred H. Baynes, Secretary of the Baptist Missionary Society."

The Committee furnished me with the means to return home, and Mrs. Spurgeon made me a present of books, and Mr. Spurgeon of £10. Mr. Spurgeon's kind words to me as I took leave of him gave me great cheer: "If you don't get on, let us know. We will not forget you."

Then he gave me the following letter—

Nightingale Lane
Balham, Surrey
May 26. 80

Mr Thomas L Johnson passed through the Pastors' College with honour, & was sent forth from us to Africa under the auspices of the Baptist Mission. His wife died & his own health failed & he returned. It is evident that he cannot live in our station at Africa & it is judged best that he should return to America. He retains the respect & esteem of all our friends & I am happy to give him this letter to recommend him to all

brethren in Christ among
whom he may settle. He has
the advantage of being like
the spouse in the Song "black
but comely", & perhaps he will
therefore be more at home among
his coloured friends — but
be his complexion what it may
he is a beloved brother in the
Lord & should be received
as such. May the God &
Father of our Lord Jesus Christ
be ever with him

C. H. Spurgeon
Minister of the
Metropolitan Tabernacle

On arrival in Manchester, my kind friends, Mr. and Mrs. Stroud Smith and Rev. J. J. Irving, thought I would be better for a few weeks at Dr. Briden's Hydropathic establishment at Saltcoats. My stay there did me much good. I sailed August 4th, 1880, on the steamship "Spain," from Liverpool for New York. The officers and many of the crew remembered that I was a passenger with them to England in August, 1876, and they displayed much kindness. At the Sunday morning service I was invited to give the address. During the week the passengers invited me to give the story of my life, and also to take part in an evening's entertainment for the benefit of the Saiior's Orphanage Home.

We reached New York safely, and on the way from there to Chicago I became acquainted with a gentleman who took a deep interest in me and in all I could tell him about Africa, and in Mission Work generally. At each place of stopping he paid the refreshment bill. This was Mr. S. L. Morshon, of Chicago, one of the great workers in the Y. P. S. C. E., and he became a great friend. We arrived in Chicago August 18th.

Before leaving England I had written the Rev. R. de Baptiste to say that I expected to return home soon. He was much concerned about Foreign Missions. He wrote to a large number of ministers, urging them to attend the annual meeting of the Wood River Association, as he expected I would be present to give some information about Africa. Soon after I arrived in Chicago, I found that preparations were being made for these meetings, which were to commence on September 1st. I found that a Pullman car had been chartered, and that a company of twenty Christian workers and delegates were booked for Jacksonville, the place of meeting.

During the meetings of this Wood River Association, composed entirely of coloured people, I presented the claim of Africa, and urged upon them the necessity for their united effort to commence at once a Mission work in Africa. I told them what the English people were doing there, and of the great work already accomplished. The matter was carefully considered by the Committee appointed, and the following is a synopsis of their report which was received and adopted:--"From the shores of Africa, teeming with millions in grossest darkness of heathenism, we see more clearly than ever the prophetic picture of Ethiopia 'stretching out her hand unto God,' and praying for teachers of His Word to be sent to teach them the way of the true and living God. We advise that the Board of this Association take up and more thoroughly prosecute the work of Foreign Missions by our churches; and by correspondence and conferences with coloured Associations and conventions in the States, try to organise more thoroughly for the support of Mission work in Africa, We advise that the Board immediately appoint Rev. Thomas L. Johnson, returned Missionary from Africa, as its Missionary agent in both its domestic and foreign work," with Rev. R. De Baptiste, D. D., Chicago; Rev. Win. Troy, Richmond, Va.; Rev. R. M. Duling, of Iowa.

This was the first step, and the work of one Association only. I afterwards visited two Associations in the State of Missouri, representing 120 churches, composed of freed-men, and they also resolved to enter upon the African Mission work. In November of the same year, I met a convention in Mexico, Missouri, when the question of Foreign Missions was thoroughly discussed, and the cooperation effected of two other Associations, representing in all a membership of over 60,000 freed-men. So anxious were the people for information about Africa, and what I had seen, that I published a little pamphlet of sixty-four pages, telling of my visit to Africa and setting forth her claims. There are thousands of freed-men to-day who are anxious to go to Africa, prevented only by the lack of means. It is indeed gratifying to know that interest in African Missions has not only manifested itself in the districts to which I have referred, but the freed-men in the far Southern States are equally alive to the importance of the evangelisation of Africa. The work is growing in all parts, and I see the prospect of enlarged operations which will help to bring Africa to the feet of my blessed Jesus.

The enthusiasm awakened at these meetings was not destined to die out soon. The thought of Africa and her perishing millions lingered in the breast of hundreds of men and women. At the various meetings I could see strong men and women weeping as I told the story of what I saw in Africa. I received very many encouraging letters from time to time from young and old, with expressions of confidence, wishing me "God-speed" in the work, and desiring information respecting the people, their condition and needs. I can now see more than ever the hand of God in my return to America. As I travelled from place to place I suffered much.

> God never makes a mistake
> On any mission field;
> The work and workers all are His,
> He calls those whom He will.

Our object was to secure the co-operation of the coloured Christians of the North-West for the purpose of raising funds, and appointing and sustaining Missionaries of our own race among the long-benighted people in Africa. Thank God this has been accomplished.

Establishment of an African Mission

At the seventh annual meeting of the Baptist General Association of the Western States and Territories, held in the Olivet Baptist Church, Chicago, Ill., October 12th, 1881, the following resolutions were unanimously adopted:

That the coloured Baptists of the Western States and Territories establish, in connection with this Association, an African Mission. Its object being—

1. To send qualified Missionaries to Africa.
2. To establish Mission Stations on the Congo, and wherever in the dark neglected land of Africa the Lord may direct.
3. The enlistment of the interest of the coloured churches of the U. S. A. in the African Mission Work.
4. That five thousand dollars be raised, and one or more Missionaries be immediately employed, and as soon as practicable commence Mission work in Africa.
5. That the Executive Board of this body take such steps as in their judgment may be best for the prosecution of this work and suggest quarterly meetings in every church, and at all annual meetings of the District Associations in each State. That all churches and Sabbath Schools connected with the District associations form Mission circles to raise funds for this purpose.

And from the public press we notice that the action on the part of the Association attracted attention. The "Standard," Chicago, Thursday, December 30th, 1880, said:--"The Wood River Association appointed Rev. Thomas L. Johnson, formerly Pastor of the Providence Church in this city, now a returned Missionary from Africa, Superintendent of its foreign and domestic work in this State, labouring under the direction of an Executive Board. Mr. Johnson commenced his life as a slave in Virginia, which position he occupied until the fall of Richmond near the close of the Rebellion. After preaching several years in Denver and Chicago--exhibiting unusual talent--he left for England on his way to Africa. He spent two years preparing himself for his life-work in Spurgeon's College. He was taken up by the Baptist Missionary Society, of England, and sent with orders to the West Coast of Africa, where he remained one year. His wife died, and his own health broke down, and he was compelled to return to this country. On Monday evening of last week, Mr. Johnson delivered an address in the Olivet Church, to a large and enthusiastic audience, on Africa, generally, past, present, and future, and on Mission work among her people in particular-- relating many interesting and affecting incidents in his own experience of brief missionary life at Victoria on the West Coast, and in the interior at Bakundu. It was one of the best Missionary addresses to which we have ever listened. . . . . This work among our coloured. brethren can now but have a most beneficial effect upon themselves, and we are glad to see that they have entered into it with so much spirit and energy. Mr. Spurgeon says that 'Mr. Thomas L. Johnson passed through the Pastors' College with honour, and was sent forth to Africa by us under the auspices of the Baptist Mission.'"

In 1881 I was urgently requested to help my Pastor and the church of which I had been a member to save the church property. This church had suffered the destruction of its chapel, which was burned in the great fire in Chicago, 1874, and rebuilt at a cost of 15,000 dollars, borrowed money. The Mortgage expired July 1st, 1881. By the 16th January, 1882, the church was able to pay 3,571 dollars to the company, which gave them time in which to pay the balance.

I was sent out by the authority of the Church, and was commended by leading men in the district, among whom were Mr. Harrison, Mayor of Chicago; Mr. Pullman, of the Pullman Palace Car Company; Mr. Hall, City Editor of the "Chicago Tribune"; Mr. Bradley, Editor of the "Conservator"; Mr. A. T. Hall, City Editor of the "Conservator"; Mr. Barnett, of the Chicago Bar; and Rev. J. W. Polk, Secretary of the Wood River Association. Mr. Bradley, of the "Conservator," wrote very kindly:--To whom it may concern. The coloured Baptists of the City of Chicago have suffered several losses during the past ten years by providential visitations entirely beyond their control, and as a result the church is burdened by a debt which, by their own unaided hands, they can hardly expect to pay. They call upon those who love the cause for assistance, and have deputised the Rev. Thos. L. Johnson, one of the most eminent and honourable Pastors of the denomination, to solicit aid. As a Christian he is worthy of all confidence, and as a faithful labourer he is entitled to every consideration. Every cent contributed will be faithfully applied."

This work considerably altered my plans for the time. The "Conservator" referred to my fresh trip to England for deputation work, and also put in the following interesting item, July 28th, 1881:--

The Rev. Thomas L. Johnson was married at three o'clock yesterday afternoon to Miss Sara A. McGowan, 287, Walnut Street. Rev. R. De Baptiste, Pastor of the Olivet Baptist Church, performed the ceremony. Miss Ora McGowen assisted as bridesmaid, Mr. J. B. French as groomsman, and Mr. James Smith as usher. The bride was tastefully dressed in a sage-green travelling dress with cord and tassel garniture and pearl jewellery. After the ceremony a large and genial reception was held until the departure of the bride at five o'clock for Washington, Philadelphia, and New York.

The presents were numerous and useful, while many of them were costly. The wedding created a good deal of notice in the circles of coloured society on account of the extensive acquaintance and connections of both parties. Rev. Mr. Johnson was formerly Pastor of the Providence Baptist Church on the West Side. He afterwards went as a Missionary to Africa. Mr. and Mrs. Johnson will sail August 1st on the 'Spain' for England."

Mrs. Johnson--Correspondent

Writing to the "Conservator," September 17th, 1881, Mrs. Johnson sends the following letter descriptive of the voyage to England:--

"Manchester, England, August, 1881.--Editor of-the 'Conservator': Dear Sir,--Before our arrival in England, Mr. Johnson's friends (knowing of his coming) had made appointments for him; more have been made since our arrival which have kept him very busy. I only hope he will be able to hold out as he has commenced. This is, indeed, all new to me, for I have never written a line for a newspaper in my life, so this is my first attempt, and I do hope due allowance will be made for all imperfections. I suppose I must first tell of the voyage. After a long ride of two nights and one day over the B. and O. R. R., we arrived on Friday morning at 7.30 o'clock, in Jersey City, and had to take a ferry boat to New York City. While on the boat we met Mr. Joshua Troy, son of Rev. William Troy, of Richmond, Va. Mr. Troy had come on from Richmond to join us in New York to sail with us to England; he expects to go to Edinburgh, Scotland, to complete his medical studies. By 9 o'clock we were at Earle's Hotel, corner of Canal and Center Streets, near Broadway. After breakfast, Mr. Troy and Mr. Johnson went out to attend to some business while I remained in the hotel. After they returned, and we had dinner, we had the pleasure of a ride on the Elevated R.R. to Central Park, where we spent a very pleasant afternoon. There were many interesting objects of attraction, the most noted of all was that of Cleopatra's Needle, or the Obelisk, as it is called, which recently came from Africa. To prevent the rush and confusion, on Friday evening, at 8 o'clock, we went on board the Steamship 'Spain,' of the National S. S. Company. On Saturday morning at six o'clock we were up. The wharf was soon crowded with people bidding their friends good-bye, who were about to depart on a voyage to the Old World along with us, waiting to wave their last adieu. At 7.30 o'clock the anchor was up, our moorings were loosened, and we sailed out of New York Harbour. The bridge being erected across the river between Brooklyn and New York, Coney Island, Castle Garden, and other places attracted much attention as we passed out of the harbour. Mr. Johnson told me we should soon be out of sight of land; my thoughts were turned to the ship on which we had taken passage--S. S. 'Spain'--and he assured me that it was perfectly safe. I soon felt at home as I saw first one and then another of the officers, including the Captain and Stewards, greeting my husband, and seeming so glad to see him. I was much struck with the size of the 'Spain.' The Company had twelve steamers running between New York and England; the largest is the 'Egypt,' the second in size is the 'Spain.' She was built in the year 1871, in England; she is 425 feet in length, 43 feet in breadth; tonnage 4512, horse power 600. In sailing across the Atlantic, this Company takes the most Southernly route to avoid icebergs and headlands. The outward track is 3,082 miles from New York to Liverpool. We had 54 saloon passengers on board. It was very pleasant from Saturday until Tuesday; then we had it quite rough until Thursday morning, the 4th. There were passengers on board both from England and America. As we became acquainted the time passed off very pleasantly indeed. I was anxious to see a whale; two were seen by some of the passengers, but I was deprived of the pleasure. Every evening we had singing either on the deck or in the saloon. Professor J. Lalor, of Mass., entertained us by his sweet singing and performing on the piano. Each evening before we arrived at Queenstown we had a concert on board for the benefit of the Seaman's Orphan Asylum at Liverpool. Mr. Johnson and Mr. Troy were invited to take part. On Monday morning, August 8th, soon after breakfast, we came in sight of land. Oh, how delighted we all were to see land once more. How joyfully the cry sounded over the ship, glasses were at once brought into requisition for a fairer view. This was the coast of Ireland; at 2 o'clock we arrived at Queenstown, and after landing passengers and sending off mail and telegrams, we steamed up St. George's Channel, having Wales on our right hand, Tuesday morning, August 9th, about 7 o'clock, we passed Holyhead, where Mr. Johnson spent a day and night when on his way to Africa in 1878. By 12 o'clock we arrived at Liverpool; soon letters were sent on board to passengers from their friends. Among them was a letter of welcome sent to us from Mr. and Mrs. Stroud Smith, our friends in the Isle of Man. All was confusion on preparing to land. As soon as we landed officers stood ready to examine our baggage, after which we were soon seated in an English cab and off to the Station (depot) to take cars for Manchester. We were too late for the 2 o'clock train, so we went to an hotel for dinner; by 3 o'clock we were off for Manchester, where we arrived at 4 o'clock. I enjoyed the ride very much. The scenery along the way

115

was, indeed, most picturesque. Here we took a cab (being the observed of all observers), and we soon found ourselves at Mr. Smith's, in Ackers Street-- dear friends of Mr. Johnson's--who invited him to stop at his house until we got settled. I have already written more than I expected. Friends writing will please address:

Y. M. C. Association, 56, Peter Street, Manchester, England."
"S. A. J."

Deputation Work

Before leaving America we received a very kind letter from Mr. and Mrs. Geo. F. Smith, of Manchester, extending an invitation to visit them. On our arrival they gave us a very hearty welcome, and invited us to make their house our home until we had decided upon where our headquarters should be. We remained with them several weeks, and through their kindness and influence, with other kind friends in Manchester, I was soon well into the work, and met with considerable success. God was indeed very gracious to me, in raising up many friends. I struggled on through the wet and cold in Manchester from September to January, 1882, when by the earnest efforts of the members and friends of the Church in Chicago, with what help they re- ceived from abroad, they were able to pay 3,571 dollars to the Company who had kindly given them time in which to pay the balance.

Among the many kind friends who helped me I will name the late Rev. J. A. MacFadyen M. A., whose interest in my Mission resulted in a letter express- ing thanks to him from Rev. R. De Baptiste, Pastor O. B. Ch., Chicago.

The African Mission

I received a letter from the Rev. R. De Baptiste informing me of what had taken place at the Chicago meeting, as a result of my return from Africa. I cannot describe the joy of my soul, when I received this letter; with it also came a request from the Committee of the newly organised African Mission, requesting me to accept the office of Financial Agent. I consulted my friends Mr. and Mrs. Geo. F. Smith and Mr. and Mrs. Stroud Smith, of the Isle of Man; also Mr. and Mrs. W. Hind Smith, of London. I wrote accepting the office, and at once began preparations for the work. In due time the following letter of authority reached me:--"To all whom it may concern,--This is to certify that at the regular meeting of the Executive Board, held in the City of Hannibal, in the State of Missouri, March 14th to 16th, 1882, the Rev. Thomas L. Johnson was regularly and duly appointed a Missionary and Financial Agent of the Baptist General Association of the Western States and Territories, and is au- thorised to present the claims of its work and receive contributions for Mis- sion work in Africa. He is required to make regularly quarterly reports of his work, and correct returns of all funds received by him under this appointment to the Corresponding Secretary of this body.--Rev. R. M. Duling, Moderator and Chairman of Board; Rev. R. De Baptiste, Corresponding Secretary of Board."

Reference was made in "The American Baptist" and in "The Freeman," to this appointment.

God answered prayer and gave me better health, and I was thus enabled to proceed with my work for Africa. I left Manchester, May, 1882, for London, after consulting my friends, and I began my work by giving some lectures on the condition of the Freedmen in the United States, and on Africa, and by telling the Story of my Life.

In the course of my work many important societies began to spring up, and I became very closely identified with them. Here is a card that I carry in my pocket:--

CHRISTIAN POLICEMEN'S ASSOCIATION MEMBER'S CARD
WESTERN BRANCH, LONDON

On the inside of the card are the words--

Name: Thos. L. Johnson. Division: Hon. Member. Date: December, 1883. "Kept by the power of God." - 1 Peter i. 5. RULE.--That all Policemen be invited to join this Association who can truthfully say that they believe on the Lord Jesus Christ with the heart, are willing to confess Him with the mouth (Rom. x., 9, 10), and are determined by His grace to follow Him in their life (John xii. 26).

I was a member of this Society when there were only ten members. Many policemen in London now speak of blessing received through the messages which God helped me to deliver. It was a great privilege afforded me by Miss C. Gurney to take part in the organising of the Christian Policemen's Association in Glasgow, when I gave the first address.

In all my work I kept the African Mission to the front, and God so graciously manifested Himself to me from the commencement that I felt encouraged to go forward. The names of the following gentlemen who spoke with appreciation of my work at that time may be known to the reader:--The late Sir S. A. Blackwood, Esq., K. C. B., Secretary of the General Post Office; Robert Burn, Esq., Secretary Y. M. C. A., Aldersgate Street; Professor A. Fergusson, Pastors' College, London; Principal Gracey, Pastors' College, London; M. H. Hodder, Esq. (Messrs. Hodder and Stoughton, London); Spencer T. Hall, Esq., Ph. D., M. A., M. D., Blackpool; Rev. Walter J. Mayers, London; Rev. S. Pilling, Blackpool; A. Plummer, Esq., Y. M. C. A., Eastbourne; J. E. Taylor, Esq., Mobwell House, Great Missenden, Bucks; the late Sir George Williams, Founder and President of the Y. M. C. A., London; A. H. Wheeler, Esq., Brighton; Albert D. Shaw, Esq., United States Consulate, Manchester; W. Wilson Hind Smith, Esq., F. R. G. A., London; Sir Algernon C. P. Coote, Esq., Norwood, S. E.; Geo. F. Smith, Esq., Beckenham; James Boyd, Esq., Manchester; Edward Stroud Smith, Douglas;

W. Hind Smith, Esq., Y. M. C. A., Exeter Hall, London; Arthur Burson, Esq., Y. M. C. A., Exeter Hall, London; Rev. Henry O. Mackey, then of Portland Chapel, Southampton; James R. Smith, Esq., Solicitor, Southampton; and many others who testified to the work and to myself.

Police Orphanage, Redhill, Surrey

After getting to the work I discovered what a grand opportunity I had of doing good in two ways at the same time, by gaining friends for Africa, and by winning souls for the Saviour in England.

119

Setting out with this determination I had some rare experiences among both rich and poor, learned and illiterate. To succeed in this I attended all kinds of Missions and Meetings in England, Ireland, Scotland, and Wales. I visited Ragged Schools, Mission Halls, Mothers' Meetings, Working men's Meetings, Bible Classes, Band of Hope Meetings, Blue Ribbon Meetings, Gospel Temperance Meetings, Meetings for Railway Men, Meetings for Postmen, in which the late Miss Ethel Tritton was deeply interested, theatrical missions with Miss H. Beauchamp, Y. M. C. A. and Y.W.C.A. Meetings, warehouse meetings, noon meetings in great workshops and foundries in different parts of the Kingdom, and meetings of the Christian Policemen's Association, concerning which I have already presented the reader with membership card. To-day there are Christian Police Associations on the Continent, and in Asia, Africa, and America.

In connection with this Association we have the Police Missionary Union. Extract from Report:--

We are thankful that our hope has been realised concerning "our own Missionary for Japan," in the persons of Mr. and Mrs. Taylor, of Tokio, who need and will surely receive our prayerful and substantial financial support. We trust they may be used for the glory of God and the good of our Japanese comrades, and that many in that far-away, beautiful land may be brought to a saving knowledge of Jesus Christ.

In the Annual Report of the Executive Board to the General Association of the Western States and Territories, my deputation work for the African Mission is referred to with much satisfaction to the authorities. The organisation and objects of the work are set forth, my appointment and service spoken of, the need for young consecrated men and women as Missionaries stated, the organised and systematic effort of the people proposed, and the encouraging openings in the Mission Field are pointed out.

In June, 1884, I visited Scotland. The Rev. W. Fulton, of Airdrie, had invited me to come and conduct a week's mission in his church. He, with his good wife and people, gave me a real hearty welcome. I was much encouraged, souls were saved and more friends were secured for Africa. The Rev. W. Seaman, a fellow-student, settled at Hawick, kindly invited me to visit his church, where he and his people would do all in their power to help the African mission. On the Sunday afternoon we had a great company of young people. My visit happened on the Sunday of their missionary collection. With what was collected, on the Sunday they had in hand £10. Some one said that they usually gave the quarterly collection to the Baptist Missionary Society, but he moved that they give it on that occasion to Mr. Johnson for his African Mission. I at once declined this kindness, and told my friend that I would rather they augmented the B.M.S. fund by that collection than that they should enrich another fund thereby. Smaller sums offered in a similar way on other occasions had been refused. My friend feared we could not be very successful. But he called on the Presbyterian minister, and explained how much better it would be to have a larger place for the lecture on the Monday night. He at once consented for me to lecture in his church. The collection amounted to £10 10s.

I shall never forget the happy time I had with the happy young people where I was entertained. The first morning after my arrival, and before I came downstairs, there was a continual running up and down stairs, and sometimes a halt at my door, and a little whisper. When I came out there was a general flight of all; but the tittle folk soon returned. I heard such laughter quite awhile after. I heard that they were anxious to see what the bed-clothes looked like! They had never seen a black man before, and were quite sure the black would come off on the sheets.

From Hawick I went to Glasgow to commence work under W. M. Oatts, Esq., Sec. Y. M. C. A., arrangements having been made for this by Mr. Hind Smith. Through the kindness of Mr. Oatts I was not only happily engaged for the Y. M. C. A., but many ministers in Glasgow invited me to visit them. It was in the month of July, when many of the families who could help were away. Mr. Oatts advised that I returned again in September or October. While in Glasgow I received a communication from the late Charles H. Allen, Esq., Secretary of the Anti-Slavery Society, inviting me to attend the 50th Anniversary Meeting of the Abolition of Slavery in the Colonies, to be held on the 1st of August, 1884.

Great Anti-Slavery Jubilee Meeting

Mr. Allen requested me to bring my relies of slavery,--the slave chains which had been used on the necks of twenty slaves, and other things. I returned in time for the meeting. I was honoured with a platform ticket, of which the following is a picture:--

Long before the hour of meeting, the Great Hall was well filled. Promptly at four o'clock H.R.H the Prince of Wales, now our beloved King, came to the platform, followed by the leading noblemen and gentlemen of the realm, and the great company assembled rose to their feet.

The following report of the meeting is taken from the "Anti-Slavery Reporter," a similar report appearing in "The Times" on the next day:--

"The Guildhall of the City of London on Friday afternoon, August 1st., presented a remarkable scene in the gathering, under the presidency of the Prince of Wales, of persons of all ranks, of different creeds, and of both political parties, to celebrate the jubilee of the Abolition of Slavery in the British Colonies, to pass in review the work of the British and Foreign Anti-Slavery Society during the last half century, and to consider the subject of existing Slavery in various parts of the world. Lord Shaftesbury, who had promised to attend, had dictated from a sick bed a letter declaring his satisfaction with the changes which he had lived to see. There were present the Right Hon. the Lord Mayor, M. P. (Alderman Fowler), Earl Granville, the Earl Derby, the Archbishop of Canterbury, Cardinal Manning, he Right Hon. W. E. Forster, M. P., Sir Stafford Northcote, Bart., M. P., Sir H. Verney, Bart., M. P., Sir J. W.

Pease, Bart., M. P., Sir George Campbell, M. P., Sir. W. M'Arthur, M. P., Mr. Causton, M. P., Sir Wilfrid Lawson, Bart., M. P., Sir H. T. Holland, Bart., M. P., Mr. G. Palmer, M. P., Mr. Sergeant Simon, M. P., Mr. F. W Buxton, M. P., Mr. Henry Richard, M. P., Mr. James Cropper, M. P., Mr. Sydney C. Buxton, M. P., Mr. Villiers Stewart, M. P., Mr. J. Errington, M. P., Sir T. D. Acland, Bart., M. P., Mr. T. D. Potter, M. P., Mr. C. Villiers; M. P., Sir J. Eardly Wilmot, Bart., M. P., Mr. J. Bryce, M. P., Mr. Thomas Loveridge (Chairman), and several members of the City Lands Committee, Mr. F. W. Chesson (Secretary of the Aborigines' Protection Society), the Hon. T. W. Ferry (late Vice-President of the United States), the Rev. Canon Wilberforce, Arch-deacon Farrar, Senor Zorilla (late Prime Minister of Spain), Sir F. Goldsmid, Sir John Gorrie (Chief justice of the Leeward Islands), Mr. G. Baden-Powell, M. A., G. M. G., Sir S. M. Peto, Bart., Mr. A. R. Scoble, Q. C. (son of the late Mr. John Scoble), Mr. E. N. Buxton (Chairman of the London School Board), Alderman Cotton, M. P., the Baroness Burdett-Coutts, the Rev. Canon Garratt (grandson of the late James Stephen), Edward Lushington, Esq., son of the late Dr. Lushington), the Misses Frere, Lady Buxton, Miss Gordon, Mrs. Foster, Mrs. Pease, and many ladies and gentlemen from all parts of the world.

ANTI-SLAVERY · JUBILEE.

THE LORD MAYOR

Requests the Attendance of *Rev. J. L. Johnson*

MEETING OF THE BRITISH & FOREIGN ANTI-SLAVERY SOCIETY,

GUILDHALL OF THE CITY OF LONDON,

On FRIDAY, the 1st day of AUGUST, at 4 p.m.

The Objects of the Meeting are to commemorate the 50th Anniversary of the Abolition of Slavery in the British Colonies; to pass in review the work of the Society during the past half century;

AND

To consider the vast amount of Slavery still existing in Africa, and other portions of the World.

HIS ROYAL HIGHNESS THE PRINCE OF WALES

(By Invitation of the Lord Mayor)

Has graciously consented to preside on this occasion. His Royal Highness will be supported by—
The Right Hon, the Lord Mayor, M.P. His Grace the Archbishop of Canterbury,
The Earl Granville, K.G., Secretary of State for Foreign   The Earl of Derby, K.G., Secretary of State for the Colonies,
Affairs.   The Earl Cairns.
The Earl of Shaftesbury, K.G.   Right Hon. W. E. Forster, M.P.
His Eminence Cardinal Manning.   Sir J. H. Kennaway, Bart., M.P.
Right Hon. Sir Stafford Northcote, M.P.   Rev. Canon Basil W. xxxxxx.
Sir Harry Verney, Bart., M.P.   Andrew Pease, Esq., M.P.
Sir T. Edward Buxton, Bart.   James Cropper, Esq., M.P.
Sir Joseph W. Pease, Bart., M.P.   Mr. Alderman Nottage.
George Palmer, Esq., M.P.   Sir Wm. McArthur, K.C.M.G.
Sydney C. Buxton, Esq., M.P.   John Simon, Esq., M.P.

And many other Noblemen and Gentlemen.

CHAS. H. ALLEN, 55, New Broad Street, London, E.C.

PLATFORM.

The Anti-Slavery Society was officially represented by Mr. Arthur Pease, M. P., President, Mr. Edmund Sturge, Chairman, Mr. Joseph Allen, Treasurer, Sir

122

T. Fowell Buxton, Bart., Mr. James Long, M. A., Mr. E. Harrison, Mr. Stafford Allen, the Rev. Horace Waller, the Rev. J. O. Whitehouse, Mr. J. G. Alexander, and Mr. Charles H. Allen, Secretary.

On the dais, behind the Prince of Wales and the distinguished company were two busts of Granville Sharpe and Clarkson. These busts were decorated with flowers, by the order of the City Lands Committee, and in front of the dais were placed the chains of slavery brought home from Zanzibar by the late Sir Bartle Frere, and kindly lent for the occasion by Lady Frere. There were also prominently displayed wooden yokes to which the necks of slaves are fastened in the march of slave caravans across the desert, and a long chain to which were attached twenty taken from a gang captured by H.M.S. "London." The gang contained 170 slaves, who had no water for three days. The chain was lent by the Rev. Thomas L. Johnson, who had himself been a slave for 28 years, and was present on the platform.

The great hall was densely crowded end to end, and the audience was most enthusiastic from the beginning to the close. The Prince met with a cordial reception.

The Secretary of the British and Foreign Anti-Slavery Society (Mr. Charles H. Allen), read a list of names of those who were unable to attend, including Mr. Herbert Gladstone, Lord Salisbury, the Marquis of Lorne, the chief Rabbi, the Duke of Argyll, the Duke of Norfolk, the Duke of Sutherland, Lord Morley, Lord Carnarvon, and Lord Shaftesbury.

The Lord Mayor having, according to civic custom, taken the chair for an instant, then vacated it, and invited His Royal Highness to preside over the meeting.

The Prince of Wales then rose amid enthusiastic cheers. He said:--

"My Lords, Ladies, and Gentlemen,--At the express wish of the Lord Mayor, I have been asked to preside on this auspicious occasion. I need hardly tell you that in such a cause it gives me more than ordinary pleasure to occupy the chair at so great and influential a meeting as this. (Cheers). I confess I had some reluctance in presiding to-day, feeling that others would accomplish the task far better than I should. (No, no.) But I also felt that possibly I might have some slight claim to occupy the chair on such an occasion as that of to-day, as so many members of my family have presided on former like occasions in connection with Anti-Slavery movements. (Cheers.) Let me say that my excuse for standing before you to-day may be given in the words used by my lamented father--(cheers)--on a similar occasion forty-four years ago. They were these: 'I have been induced to preside at the Meeting of this Society from the conviction of its paramount importance to the greatest interests of humanity and justice.' (Cheers.) This is a great and important Anniversary. To-day we celebrate the jubilee of the emancipation of slavery throughout our colonies, and it is also a day which has been looked forward to with pleasure and satisfaction by this excellent Society, which has worked so hard in this great cause of humanity.

(Cheers.) As I said before, I feel, perhaps, I may have some slight claim to stand before you, as members of my family have occupied a similar position. In the years 1825 and 1828, my uncle, the late Duke of Gloucester--(cheers)--presided at meetings of the Society, which were numerously attended. The Duke of Sussex--(cheers)--did so in 1840, and you are well aware of the interest they took in promoting the objects of the Society in bringing forward questions concerning it in Parliament. (Hear, hear). In the same year my lamented father occupied the chair at a very large and crowded meeting at Exeter Hall, and I believe that occasion was the very first on which he occupied the chair at any public meeting in this country. We may all be proud, ladies and gentlemen, that England was the first country which abolished Negro slavery. (Cheers.) Parliament voted and the nation paid twenty million pounds to facilitate this object. (Applause.) Our example was followed by many other countries, though I regret to say that in Brazil and Cuba slavery still exists, as well as in Mohammedan and heathen countries. It is a very natural temptation that, in newly-peopled countries, and especially when the climate prevents Europeans from working, forced labour should be introduced. The Duke of Gloucester very properly said that 'The Slave Trade can only be abolished by the abolition of Slavery; that while there is a demand there will be a supply; this is the keynote of the Society during its existence." (Hear, hear.) Principally owing to the indefatigable exertions of the undaunted Thomas Clarkson and his great Parliamentary coadjutor, William Wilberforce, the Slave Trade and the untold horrors of the Middle Passage were as far as Great Britain was concerned, put an end to in the year 1807. The majority, therefore, of the slaves in the West Indian Islands who received the benefit of the Emancipation Act were descendants of those Africans who had been originally torn from the forests of Africa. Speaking of the proclamation of the emancipation of the Slaves in the Colonies, Mr. Buxton said: 'Throughout the colonies the churches and chapels had been thrown open, and the slaves had crowded into them on the evening of the 31st of July, 1838. As the hour of midnight approached they fell upon their knees, and awaited the solemn moment, all hushed, silent, and prepared. When twelve o'clock sounded from the chapel bells they sprang upon their feet and throughout every island rang glad sounds of thanksgiving to the Father of all, for the chains were broken and the slaves were free.' (Loud cheers.) I may mention that I have within a short time ago received a telegram from the President of the Wesleyan Methodist Conference of Burstein, congratulating me and you on the meeting of to-day, and stating that it was during the session of the Conference in 1834 that the abolition of slavery in the West Indian Colonies became an accomplished fact--a consummation for which, as Wesleyan Methodists, they had universally prayed and laboured. They cannot, therefore, but profoundly rejoice at the jubilee of the great event, with its incalculable benefits, not only to the West Indies, but to all other peoples through the world. (Cheers.) It may not, perhaps, be generally known to you that slavery was abolished in India in 1843 by the simple passing of an Act destroying its legal status, and putting the free-man and slave on the same footing before the law. The natural result took place, and millions of slaves gratuitously procured their own freedom without any sudden dislocation of rights claimed by their masters. A plan similar to this would be found a most effectual one in Egypt and other Mohammedan countries. (Cheers.) This example was followed by Lord Carnarvon in 1874 on the Gold Coast of Western Africa, where he was able to abolish slavery without any serious interference with the habits and customs of the people. (Hear, hear). Under the influence of England, the Bey of Tunis issued a decree in 1846 abolishing slavery and the slave-trade throughout his dominions, which concluded in the following simple and forcible terms: 'Know that all slaves that shalt touch our territory by sea or land shall become free.' In connection with this there are two names which I cannot do otherwise than allude to-day, that of Sir Samuel Baker, and one which is on everybody's lips--that of General Gordon. (Loud cheers.) You are well aware that during the term of five or six years that they were Governors of the Soudan their great object was to put down the slave trade on the White Nile. They were successful to a great extent, but I fear they had great difficulties to contend with, and when their backs were turned much of the evil came out again which they had found on their arrival. I will now turn to Europe. The great Republic of France in 1848, under the guidance of the veteran Abolitionist, M. Victor Schoelcher and his colleagues, passed a short Act abolishing Slavery through the French Dominions: 'La Republique n'admet plus d'esclaves sur le territoire Francais.' (Cheers.) In Russia the emancipation of twenty millions of serfs in 1861 by the late Emperor of Russia must not pass unchronicled in a review of the history of emancipation, although, strictly speaking, this form of slavery can scarcely be classed with that resulting from the African Slave-Trade. In the United States of America in 1865 the fetters of four millions and a half of slaves in the Southern States were melted in the hot fires of the most terrible Civil War of modern times. (Cheers.) Passing on to South America, and looking to Brazil, it may be noted with satisfactlon that all of the small republics formerly under the rule of Spain put an end to slavery at the time they threw off the yoke of the mother country. The great empire of Brazil has alone, I regret to say, retained the curse which she inherited from her Portuguese rulers. At the present moment she possesses nearly a million and a half of slaves on her vast plantations, many of whom lead a life worse than that of beasts of burden. (Hear, hear.) Now, having taken this glance at the condition of slavery to-day, I will add in the words of the Society that 'the chief object of this jubilee meeting is to rekindle the enthusiasm of England and to assist her to carry on this civilising touch of freedom until its beneficent light shall be shed over all the earth.' (Loud cheers.) The place in which this meeting is held, the character of this great meeting, and the reception these words have received assure me that I have not done wrong in stating freely these objects. (Cheers.) One of the objects of the Society is to circulate at home and abroad accurate information on the enormities of the slave-trade and of slavery, to give evidence--

if evidence, indeed, be wanting--to the inhabitants of slave-holding countries of the pecuniary advantages of free labour, and to diffuse authentic information respecting the beneficial result to the countries of emancipation. The late Duke of Gloucester, in the course of a speech made by him in 1825, said that 'his family had been brought to this country for the protection of the rights and liberties of its subjects, and as a member of that family he should not be discharging his duty towards them if he did not recommend the sacred principles of freedom by every means in his power.' Most heartily and most cordially do I endorse his words. (Cheers.) I rejoice that we have on the platform the eminent sons of two eminent fathers in the work of abolishing the slave-trade and slavery. Lord Derby and Mr. Forster, whom I rejoice to see here, have a hereditary connection with emancipation. The late Lord Derby, then Mr. Stanley, was Colonial Secretary to the Liberal Government of that day, which had set before it the task of carrying through Parliament a measure which was to put a term to slavery in all the dependencies of the United Kingdom. Mr. Forster's father having taken his full share of the agitation which led to the abolition of colonial slavery, went to Tennessee on an anti-slavery errand, and died in that State. There are glimpses, ladies and gentlemen, in Mr. Trevelyan's Life of Macaulay of the devotion with which this great movement was carried on. Zachary Macaulay, father of our great historian, was one of the chief workers in the cause, and it is said of him that for forty years he was ever burdened with the thought that he was called upon to wage war with this gigantic evil. In some of the West India Island, the apprenticeship system produced worse evils than the servitude of the slave. The Negroes were theoretically free, but were practically slaves. The masters had been paid for their emancipation, but still held them to service. In a year or two the term of apprenticeship was shortened, and soon afterwards public opinion at home demanded and effected its complete abolition. There were four years of disappointment, trouble, dispute, and suffering in all the West Indies, except the island of Antigua, where the planters had to be enforced in 1838 by another Act, which abolished the transition stage, and proclaimed universal and complete emancipation. This Act only completed the work which 1838 began. The battle in which so many noble spirits had been engaged was practically won when the name of slavery was abolished. The Negroes of the West Indies look back to the 1st August, 1834, as the birthday of their race. The Emancipation Act, which on that day came into force, spoke the doom of slavery all round the world. I have ventured on this occasion to touch on different topics and dates which I thought would be of interest, but it is not my wish to weary you with longer details. Allow me to thank you for the kind way in which you have listened to the remarks I have made, and to assure you how deeply I am with you on this occasion, both heart and soul." (Loud cheers.)

Other speeches followed by Earl Granville, Sir Stafford Northcote, M. P., the Archbishop of Canterbury, Sir Harry Verney, M. P., Lord Derby, Mr. W. E. Forster, M. P., Cardinal Manning, Mr. Henry Richard, M. P., Canon Wilberforce, Sir

Thomas Fowell Buxton, Mr. A. Pease, M. P., Alderman Sir W. M'Arthur, M. P., Mr. Sturge, and Mr. James Cropper, M. P.

The Prince of Wales and the Lord Mayor replied to votes of thanks so very cordially expressed. The Prince in his reply said:

"I am not likely to forget this important day, and most sincerely do I hope that important results may accrue from it. We have to-day celebrated the past, but we have the future to look to, as many speakers have said, and I cannot do better than agree with my right hon. friend on my left (Mr. Forster) that we must act with caution. But with due caution, and with the advice and good example which have been set, I feel sure that in time all countries will follow in the footsteps of England. (Cheers.) The best chance of a complete abolition of slavery will lie in civilisation in opening up those great countries, Asia and Africa, many parts of which are now known to but few Europeans, and in in disseminating education. (Cheers.) In time people will see that they have derived no benefit from having slaves, that the free-man will do his work far better than the one who is forced to labour."

The prince then concluded with kind reference to the late Sir Bartle Frere's services, and to his widow.

As I sat upon that platform, with the heir to the British Throne, and now the occupant of that Throne, and with many of the leading men in the Kingdom, and before me hundreds of ladies and gentlemen of rank, of learning, talent, and wealth, and of moral and religious worth; and as I thought of the great transformation that had taken place regarding even myself, I was greatly moved indeed; from being a poor slave, ignorant and helpless, by the law of the land "a thing, a chattel," now considered a man, a brother, and treated as such, and on this occasion treated with such favour; this impressed me profoundly. Although all these years have passed away since that event the whole scene is vividly before my mind at this moment, and shall ever remain so.

In the evening of that same 1st of August, I presided at a meeting of "The Balloon Society," held at the Royal Aquarium, the subject for discussion being the Jubilee of the Emancipation of the Slaves. There was a report in the "Westminster and Lambeth Gazette," in which it was stated that:--"The Rev. Thomas L. Johnson, a coloured gentleman, formerly of Mr. Spurgeon's College, presided. The President, Mr. Lefevre, C.E., said they had celebrated a Centenary in that room, and now they would celebrate a Jubilee. It was a red-letter day since they were the pioneers of emancipation. After referring to the Guildhall meeting, the speaker called on a coloured lady to sing one of the well-known 'slave choruses.'

"The Chairman, in an interesting speech, gave an account of his experience as a slave. He had never felt the value of life until the proclamation of President Lincoln freed him. As he sat in the Guildhall he thought of years ago when the Prince of Wales rode into Richmond, Virginia, and was received with loud approval, and he hoped then to have been able to ask His Royal Highness to free him, but he lost the opportunity. In this land of freedom--not in words only, but in facts--he felt that he was a man indeed. When he thought of the great society and noble men who had given millions their freedom, and the sympathy of the British nation, he had not words to express his feelings; but he said, 'Praise God from whom all blessings flow.' Many wonderful events had taken place in the nineteenth century, but the greatest event was that which they celebrated that day.

"Mr. Kelly moved and Mr. Peters seconded a resolution expressing 'Sincere satisfaction at the enthusiastic feelings which have been manifested this day throughout the entire Kingdom in celebrating the Jubilee of the Emancipation of the Slaves in all the British Colonies, which was the noblest act known in the history of Christian and civilised nations.'

"Miss Vance, a coloured lady, sang with much feeling several selections. The singing of the National Anthem closed the meeting."

The Campaign Continued

In September I returned. to Scotland in the interests of the African Mission, and remained five months, with head-quarters in Glasgow, during which time, through the kindness of Mr. Oatts and Mr. Hunter Craig, Mr. Macfarlane, Mr. William Sloan, Mr. and Mrs. Peter Mackinon, and others, doors were open to me, and I was kept busy from week to week, in one Mission Hall or another, in and about Glasgow. Many of the ministers cordially invited me to visit their churches, where I received a real hearty welcome and help for Africa.

On December 27th, 1884, the following appeared in the "North British Daily":--"The African Mission--Last night the large hall of the Christian Institute, Bothwell Street, was crowded to hear addresses from Rev. T. L. Johnson, Rev. James Newby, and Dr. T. E. S. Scholes (coloured men), on African Missions. Mr. Oatts presided, and the speakers eloquently and earnestly pleaded for aid for the establishment of new Mission Stations on the dark continent. They pointed out that if the vast continent of Africa was to be Christianised, as they believed it would be, it could only be done by the people of that country. A collection, which was liberal, was made on behalf of the Mission."

During the winter and spring I was privileged to conduct meetings in Carrubbers Close Mission, and in other places in Edinburgh, Hellensburgh, Alexandria, Campbeltown and neighbouring places.

First Visit to Ireland

In January, 1885, I received a letter from Mr. Hind Smith to say that appointments had been made for me in Ireland, and that I would hear from Mr. Robert McCann, travelling Secretary of the Y. M. C. A. in a few days. I was glad to hear this; for a long time I had a wish to visit Ireland, but I did not care to go just at this time, for wherever one went the talk was about Ireland, and ominous things were said.

Soon the letter came concerning appointments due in February. I told a gentlemen of the letter; he shook his head and expressed surprise that my friends should have made appointments for me in Ireland just then. He expressed his good-will by hoping that I would get on all right over there. His observations perplexed and troubled me. With many misgivings therefore, I made preparation for the journey. I prayed over the matter, and made up my mind to trust the Lord who had never failed me. In a short time I was ready, and I took the steamer from Glasgow to Belfast where I arrived the next morning about sunrise. As I went on shore all eyes seemed turned on me. The first thing that took my attention was the number of Irish cars. Several drivers sought my patronage at the same time. I soon found that it was a very difficult thing for me to keep my balance on the car which I ascended. The driver with a merry twinkle in his eye, would call attention to me with a jerk of his head or the turn of his thumb, as he passed anyone whom he knew. As he turned a corner he would say to me quickly--"Houle tight now," or "Houle on." I assure the reader that the advice was very necessary, and that it was readily taken. I saw but little of Belfast that morning as we drove to the station, for I was fully engaged in "houling on" by the car. I was greatly relieved when I arrived at the station, and when I was able to get off instead of being thrown off the vehicle.

As I followed the porter into the station there was quite a commotion. Soon I was seated in a railway carriage and off to Lisburn, my destination. The late Rev. Mr. Bigger met me, and at once made me feel happy in his company. On our way to the Manse he called at the post office and at several shops, where he introduced me to members of his church. On arriving at the Manse Mrs. Bigger gave me a very cordial reception. We then had breakfast, and I began to make enquiries, and some of my questions must have amused my good friends. I asked them if they were really Irish. "Oh, yes, Mr. Johnson," was the reply. "And were those people in the post office and in the shops Irish?" With surprise they said: "Yes, Mr. Johnson. Why do you think we are not Irish?" "Well, you differ but little if any from the English and Scotch," I said. Here in Lisburn my first impressions of the Irish people were received. I stopped here for over a week, and I shall never forget the kindness of the late Rev. Mr. Bigger and his most estimable wife, who sought in every way to make me comfortable and happy; and everywhere in Lisburn I was entertained with much cordiality. From this time I began to think that much that had been said unkindly about the Irish might have been left unsaid, and no doubt it would have been had more been known about the people. I have heard even intelligent folk talk about Ireland and the Irish without making distinctions, and saying what ought to be done; but their ignorance of the place and the people is the only way to account for the remarks of these good friends. Some speak of the emancipated Negroes and their descendants in the same way. As a general thing the defects of the worst samples from among the Negroes are taken, unfairly, and then judgment is passed upon the race. Since 1885 I have been privileged to meet with all classes in Ireland, among whom were to be

129

found thousands of as noble-hearted consecrated, God-fearing, and God-honouring men and women as could be found in any other part of the world.

After ten days in Lisburn I left for Belfast, where I arrived in the evening. The next morning when I went out, I thought--Now I will have it. For I expected some merriment, among the children, at least. But to my great surprise all that I could hear them say was, "The Lord save us." "Look at him; look, look at the man"; and this was said in almost a whisper. I had provided myself with a little book and pencil, to get all the Irish wit I could, for I expected to hear lots of it, even from the children; but I seemed to have frightened all the wit out of them, for all I could hear was "Lord save us; look at the man." I went into Great Victoria Street to get some paper and envelopes. A crowd followed me. Nothing was said that one could take offence at; but the shopkeeper said to the crowd at the door, "Be off there; you should be ashamed of yourselves." I said, "Let them alone, it's all right." After a little while I saw a lad watching me from across the street; presently he ventured over. When he got a better sight of me and standing on tip-toe, he called to his companion in a tone of amazement, "Bill! Bill! come here, come and see the divil!" This was rather a rough note with which to commence my little book.

During my visits to and lectures in Belfast and Cork, and wherever I presented the claims of the heathen I was much encouraged. But some of my experience in Ireland I shall never forget for the oddness of it as well as the anxiety of it. One night when returning from a meeting at Carrick-on-Suir, with Mrs. Grubb, my good friend, a company of lads followed, and soon began to make remarks and afterwards to throw stones. One struck me on the shoulder. Mrs. Grubb at once opened the door of a house we were passing, and walked in. She knew the people. There we remained for over an hour. I felt a little anxious, but knew I was safe in the Lord's hands. The friends in the house kept watch until the lads were gone, and then I went on to the house of Mrs. Grubb's son safely.

While I live I shall never forget my experience at New Ross. When I arrived in the town in a bus the people gathered around and looked at me with the usual remark, "The Lord save us," or "The Lord bless him." One woman came up and gave me a welcome to the town. A man came to me, spat upon his hand--a common custom in some parts in striking a bargain--and then gave me a hearty welcome. I was taken to an hotel and was fixed up quite comfortably. Many people gathered around in front of the hotel looking up at the window. After tea a friend came with a minister of the Gospel to see me. I was asked how I intended to conduct the meeting and I replied by asking how the Y. M. C. A. meetings were conducted. He said they were conducted in the usual way, but as the meeting was to be in the town hall that all classes might feel free to attend they did not intend to make it a religious service, but to just have the story of my life told. "But you will have prayer and a hymn," I suggested. "I think not," said he. I hardly knew what to say; I could see the difficulty of these gentlemen. The minister who was to take the chair said: "I will just introduce you, and you will then tell the story of your life as a slave." I then agreed that he should simply introduce me. When these gentlemen left I wrote a letter to my wife and explained all to her. The hour for the meeting came. There might have been forty or fifty Protestants present, and about twenty or more young men who were Roman Catholics and who sat by the door. The platform was large with seats at the back. I said, just before the meeting commenced, "Will those young men come up here, there is plenty of room." One or two started; soon they all came. They seemed much amused among themselves. The Chairman made a few appropriate introductory re-marks and called on me. Now before leaving the hotel I had been on my knees, and now while they were clapping their hands and giving me a hearty welcome I was lifting up my heart in prayer. As soon as all was quiet I said "Let us pray." What might follow this act I did not know, but I had made up my mind to honour God whether it was offensive or not. After prayer I com-menced my address and in my way praised God for His goodness, told of my conversion and how it came about. At the close a collection was taken, but the plates were not passed to these young men. One of them rose up in his place and said, "We want to give this man some money." And I believe all the young men gave something to the collection. At the close of the meeting I had many a hearty shake of the hand.

One night, when lecturing in Cork, the doors being closed, some men com-menced knocking for admission. All eyes were turned from the platform to the door. When the door was opened, some ten or twelve young men came in. There being no room in the body of the hall, I again thought of all the room I had on the platform. I had a large map of Africa stretched across. I went to one side, untied the cord, let the map down, and then invited the young men up to the platform; and they came up and took their seats on the platform and we had a real quiet time.

I had many kind and friendly receptions in Ireland, but of no place can I say more so than the great reception in Bessbrook. The late Mr. John Grubb Rich-ardson took me for a drive. The news had been circulated that a coloured man was in town. The mill was closed that afternoon; when hundreds of men, women and children lined the streets, and they gave me a great shout of welcome.

In the evening the large hall was quite full of people for the meeting. Mr. Richardson presided. I think this was my first visit to the teetotal town of Bessbrook. I cannot tell how many times I have been there since.

I conducted a mission for ten days in the Skating Rink, Rathmines, Dub-lin, under the auspices of the Rathmines Y. M. C. A. A choir had been orga-nized, and there were some twenty young men,--I think they were from the college,--who assisted each night, some inside and some outside, distributing leaflets and bills, others with lanterns at the corners of the streets and with notices of the meetings. This naturally brought large crowds of people to-gether; some, like Zaccheus, came out of curiosity, but thank God, many, we believe, who came thus received a blessing. Mrs. Johnson, and her sister, Miss

Ora L. McGowan, who was on a visit to this country, sang with me the Gospel each night, Mr. R. McCann and the late Mr. Ernest Lloyd, with other workers took part with me in the meetings each night. The notices on the lanterns and exhibited in other ways, contained the announcement, "Come and hear the Liberated Slave--28 years a Slave--The African Missionary," etc.

BIBLE PRESENTED BY THE COMMITTEE.

At the close of the mission the Committee presented me with a nicely bound Bible and two volumes of Van Doren's works on the Gospel by St. Luke, and which I prize very highly. The following appears as a little testimony of fraternal appreciation and imprinted in gilded lettering in the Bible:--

Testimonials of my services were collected by my very kind and helpful friend, Mr. R. McCann, the travelling Secretary of the Y. M. C. A. in Ireland. Through the kindness of this gentleman many friends were secured in Ireland for the African Mission, for which I thank God. Many readers may know some of the names which we give in memory of the kind and encouraging testimony while I was engaged in deputation work:--Rev. J. Duncan Craig, D. D., Minister of Trinity Church, Lower Gardiner Street, Dublin, wrote:--"Rev. T. L. Johnson delivered a very pathetic and most earnest lecture in the hall of Trinity Church. Mr. Johnson riveted the attention, and fully enlisted the warm sympathy of his audience. I look upon Mr. Johnson as a devoted minister of Christ, who is possessed of much power over an assemblage, and who seeks to exalt the Blessed One."

Similar letters were received from: Mr. Richard Allen, Rev. D. R. Moore, Hollypark, Blackrock; Rev. James Meek, First Presbyterian Church, Larne; Mr. David Black, Hon. Secretary Y. M. C. A. and Literary Association, Dundalk; Mr. David Murray, Hon. Secretary Y. M. C. A., Rathfriland; Rev. Henry Montgomery, Albert Street Presbyterian Church, Belfast; Mr. David Logan, Hon. Secretary Y. M. C. A., Cloughougue; Mr. Arthur Pim, Hillsborough; Rev. T. Hamilton, York Street Presbyterian Church, Belfast; Rev. Thomas Hamill, Presbyterian Church, Lurgan; Mr. H. Kirker, Hon. Secretary Y. M. C. A., Banbridge; Rev. James L. Bigger, Professor Magee College, Londonderry; Rev. W. Fleming Stevenson, Lecturer Christian Union Buildings, Dublin; Mr. Robert Cotter, Secretary Dublin United Services, Dublin; Mr. John Grubb Richardson, Moyallen House, Gilford; Rev. J. Hoffe, Church of Ireland, Arklow; Rev. William Maguire, Methodist Church, Dublin; A. D. Martin, Esq., Newry; Mr. J. Ernest Grubb, Carrick-on-Suir; Mr. H. Ed. Richard, Secretary Y. M. C. A., Wexford; Mr. David Black, General Secretary, and Mr. W. S. Mollan, Hon. Secretary, Y. M. C. A., Belfast; Mr. Robert McCann, Travelling Secretary Y. M. C. A., in Ireland. Press notices were also given in the "Daily Express," Dublin; the "Christian Advocate"; the Belfast Y. M. C. A. "Monthly Bulletin'; the "Sunday School Chronicle"; the "Manchester Guardian," and "The Christian," and a very kind letter was sent to the Rev. S. Pilling, of Blackpool, from a medical and literary gentleman, who had listened to my lecture at Blackpool, Mr. Spencer T. Hall, Ph. D., M. D., M. A.

On one of my trips to Ireland Dr. Theophilas E. S. Scholes, M. D., accompanied me. I shall never forget the hearty reception he had everywhere he went while in Dublin. We made our home with our dear friend the late Mr. E. F. S. Lloyd, Rathmines. One cannot forget how this good man, now in glory, threw himself heart and soul into our mission on behalf of Africa. He seemed never to tire. Through him many friends were made for Dr. Scholes and myself. Rev. William Maguire, then in Dublin, invited Dr. Scholes to visit his church, and this resulted in a present of a valuable box of tools and other useful things for the work in Africa.

February 3rd, 1886, was indeed a very happy day to me, a day of great relief, a day of praise to our Father God for answer to prayer. On that date Dr. Scholes and Rev. J, S. Ricketts sailed from Liverpool for the Congo.

Departure of Missionaries for Africa

The following piece of information appeared in the "Belfast Witness":-- "African Mission sending Coloured Men as Missionaries to Africa.--On Wednesday the 3rd inst., Dr. Theo. E. S. Scholes and Rev. J. E.. Ricketts--both black men--sailed for the Congo on the SS. 'Ambriz.' Dr. Scholes goes out as agent and medical Missionary of the above Society. He has studied seven years in Britain, and is a graduate of Edinburgh University. Dr. John Lowe, F.R.C.S. E., Secretary and Superintendent of the Edinburgh Medical Missionary Society, says of Dr. Scholes:--'I believe him to be thoroughly well qualified professionally. He possesses gifts and qualifications, which, with God's blessing, will enable him to do a great work for his Master.' The Rev. John E. Ricketts was educated in Jamaica--the birthplace of both these brethren. He is a carpenter by trade. We ask the prayers of God's people for these brethren, who go to the land of their fathers with the good news and glad tidings. Rev. Thomas L. Johnson, financial agent of the above society, wishes to thank the friends in Ireland and Britain, not only for the contribution to send these brethren to Africa, but for valuable articles of cutlery, beads, and stationery sent to the Christian Union Buildings, Dublin, for these brethren."

Dr. Scholes wrote from the Congo Hotel, March 25th, 1886, concerning his progress on the journey, and his letter gave me great joy and led to praise. An extract is as follows.--"Dear friend,--I hail this opportunity of writing from this stage of our journey. In answer to prayer, no doubt, our Heavenly Father brought us hither in safety yesterday morning. You will be curious to know the kind of reception we had after the pictures we had presented as to the manner we should be received owing to our colour. I frankly confess that after taking into consideration the fact that we came without any introduction to the agent of the Dutch House, our reception by gentlemen in connection with that firm, and others whom I have met since arrival, was most courteous. We shall be two days here, as the Dutch House steamer leaves for the river in the forenoon to-morrow (D. V.). I had an interview with Mr. De Bloeme respecting the receiving and forwarding of our goods, etc., henceforth. He has agreed to do it at a premium of ten per cent of mail rates. This, I understand, is a new arrangement which is to apply to missions alike."

In the annual report of the General Association of the Western States and Territories, Chicago, Ill, September 22-26, 1886, the following occurs:--Under date of February 22nd, 1886, Rev. Thomas L. Johnson wrote that Dr. Scholes and Brother Ricketts sail February 3rd in steamer "Ambriz" for the lower

Congo river, south-west coast of Africa; and again under date of May 4th the letters received from them informed him of their arrival at Banana, March 25th, and that they had sailed up into the interior March 26th. It was a relief to know that Brethren Scholes and Ricketts were in Africa, the field of their future labours. And it is just to say here, that while our work this side the water was not much considered, but much criticised, because but little understood by our friends in Britain, that we should put on record our appreciation and thanks for the liberal, steadfast and disinterested support they gave to our Financial Agent, Rev. Thomas L. Johnson, and for all they have done to help on our small beginning in trying to give Africa the Gospel through her own sons and daughters. Our small and very feeble beginning in a work whose importance in incalculable, and whose immense proportions are all but overwhelming, may have some point of analogy to another even in Evangelical Christianity that has now become historical, and which is thus described by a recent English writer: A hundred years ago, only a few hundred pounds were raised,--for Christian missions to the heathen world--chiefly by Continental Christians, feebly assisted by our "Society for the promotion of Christian Knowledge." When England, in the language of the day, "sent out a cobbler to convert the world," it was with great difficulty a few hundred pounds could be collected to pay the passage of Carey and his co-adjutors. For many years the funds of missionary societies were summed up in hundreds of pounds. They slowly rose to thousands and tens of thousands."

Visit to the St. Louis Convention and the States

Having been successful, through the help of God, in getting our Missionaries off, the following August our Advisory Committee at a meeting held at Aldersgate Street Y. M. C. A., strongly recommended me to accept an invitation to visit the National Baptist Convention of coloured people meeting in St. Louis, Mo., U. S. A., at the end of August. In a few days I sailed on the Umbria from Liverpool. I cannot describe the hearty welcome I received on my arrival in St. Louis. Having been away from my people for years I was deeply interested in all their deliberations and progress. I soon discovered that I was in the midst of hundreds of delegates from all parts of the United States, and that most of them were far ahead of me in education and ability, and yet I was given a place and a welcome amongst the most clever. But this was greatly accounted for by the fact that I had been to Africa and that I had been to London and other places in England, and my story was of great interest to them. I was conscious that I was neither clever nor eloquent like some of those to whom I had listened; but I had one thought, one idea to present in the most forcible language I could command, to these delegates, representing a quarter of a million of Coloured Christians, and that was,--

Africa for Christ, and Christ for Africa

I soon saw that all I had to say was listened to with much attention. I had every reason to conclude that my visit was not in vain, but that greater interest had been awakened for poor Africa.

One of the delegates moved that I be chosen as one of the Vice-Presidents of the National Convention; and this was adopted. At one of the sessions I was requested to give a Bible Reading to young men, and this Service was attended with considerable interest. After the Convention I was desired to visit six Associations in the Western States, and to present to these bodies the claims of Africa. At each Association the principal topic was Africa. Men and women young and old, were anxious to catch every word that might be said, not only at the public meetings, in churches and halls, but also in their homes.

Co-Operating with the A. B. M. U.

The thirteenth annual session of General Association of the Western States and Territories was held at Chicago, September, 1886, and at that meeting it was unanimously resolved that the Association co-operate with the A. B. M. U. in mission work on the Congo, and secondly, that Brother Thomas L. Johnson, should be re-called from England as Financial Agent, and be appointed Corresponding and Financial Secretary of the General Association of the Western States and Territories, with headquarters in Chicago.

The following extract from the report of the Executive Committee embodies this resolution: "On the 26th of March this year, under the auspices of the African Mission of the General Association of Western States and Territories, the Rev. Dr. Theo. R. S. Scholes, Medical Missionary, and the Rev. J. R. Ricketts, mechanic, arrived at Banana point, Congo River, there to commence mission work. At the thirteenth regular meeting of the General Association, held with the Bethesda Baptist Church of Chicago, Ill., September 22-28, great interest was manifested in the work of the Association carried on in Africa. And in order to facilitate this work in Africa, and more adequately provide for those brethren now engaged there, terms of co-operation were entered into between this Association and the A. B. M. U. by which the work for Africa might be carried on in perfect harmony. Brother Thomas L. Johnson, a returned Missionary, and for some time the Financial Agent of the African Mission of the G.A.W.S. and T. in Great Britain, was present at the meeting and heartily favoured the measure and terms of the co-operation. He also spoke warmly of his reception and encouragement from the National Convention of Coloured Baptists held in St. Louis in August, also at the Wood River Association at East St. Louis, Ill., the Mount Olive Association at Metropolis, Ill., the Union Baptist Association of Ohio at Cincinatti, O., and Second District North Missouri Association at Tipton. The enthusiastic spirit manifested at these different gatherings, as well as that of the Chicago Association, undoubtedly affords new hope and life to the friends of African Missions in this country and the world.

To foster this spirit in America it seemed good to the brethren of the Association that Brother Thomas L. Johnson, who has met with such signal success as the Financial Secretary of the Association in Great Britain be re-called to America and be appointed the General Financial Secretary of the Association for this country. By direction of the Executive Board he goes South to spend six or eight weeks in the Southern States in stirring up the brethren in that section in the interests of African mission work. After this visit he will return to England to close up his business there and bring his family to America, where he will engage permanently in the work of his office as the Association's Financial Secretary. The Association expresses its profoundest gratitude to the people of Great Britain and Ireland who so kindly helped it through its earnest agent, the Rev. Thomas L. Johnson, when the Association was getting its first Missionaries on the field. And among the other kind friends worthy of special mention we cheerfully express our indebtedness to Mr. W. Hind Smith, and wife, Mr. George Williams, of London, President Y. M. C. A., Mr. W. M. Oatts, of Glasgow, and Mr. R. McCann, of Belfast, for valuable assistance rendered our agent."

The above was unanimously adopted as the sense of the body, of which the Rev. R. De Baptiste was President, and R. J. Temple, Secretary of the National Board.

Acting upon the advice of the Committee I visited the States of Missouri, Kentucky, Tennessee, Louisiana, and Mississippi. I was simply charmed with the sympathetic interest by which I was received everywhere by the thousands of my people as I spoke to them of Africa. At that time it was estimated that a quarter of a million of our people wanted to go to the land of their fathers; to-day we are told that quite a million are anxious to go to Africa.

On my way South I had an opportunity of judging of the strong prejudice against the Negro and the colour line. When travelling I usually wore a "Fez," and when I had this on I was looked upon as from the East. On my way to Louisville, Ky., the conductor on the train on passing through eyed me closely. Finally he came to me and asked if I were from the East. I said, "From England, if you call that East." Then he wanted to know my nationality. I told him I was a Negro. We had quite a pleasant talk about England and Africa. When he asked how I liked the country, I told him that I liked it and knew it quite well. At this he was surprised. I then told him that I was born in Virginia. He said, "You are not one of this country 'niggers?'" "Yes," I said; I could see at once that it would not do for me to correct him in the word "nigger." He looked round as though something wrong had taken place, and then he went out. On the other side of the car sat two white men; one said, as he looked across at me, "That conductor must know what he is or who he is." I could not catch the word. When the conductor returned, he came to me, and in a low tone said that he believed that there were just as nice coloured men as there were white. He did not like to make any difference, but the Company did. Perhaps a little explanation is needed here, The Civil Rights Bill passed in the Congress of the U. S. A., 1875, gave the coloured people the right to enter public places and ride in first-class railway carriages if they wish so to do.-- See Johnson's History of the Negro Race in America.

From 1875 to 1884 this law was the Negro's only protection in the South. in 1884 the United States Supreme Court declared the Civil Rights Bill unconstitutional, and this at once gave the open door to "State's Rights."

The Southern States proceeded at once to make laws which step by step diminished these rights. In many of the States laws have been passed by the Legislators prohibiting the coloured people from riding in railway car with whites. From what I see in the papers it seems more binding now than when I travelled in the Southern States in 1876. In the East, West, and North there is no difference made in travelling on the railway, any more than there is in England, but, going South, as soon as the Mason and Dixon line is crossed,-- that is the dividing line between North and South--the coloured lady or gentleman must travel in a car provided for "coloured people." Hence the conductor referred to above said, "I do not make any difference, but the Company does."

After this he was very busy, and had no time to seek further information. However, he did not ask me into the next car. On arriving at Louisville, Kentucky, I received a hearty welcome from W. H. Stewart, Esq., Editor, Rev. C. H. Parish, and the Rev. Wm. Frank, and the late Rev. Wm. Simmonds, D. D., President of the State University, who had invited me. When giving an address at the University, Dr. Simmonds requested me to say something about England and the English, and how I was received in England. This I was pleased to do.

While hanging up my map in a chapel to lecture on Africa in the evening, two young "coloured" men were talking very quietly yet very earnestly. One seemed a little excited as he raised his hand and his voice, and I overheard him say, "I tell you, there are only two places on 'earth' where a coloured man can get justice, that's England and Heaven." When I told Dr. Simmonds how I was received as a foreigner when I wore my "fez," and as a "nigger" when I did not, and that with the "fez" I could travel as a general thing unmolested, he advised me to keep it on all the time. This I made up my mind not to do. I wanted to be identified with my own race, and no other, though by doing so I might suffer. Through the influence of the Rev. W. H. Stewart, of Louisville, I was able to secure a minister's half-fare ticket, and to this I had to sign my name as a returned Missionary from Africa. On presenting this ticket at the station I would be required to write my name in the ticket agent's book.

On leaving Louisville to go South about 4 o'clock one morning, I found that there was a separate waiting room for coloured people, also a separate window for them to receive their tickets. It was quite cold. When I presented my ticket to show I was entitled to a half-fare, the agent looked me up and down and then asked me, "Are you from Africa?" I replied that I had been there, but was now from England. After giving me a ticket, and asking some questions about Africa, he asked if I were cold. I replied that I was. He said, "Come round to the sitting room to the fire." There was no fire in the waiting room for coloured people. I did not wait for a second invitation, for I felt the cold very much. I had hardly got warm when a white porter came in and told me that was not the place for me; round there was the place for coloured people. The ticket agent heard him and said, "I gave him permission." When the train came, I at once entered the car provided for coloured people; this was nothing more than a smoking compartment. A coloured lady, however refined and respectable, must first pay the same fare as the white ladies, but is compelled to sit in this car, where (at that time) white men would come in and smoke and spit and use bad language, and no one dared to say a word against it. On my way to New Orleans, Louisiana, where the train stopped for dinner, I went into the dining room. I did not think of going to the table, but went to the lunch counter, when I was told I could not have it there, but if I chose to go round to the back part of the Hotel to the kitchen, someone might accommodate me there. I was hungry, but did not wish to be left at this Station and my luggage in the car, so I returned to my seat. I had many experiences in the South that would take up too much space to tell.

In September, 1889, the National Convention of Coloured Baptists was held at Indianapolis. Delegates attended from all Parts of the U. S. A. and Canada. The delegates from Georgia travelled by the East Tennessee, Virginia, and Georgia Railroad, having secured first-class tickets from the agent of this Road, who assured them that going North they would not be molested. When they arrived at a Station called Baxley in the State of Georgia, there were seventy-five white men armed with pistols, clubs, dirk knives, and brick-bats; and as soon as the train stopped, they jumped upon the platform, yelling like demons, and rushed into the cars, and were at every door and window; women were insulted, ministers and delegates were roughly handled, some greatly hurt, some were thrown off the train, others kicked out and made to go into what is commonly called the "Jim Crow car." When the delegates arrived at Indianapolis, Indiana, several suffered very much from the wounds and bruises they received. I was present at this Convention when the late Rev. Dr. E. K. Love, of Savannah, Georgia, stood up and told how he had been beaten over the head with a heavy piece of scantling; the Rev. G. M. Sprattling, of Brunswick, Ga., who carried his arm in a sling from the effect of wounds; Deacon J. N. Brown, of Savannah, who had several fearfully bad gashes on his head; Mrs. Jane Garrett, who was thrown to the ground by the ruffians and threatened with death if she did not stop screaming. These and others as they related their story led to words of indignation and protest that will not soon be forgotten. On my return from this Convention to Chicago I was invited to take the chair at a meeting held in Providence Baptist Chapel, when coloured men met and gave expression to their feelings, some advising that coloured men should arm themselves for protection. I opposed this course, and called their attention to the condition of Israel in Egypt, and their conduct under the circumstances. "The King of Egypt died, and the children of Israel sighed by reason of the bondage; and they cried, and their cry came up unto God, by reason of the bondage, and God heard their groaning." My advice to my people to-day is to go and seek God in prayer, as thousands of us did in the old slave days. God heard our voice and looked on our affliction and our labour and on our oppression, and at His own time, which is the best time, and in His own way, which is the best way, He answered our prayers. Let the oppressed be importunate, God is not less sympathetic than man. God, who said, "Ethiopia shall soon stretch out her hands unto God," is with us and for us; and if God be for us, who can be against us.

In the Southern States I found many of the former slave-holders greatly interested in African Missions, and I had encouragement everywhere that I went. And after issuing an appeal to the Pastors and Churches of the Baptist General Association of the Western States and Territories, pointing out that the Congo Mission was now established; that Missionaries of our own race were in the field; that good and hopeful work was being done; and that liberal gifts were needed not only to meet pressing wants, but also to keep our compact with the American Baptist Missionary Union, I then took my departure for England.

To England Again

Arriving at Pittsburgh on the morning of January 21st, 1887, I found that passengers were allowed twenty minutes for breakfast. An energetic reporter intervened between me and my meal. He was certainly very polite. He followed me everywhere, and wanted to know lots of things all at once. With notebook in hand he put question after question. Before I could answer one, he asked another. When I arrived home in Sydenham, S. E., London, I received a copy of the paper containing the reporter's article, with some mistakes. As a rule I found reporters the very best of fellows. Here is the article, and it is

A Typical American Report

It is from the "Pittsburgh Chronicle Telegraph," Friday evening, January 21st, 1887.--"Experiences of a Former Slave.--A Graphic Story of Travels in Africa, and His Efforts to Benefit His Race.--Among the passengers who stepped from the Chicago express at the Union Station this morning was a man dressed in such a peculiar and picturesque garb that he attracted general attention as he walked along the platform. The man was Thomas L. Johnson, of London, England, the coloured man who has a world-wide reputation for his long experience and trials as a slave, and in recent years his work for the bettering of the condition of his race in America and Africa. He wore a high red Turkish cap and a long flowing robe, his long, kinky hair giving him a very prominent appearance. He was en route from Chicago to London. His prominence in life is due partly to his aptitude, and also to the interest taken in him by such men as ex-Secretary of War Robert T. Lincoln, and Albert Pullman, of the Pullman Bros., of Chicago, E. S. Ishem, and H. M. Kinsley. In a conversation at the depot this morning he said: 'I have a vivid recollection of the old slavery days, which I shall never forget. I was a slave in Virginia for twenty-eight years. After we gained our freedom I went North, and my first work was as a waiter at Leland's Hotel, New York. Then I went to Chicago and was head waiter for Kinsley in 1866, and finally became a porter on a Pullman car. I was anxious to be educated, and through the help of friends I was sent to Spurgeon's College in London in 1876. I was then forty years of age, and two years later was sent to Africa for Missionary work. Yes, I had a decidedly exciting experience in that country. I landed at Victoria, on the West Coast of Africa, and after many days' hard work penetrated eighty miles into the interior, stopping at a native village called Bakundu, where I opened a new station...I returned to London and remained for a time. . . . . I came to the United States from London on the last occasion to attend the National Convention.' . . . . Mr. Johnson left at eight o'clock this morning for New York. Thence he will sail for England. After visiting Ireland he will return to this country with his wife and locate in Chicago as the Corresponding Secretary of the African Missionary Association."

Return to America

After some visitations in England and Ireland in the interest of the African Mission, I returned to Chicago in August, 1887, with my wife, and when the work began to be known more fully, I received many invitations to preach and lecture.

Entertainment Given Me by H. M. Kinsley, Esq. Chicago

December, 1887.

The following will explain the proceedings:--
HONOURING THE SLAVE.
Copy of invitation:--
- The Slave in Virginia.
- Chief Steward at Kinsley's.
- The Student at Spurgeon's College, London.
- The Missionary in Africa.

On WEDNESDAY AFTERNOON, DEC. 14th, at 3 o'clock, REV. THOMAS L. JOHNSON, formerly known as "THOMAS" at Kinsley's, in 1866-1867, will deliver a Lecture in the Banquet Hall, at KINSLEY'S, Nos. 105 and 107, Adams Street, on his personal experiences and travels in America, Great Britain, and

Africa, from the time he was a Slave in Virginia to the present. He will exhibit quite a number of African curiosities, fine maps, pictures of natives, idols, and slave chains.

Mr. Johnson will sing in the African language, assisted by Mrs. Johnson, her sister (Miss O. L. McGowan), and Mr. Price. He will also appear in African Dress.

Yourself and friends are cordially invited to be present. Admission Free.

Chair to be taken at 3 o'clock, p.m., by Rev. J. S. McPherson, D. D., supported by Rev. J. L. Withrow, D. D., Rev. P. S. Henson, D. D., Rev. W. M. Lawrence, D. D., and Rev. F. W. Gunsaulus.

The reference in the "Chicago Tribune" to this event may not be without interest to the reader, On December 11th, 1887, the following appeared:-- "An African Missionary.--Old Chicagoans will remember Thomas L. Johnson-- Kinsley's head waiter after the War, now labouring among uncivilised Negroes in the Tropics--His eventful career--Born in slavery he learned secretly how to read--Sold away from his mother--Recollections of the War-- Subsequent Progress.--When Thomas L. Johnson threw off his dress suit and took to preaching the Gospel in Africa, a good waiter was lost and a good Missionary was gained. Old-time Chicagoans will tell you that Thomas--they all knew him as 'Thomas'--was the best waiter that ever served a dinner. He was a waiter at Kinsley's in those years after the War when Kinsley had his restaurant sandwiched in among a lot of music stores in the Crosby Opera House--Robat and Cady's one side, Kimball's the other side, and Julius Bauer's next door. Then when Kinsley opened at Wabash Avenue and Washington Street, Thomas was made head waiter. Mr. Kinsley could still tell you if he pleased of the great crush in the restaurant the night General Grant was first nominated, and how Thomas, the head waiter, buckled to work with the other waiters and took twenty orders for dinner at once at one table, and brought back the twenty complete dinners exactly as ordered. He had an extraordinary memory, had Thomas. You and all your friends could order what you and they pleased, and Thomas could be depended on to remember it. But he took to studying the Bible, and became imbued with the idea that his mission was to preach to his brethren of the Negro race--perhaps the manifestly lost condition of Kinsley's waiters had something to do with that resolve, and perhaps not, but no matter--anyhow, he began preaching and soon was the Pastor of a coloured church, and thus, as stated, a good waiter was lost. By-and-by he went out to Africa to preach to the heathen.

"On Wednesday afternoon next the Rev. Thomas L. Johnson, an African Missionary, will lecture in the banquet hall at Kinsley's on his personal experiences and travels in Africa, Great Britain, and America. Kinsley doesn't usually throw his banquet hall open to Missionary Meetings--it is not remembered that he ever did it before--but Kinsley is the man who discovered Thomas, and is one of his warmest friends. There are four epochs in Mr. Johnson's life, and this is the way he marks them out:--1--The slave in Virgin-

142

ia; 2-- The chief steward at Kinsley's; 3--The student at Spurgeon's College, London; 4--The Missionary in Africa.

"Mr. Johnson, it should be stated right here, has been a most successful Missionary, and is one of the most earnest and hard-working labourers in the Gospel vineyard. His work for the heathen in Africa has had prominent recognition in Great Britain.

"'I was a slave for twenty-eight years,' said Mr. Johnson, in a chat yesterday, 'I was born in Virginia. My father was an octoroon and a free man, and my mother was a slave. My mother's father came from Africa. My father wanted to purchase my mother and myself, but Mr. Brent, our owner, would not sell us. A free man was permitted to marry a slave woman, but her children were slaves. My mother told me that my father, when he died, left money for me to purchase my liberty when I grew up, but the white people got it, I was in Richmond when the War began; after I received my freedom at the close of the War I went North. I got work first in Leland's Hotel in New York as a waiter. I then went to Rocky Point, R.I., where I saw Mr. Kinsley. I came to Chicago in September, 1866, and went to work in Mr. Kinsley's in the Crosby Opera House as a dish-washer in the kitchen. I was soon made head dish-washer. Then I was promoted to wait in the dining room. Everybody seemed to know me because of my long hair.'

"Mr. Johnson is too modest to tell all in his favour. Everybody knew him because he was the best waiter in the place, and was in every way distinguished above his fellows. He was most courteous, attentive, dignified, intelligent, and cleanly. Moreover, he knew everybody and what everybody liked. In those days the Union Pacific Railroad was being built, and when it was completed a few hundred miles beyond Omaha, excursions would be frequently gotten up by the Company with intent to boom the project. Kinsley catered for these excursions, and Johnson was always sent as chief steward. His cleverness attracted the attention of everybody, and thus it came to pass that the Pullmans, the Fields, the Leiters, the Ishams, John V. Ayer, Bob Lincoln, John Crerar, Norman Williams, George L. Dunlap, Perry Smith, Colonel Howe, and a host of other leading Chicago people knew Thomas well, and appreciated him highly. When Mr. Kinsley moved to his new quarters at Washington Street and Wabash Avenue he made Thomas head waiter.

"In 1876, through the influence of Mr. and Mrs. Stroud Smith, and Mr. W. Hind Smith, of the Y. M. C. A., Manchester, he was invited to England, where after a regular course of study in Spurgeon's College, he went to Africa. The story of his adventures in Africa would fill a volume."

"THE CHICAGO HERALD."

Thursday, December 15th, 1887.

EXALTING THE SLAVE.

"A brilliant assemblage in Kinsley's Banquet Hall yesterday afternoon pays tribute to the worth of a most deserving coloured man.

"The most brilliant company which ever assembled at Kinsley's Banquet Hall was that which a Negro entertained yesterday afternoon. The Negro is Thomas L. Johnson, whose remarkable career well illustrates the possibilities in a black man's life. Johnson is now fifty-two years of age. He was born a slave, entered the employ of Kinsley as dish-washer, was promoted to the post of head-waiter, felt himself called upon to engage in Missionary work, was successful, went to London, graduated at Spurgeon's College, and went thence into the interior of Africa as a Missionary. He returns to Chicago as the accredited agent of the African Missionary Society; he enters a hall into which, until yesterday, no coloured man had gone except as servitor; he is the honoured guest of his former employer; he entertains as select a gathering as Chicago has ever witnessed.

"Johnson is six feet in height, with pronounced African lips and nose. He has the forehead of a Caucasian, an honest eye, and a face on which energy and kindness are written. As he stood on the platform yesterday afternoon pleading for Africa eloquently and earnestly, no one gave a thought to his colour. On the westerly wall of the hall were displayed charts and maps of Africa, with heroic-sized types of the black tribes of the world, which were made by authority of the German Government. Rev. Dr. S. J. McPherson presented Rev. Dr. William D. Everette, who offered prayer, after which Rev. Mr. Johnson, his wife, her sister, and Mr. Price sang, 'A Plea for Africa.' The first verse, with refrain, is as follows:--

"Give a thought to Africa; 'neath the burning sun
There are hosts of weary hearts waiting to be won;
Many idols have they made, but from swamp and sod
There are voices crying now for the living God.

CHORUS--
Tell the love of Jesus by her hills and waters;
God bless Africa, and her sons and daughters."

"The melody was that of four finely-trained voices, and the 'Plea' was one which will be long remembered by the auditors. In introducing the speaker of the afternoon, Rev. Dr. McPherson said that the coloured man who was to entertain them represented a variety of great causes. One of these related to our own nation. The freedom of the slave had been won, and what the black citizens accomplish depends upon themselves. They must not expect to be lifted; they must lift themselves. Dr. McPherson said that slavery had been denominated a sectional question. He had not so regarded it. 'I have been told by those who ought to know,' he continued, 'that the roots of slavery were in the Constitution of the United States.' Not even New England had a right to boast on this question, for slaves had been owned there under the law, and slaves had been cattle in New York State. It had only been a question of time, however, and the Northern States were the first to renounce the stain of slavery. The speaker said Mr. Johnson represented another great cause--that of the evangelisation of Africa, which can only be effected by men with African blood in their veins. To the Christian as well as to the commercial world, Africa was the great treasure trove. Livingstone, Grant, and Stanley had agreed that there was a great future for the Dark Continent.

"The lecturer was received with a volley of applause. He said that since the libraries of the world had been opened to him that he might obtain knowledge he had enjoyed many grateful surprises. But on no occasion had they appealed to his gratitude more than the one with which he was confronted. He hoped he appreciated the full significance of the gathering. More potent than any words he could speak were the silent lessons of the afternoon, which every young coloured man in Chicago should ponder.

African Bushman.

Men and women of religious and moral worth, of wealth and talent, had assembled to show their respect for a poor ex-slave who had tried to respect himself. It was to him another link in the golden chain. The negro who improved his opportunities, who respected himself and honoured God would secure the respect, confidence, and esteem of men and women whose good opinion was worth having.

"'I am now about to treat of my humble life,' he said, 'in four phases--slave, waiter, student, and Missionary. I shall, with your permission, touch lightly on three, and enlarge on the fourth, for my heart is over the sea.' Johnson then told of his mother, the black, superstitious, ignorant Virginia slave woman, whose ebony arms were his cradle, and whose songs were to the boy as the music of heaven. 'I hardly know what I am; I am not an octoroon, a quadroon, nor a mulatto, but I believe that my grandfather looked like that'-- pointing to a large picture of the typical negro of the Guinea Coast of Africa-- woolly head, thick lips, flat nose, black negro. 'I am not as black, you see, as my grandfather, and in Africa I was always spoken of as a "white" man.' The speaker's memories of his early days in Virginia were told with charming simplicity. Then came the story of his conversion, his separation from his mother by a slave sale, their subsequent re-union, the end of the War, his journey to the North, his meeting with Mr. Kinsley, and his installation in the caterer's kitchen as a dish-washer. The steps of promotion which he bounded were chief dish-washer, dining room man, captain of the watch, and head waiter. He not only had time to attend to the duties, but every spare five minutes were devoted to study, and at night he received instruction in private. Whenever he had ten cents which he did not have use for, he deposited the dime in the savings bank. English grammar defied him; he couldn't see any sense in it, and finally, when he relinquished a position paying a hundred dollars a month for a Missionary station in Colorado, worth only twenty-five dollars a month, he believed he had just entered upon his true life work.

Modestly the black man narrated the struggles and strivings which preceded his advent in London as a student in Spurgeon's College. When he entered, the English grammar was his stumbling block, but it was finally dealt with, and thoroughly equipped for Missionary work he sailed for the West Coast of Africa, accompanied by the wife whom he had married in slavery. To hear the story of Johnson's experience was a rare treat. The man is a born entertainer. The interest of his listeners was maintained every minute. Statistics were interspersed with African songs, and the religious side of the address was relieved by recitals of personal experiences, by exhibition of African curiosities, and finally by some hymns in native costume and language. Here is a verse of 'Come to Jesus,' in the Dualla language:--

"Yana Jazu, yana Jazu,
Yana Jazu, tata nu; tata nu,
Yana Jazu, yana Jazu, tata nu."

"Johnson's experience, when taken prisoner by an African chief, proved that truth is stranger than fiction. The death of his wife was alluded to. 'She was crowned in the land of my fathers, and went up to live with our Saviour.' In the Congo Free State there are five thousand miles of fine waterway, and over 50,000,000 of people. In Africa to-day, 250,000,000 people are stretching out their hands and straining their eyes, praying for the light. Missionaries there are three to every million of inhabitants. The horrors of cannibalism and slavery were pictured. Cannibalism was dying out, but slavery remained as the curse of the continent. The speaker attributes the degraded conditions of Africans to the demoralization consequent upon slavery. Arab traders sometimes go into the interior and return with 2,000 captives, who are sold into bondage. This was enough to demoralise any people; such treatment would degrade a white nation. Africa for centuries has been a man-hunting man land, and nearly every other nation had had a hand in making slaves of Negroes. Many interesting facts were given touching the Bushman, who conversed in the 'click' language, with sounds resembling 'klik,' 'yik,' 'tock,' 'woc,' 'nic,' 'Stchu,' 'slik,' which jabber has been mastered completely by missionaries, and committed to grammar. The Hottentot, the Nubian, and the Aborigines of Australia all came in for mention, the conclusion reached being that the white man cannot Christianise Africa, owing to the climate. He showed by figures that Africa had been the Missionaries' graveyard. It was to-day the white man's cemetery. It had been written in Holy Writ that 'Ethiopia shall stretch forth her hands.' Calling his coloured friends to his side, Johnson sang a solo, and all united in the chorus. It is no exaggeration to say that sweeter music has rarely been heard in Chicago than the notes which had been fitted to these words:--

Nubian Negro.

"O Africa, thou long hast been
Of sin and ignorance the scene,
For ages trodden in the dust,
The slaves of selfish men of lust:
How long has densest darkness reigned,
And cruelty her way obtained,
O'er thy poor sons whom God designed
To worship Him with heart and mind.

CHORUS--
Ethiopia shall stretch forth her hands to God,
God hath said it, God hath said it;
Ethiopia shall stretch forth her hands to God,
Yes, God hath said it."

"Dr. McPherson said that Mr. Johnson would answer any questions that might occur to the audience. S. L. Booth after propounding some queries, said that he could heartily endorse what the lecturer had said regarding the superior intelligence of representatives of some of the interior tribes of Africa. Dr. McPherson, on behalf of the audience, thanked the lecturer for his address, and made fitting acknowledgment to Mr. Kinsley for the kindly interest which he had manifested in his former employee.

"Johnson brings from Africa a rare collection of curiosities, which he exhibited at the conclusion of his lecture. A large necklace braid of sea shells, which are the coin of certain tribes, a common shell about as large as a bean being worth eight cents. He has a cutlass once used by an Arab slave trader, and the iron neck-yoke and twenty pound shackles now worn by slaves while being driven in droves to the coast. He has the full costume of an African chief, with spear made from ironwood. He says the natives are expert in primitive manufactures. They see a towel and make its counterpart in shape and style out of grasses. A fan they imitate with straw. Their bags and baskets are more durable than ours. Of the numerous specimens of African handiwork which Mr. Johnson exhibits, there is one napkin which will rival anything of European in delicacy of texture. On the Mungo River a missionary was one day engaged in explaining the Darwinian theory to a very intelligent chief of a certain tribe. After the ex-Chicago waiter had dilated on the monkey evolution question, the chief assured him that Darwin had 'completely reversed the real facts of the case.' 'Many suns and moons ago, explained the Mungo sage, 'some of our fathers and brothers who were hunting, became separated from the tribe and wandered off into the forests. Such became their destitution that they were obliged to feed on the food of animals. By-and-by they became like brutes, and, the monkeys and apes which are found in our forests are the descendants of those who, many, many suns and moons ago, were the ancestors of our great-grandfathers.' Johnson says the Dutch have shot down African Bushmen like monkeys. The Hottentots are treacherous and ferocious, but their language is now printed, and the missionaries are now lifting them up out of the degradation which slavery has imposed. On the Mungo the people can talk to each other on their drums by a system of sound resembling the Morse telegraphic alphabet. The articles of trade are ivory, cam-wood, palm oil, dye-woods, rubber, gum, etc.

CAPS AND BAGS MADE OF GRASS, AND AN IDOL GIVEN UP BY A CONVERT.

"Johnson is labouring to evangelise Africa with the same faithful, conscientious effort which characterised him when he was a waiter in this city. His salary is seventy dollars a month. To-day the Negro missionary is not worth a hundred dollars. Speaking of his work, he said, 'My only object in alluding to my former bondage is this: I want to encourage the young coloured men of this country to persevere in the right direction. No matter what their present discouragements are, they must learn to labour and to wait. I tell you that every coloured man in the United States should be glad that he is in this country instead of the benighted land of his fathers worshipping idols. With sobriety, industry, and honesty he can win fame and name in this great Republic. I read the article printed in the Herald of Monday, relating to the toleration of coloured men in this community. It is a fair presentation of facts. But because our environments are as stated, there is all the greater need for patience, industry, and Christianity. The coloured problem in Chicago is of little concern compared with the great African problem. A Missionary can live in Africa on 500 dollars a year and live well. But to endure the African climate he must have African blood in his veins. I want the American people to understand this great truth, and govern themselves accordingly.' To-night Mr. Johnson lectures in St. Stephen's Church, 682, Austin Avenue. Before engaging in work in the Dark Continent, the Missionaries are thoroughly educated in secular and religious colleges, and well-grounded in the theory and practice of medicine."

New Missionary Paper--A Lady Printer

I soon found that the work of travelling from city to city, and to towns and villages in fifteen States and Territories of the West, was more than I could accomplish. My wife resolved that she would learn how to set up type, and then we could publish a paper which would visit the pastors in their studies, the children in the Sunday School, and the people in their homes. This we thought would plead the cause of Missions, and speak for the millions of Africa. In October, 1888, the first number appeared, bearing the following details of management:--

"THE AFRICAN MISSION HERALD."

Publishing Office, 180 S., Clark Street, Room 7.

Entered in the Post Office, at Chicago, as mail matter of the Second Class.

Address all communications to Post Office, Box 687, Chicago. Official organ of the African Mission of the Western States and Territories, U. S. A.

THOMAS L. JOHNSON, Editor, Chicago, Ill.

MRS. S. A. JOHNSON, Compositor and Manager.

My grateful thanks are ever due to the late Mr. Peter Mackinnon and Mr. W. M. Oatts, of Scotland, for their valuable assistance in the issue of this paper.

Nomination as U. S. A. Consul to Liberian Republic

The "Chicago Conservator," February 23rd, 1889, contained the following letter, dated from Evansville, Ind.:--Editor, 'Conservator.'--The coloured people of Indiana, as in other sections of this country, are deeply interested in the changes which will take place when the new administration shall take the reins of government. We are desirous that our race shall have its proper measure of recognition, both as to the positions filled and the persons named to fill them. We do not pretend to obtrude our advice upon the great leader whom our State has been privileged to send to Washington as the head of the Republic, but we do desire, as good citizens, to contribute our share in the endorsement of good men from which the President shall choose the representative coloured men of the race. For this reason, and on this behalf, the undersigned, after consultation with a number of friends, ask the use of your columns to suggest the appointment of Rev. Thomas L. Johnson, of Chicago, as Minister to Liberia. Now it must be understood that we do not pretend to say that he is the only Negro capable of filling that exalted position, but we do say, without fear of successful contradiction, that his experience, education, and extensive travel peculiarly fit him for that position. His association and acquaintance, especially his knowledge of Africa and its people, gained through missionary service, strongly commend him as one of the very best selections that could be made by the incoming administration, for the Liberian Mission.

"The subject of this sketch is a man of marked ability and national reputation. He is known and highly endorsed by men of the old and new worlds. That a man of his calibre is needed to fill posts of so high degree of honour, goes without saying.

"While in London, Mr. Johnson made many earnest friends. His earnestness, zeal, and devotion to the work of elevating the race won the sympathy and esteem of all.

"Many of the leading clergy of Ireland speak in the most commendable terms of Rev. Johnson, as also did the 'Daily Express,' 'Christian Advocate,' and 'Monthly Bulletin,' of Dublin. Rev. C. H. Spurgeon, London, at whose school Brother Johnson was educated, is among those of England who bear testimony of the most flattering character.

"Of the testimonials from leading men and journals in the United States it is unnecessary to speak; Rev. Johnson has travelled and lectured so extensively that he needs no introduction.

"In conclusion Mr. Editor, it is the wish of every patriotic coloured man that our strongest hands and bravest hearts are at the helm. In dealing with Africa no candidate for appointment to Liberia will have had experience on the Continent of Africa, as Rev. Johnson has had. No one will more faithfully discharge every duty, and no one will bring more universal approbation to the new administration than Mr. Johnson."

For Liberian Mission

"Rev. Thomas L. Johnson has been announced as a candidate for the Liberian Mission, his sponsors being a number of influential ministers of our sister state, Indiana. Their letter, endorsing him, shows that he was highly regarded on the continent while preparing for his work in Africa.

"All who know Rev. Johnson can testify to his strong Christian zeal in the work of elevating the African race. He has devoted the last fifteen years of his life to that work, and is still earnestly engaged in the work. It is believed that his experience in the missionary work, his active service in Africa, make him a more efficient and acceptable representative.

"Of one thing we are certain. He could make an official against whom there would never be a word of blame; intelligent, capable, and of sterling integrity, he would make a record honourable to the nation as well as his race. He has lived in Chicago, and has the universal regard of every man, woman, and child in his large circle of acquaintances. Among the best class of our white citizens for whom he was engaged in a position of trust, he enjoys the highest esteem, and they may be depended upon to commend him when and wherever it is needed. The 'Conservator' cordially endorses the letter which presents his name, and will add that Illinois has no coloured citizen more acceptable as a representative than the distinguished traveller, Rev. Thomas L. Johnson."

Another letter of a very kind and commendatory nature was sent to the same paper from Augusta, Ga., by John W. Dundee, who described himself as an old friend of Mr. Johnson's since before the War, and went on to state that: "Certainly the new administration would hazard nothing in appointing such a man minister to Liberia. His experience and knowledge of the people and their needs would make him most valuable to the United States as an officer, and to humanity as a valuable aid and blessing. We think beyond question that Mr. Johnson is the posted coloured man in America on matters relating to the African people, and I hope the friends of the cause of bleeding Africa will support such a man for the place as will be serviceable to the U.S. Government and the race."

When the above was published I was in the far South. It was altogether the effort of my friends who had heard me tell the story of Africa and her neglected millions, and the publicity given through the press of the reception referred to at Kinsley's Banquet Hall. I never made application to the Government for this position, neither did I write a line to any of the papers advocating the appointment. I simply felt that if it was God's will, I should be appointed. It came about without my interfering in the matter. Indeed, I protested against rushing me into such a prominent and important position, and in any case begged the friends to be careful in their enthusiasm to avoid a fanciful and misleading representation of my abilities and qualifications. I felt that I could not assume such an important Government position. There were, I heard, fifty applications for the post. The man who was eventually chosen, who was a scholar, afterwards came to me for some information about the place to which he was appointed, and I was glad to give him all the information I could, for truly he was far superior to myself and better fitted for the post.

Health Considerations

For nearly three years, from August, 1886, to July, 1889, I travelled extensively in America and in Great Britain and Ireland, preaching and lecturing night after night, with the anxiety of the Mission ever on my heart; struggling on with great difficulties, and in much weakness. I was finally compelled to offer my resignation, owing to the precarious state of my health. I felt I could do no more when I returned from Africa in 1880 in bad health. I prayed to God to let me live to do something for Africa since I could not live in Africa. God graciously answered this prayer indeed. Through His help I was enabled to awaken a deeper interest in my people of the Western and Southern States of America, in the African Mission work, and also to raise the necessary means to furnish outfits for the two missionaries and meet other expenses to Africa; and since the co-operation agreement with the A. B. M. U. and the B.G.A., of the Western States and Territories had been satisfactorily settled, I felt greatly relieved from the responsibility which rested heavily upon me. I felt I had done all I could do. God had graciously answered my prayer in enabling me to get the Mission started. I made the subject a matter of prayer. I shall never forget how that before God I wept bitterly. A very strange feeling seemed to lay hold of me, and I was led to the composition of the following lines:--

Africa for Christ, shall be my theme,
Wherever I may go;
Africa for Christ, who reigns supreme,
'Tis life His love to know.

Africa for Christ, His saints should say,
Who love His holy name;
Africa for Christ, whose throne is high,
His mandate I'll proclaim.

Africa for Christ, I will proclaim,
In sickness or in health;
Africa for Christ, that precious Name
To know indeed is wealth.

When I tendered my resignation, the Committee accepted it only on the understanding that it was until my health improved. But my own conviction was that, so far as I was concerned, it must be final. Then the Committee were perplexed about the £100 that was owing to me as their financial agent. I relieved the Committee by giving them a full receipt for the amount due. In the meantime I would help myself by selling my books and photographs, so that the Mission would not be hampered.

In the "Herald" there appeared a statement recording the fact about my health and appealing for further assistance for the funds of the work.

The little Church of which I had been Pastor before going to England in 1876, referred to, addressed a call to me to become its Pastor again. But the position was rather singular, for, being divided, the party withdrawing had asked me to become their leader, while the other party gave me a very decided call, which I accepted, and the result was that the parties were re-united.

But my health continued to fail and a trip to Denver was arranged This city had grown immensely since the time I lived there before, the inhabitants having increased from 16,000 to 125,000. Here I was cordially received by old friends, and was enabled to do something for the Mission.

The daily paper gave a kindly notice of my presence, stating that: "Rev. Thomas L. Johnson, well known in this city as a coloured missionary, has returned to Denver after an absence of some years, and will remain several months at least on account of his health, which has become considerably impaired by reason of his severe labours. He has been greeted warmly by all of his old acquaintances, who recognise in him a man of worth."

I returned to Chicago after a time, nothing improved, and the Chicago "Conservator" said of this, that: "Friends of Rev. Thomas L. Johnson will regret to learn that he has returned from his trip to Colorado, no way improved in health, but unfortunately weaker and less capable for work than when he left. The principal trouble thus interfering with him is a stubborn case of sciatic rheumatism, which seems to baffle the best medical skill. It came as the result of hard work and exposure while in the Army, and has grown worse continually, compelling rest from work.

After eighteen months, thank God, my health began to improve, then the Committee requested me to resume work for Africa. Having been greatly impressed by the earnest appeals of Dr. H. Grattan Guinness, D. D., during his visit to Chicago, when he awakened such deep interest respecting the Great Soudan Country; I conceived the idea that there was another opportunity for me to do a little more for the millions in the Land of my Fathers. With this in view, I considered the Committee's request, agreed to enter upon the work, providing the Committee would consider the following: (i.) Seek the co-operation of the Native Christians in Liberia. (ii.) Should this succeed, at once make efforts to plant a chain of Stations from Monrovia, the Capital of the Republic, to the great Soudan. This was thoroughly considered and adopted by the Executive Committee.

The Great Soudan

The visit of Dr. Grattan Guinness to America aroused much enthusiasm for Africa, and especially in the Soudan, and in December, 1889, appeared in Chicago the first number of the monthly journal, "The Soudan and Regions Beyond." Through the addresses of Dr. Guinness the idea of making efforts to reach the Soudan was deeply impressed upon me.

"Where is the Soudan? What is it? Who cares about it? Yet its people number eighty to ninety millions; more people than in all the United States, and in all North America.

Everybody knows about the Congo. Stanley has made it famous. To most the Congo is the 'New World of Central Africa.' Yet the Soudan is greater than the Congo region in extent and population. It is a newer world in Central Africa, and none is older. It is less known and less explored than the Congo region, but it was peopled earlier. It is far more civilised than the Congo. It is not wholly heathen. Half its people worship in their way the one living God; they are Monotheists-- Mohammedans; the other half, the lower, subject, conquered half, are heathen. Arab monotheism and Negro fetishism are mingled in the Soudan. Its people are of mixed blood and mixed religions.

"The Soudan lies between the great Sahara and the vast Congo basin, bounded on the east by the Indian Ocean, and on the west by the Atlantic.

America is three thousand miles broad from New York to San Francisco; the Soudan is half as broad again--four thousand five hundred miles.

"The name of the Soudan is Arabic, and means the 'Land of the Blacks.' It is a witness that the Land of the Negro has become Arab. The Semite and the Hamite dwell together in its sunny plains.

THE GREAT SOUDAN

"The men of the world are the heroes of the Soudan, Travellers have been regarded as heroic. Distance has been no barrier to them. Disease and death have been proved as unable to affright them. Neither love of friends nor fear of foes has been able to turn them from their fixed resolve to open the country to the world, and to bring its people into contact with the civilisation of surrounding lands. But the heralds of salvation have feared or forgotten this mighty heritage of a host of heathen nations. They have left them all these ages to the reign of darkness and unmitigated depravity. How long will the great commission to preach the Gospel to 'every creature,' be neglected, so far as the millions of the Soudan are concerned?

"We plead for these neglected millions. We raise our voices on their behalf. They cannot speak for themselves. Distance makes them dumb. Strangership silences them. They wander in moral midnight. They know not what they do. Year after year, age after age, they fall and perish, as though of no more worth than the withered leaves of autumn. They have fallen by millions, and

154

they have not been cared for. Torrid sun and sweeping rain have bleached their bones, or their sepulchres. Melancholy winds have moaned their requiem. Relentless time has rolled over their generations the billows of oblivion. They have perished from the earth, gone into a dark and dread eternity, without ever having heard of Him who died and rose again that men might live. Who was lifted up from the earth to draw all men unto Him, and who cries aloud to a ruined humanity, 'Come unto Me, all ye that labour and are heavy laden, and I will give you rest.'

"We plead for the neglected millions of the Soudan. We say to the Church of Christ, 'Behold them. They are our own brothers and sisters in a common humanity. They are one with us in sin and ruin, let them be one with us in the knowledge of salvation. Awake, O selfish, sleeping, forgetful Church; arouse thee to thy neglected duties; fulfil thy solemn mission; bear thy testimony; send forth thy sons; proclaim thy glorious message; gird thyself and give thyself, in the name of Jesus Christ, to the tremendous task of evangelising at last this greatest and most populous of all the wholly neglected and benighted regions on the surface of the globe.'"

Since the publication of the above pathetic and powerful appeal of Dr. Guinness practical interest has been taken by Christians in Great Britain and America in the evangelisation of the Soudan, for which we praise God.

Labour Resumed

At the next meeting of the Committee I was requested to visit Liberia with the object of effecting co-operation among the native Christians. The local press referred to the matter in the most kindly way, and made mention of the many tokens of goodwill given me by the people of Chicago on my starting once more for Africa.

Resolutions of Respect

At the close of a lecture on 'Africa,' delivered by Rev. Thos. L. Johnson, at the Second Baptist Church in Jefferson City, Mo., U. S. A., Tuesday evening, September 29th, 1891, a Committee was appointed to draw up a set of resolutions to be presented to the lecturer prior to his departure from this country in November. The Committee, on behalf of citizens and friends present the following resolutions:--

"Whereas, we recognise in Rev. Thomas L. Johnson, a man whose heart and soul are thoroughly devoted to the work of evangelising Africa; and

"Whereas, His great love for this benighted continent is so deep, so earnest, that notwithstanding the temporary failure of his health and the loss of a devoted companion, he is still willing, yea, eager to sacrifice home and friends and enter, the Mission field to give light where darkness now reigns supreme; and

"Whereas, His services as Financial Agent in Great Britain have won for him many strong and devoted friends, both abroad and at home, who are ever ready to assist him in his work; be it

"Resolved: That we, as representatives of Lincoln Institute and of the citizens of Jefferson City, do hereby express our appreciation for this Christian friend and brother, whose patient endurance, earnest zeal, and Christian fortitude have made him worthy of our deepest love.

"Resolved: That we commend him to the Christian world as a worker whose unswerving fidelity to the cause of Christ embodies a spirit of self-denial and an ever implicit faith in the guidance of his Heavenly Father.

"Resolved: Further, that we do hereby convey to him and to his beloved family our most sincere wishes for a pleasant and safe journey across the deep, with the assurance that our prayers for his continued success may ever attend him.

"Resolved: That a copy of these resolutions be published in the "Jefferson City Tribune," and some of the leading Afro-American papers.
PROF. S. D. FOWLER.
MINERVA J MATLOCK
ZELIA R. PAGE.
PROF. W. R. LAWTON.
GEORGIA M. DE BAPTISTE."

Africans to Evangelise Africans

As Moses and Luther and Knox and Whitefield were potent forces among their own people, so, as we have the example of the Ethiopian eunuch, the African must take the Gospel back to Africa. The Ricks' Institute, Liberia, was founded in 1887 by Native Christians, having for its object the proper training of the youths of the Republic to become guides and counsellors and Missionaries in the interest of their own country and people.

Mr. Ricks, who was emancipated and went out to Liberia, was a relative of Mrs. Martha Ricks, who, in 1892, visited England at the age of 76 for the purpose of seeing the greatest of Queens, the universally beloved Queen Victoria, who kindly received her. The papers at the time recorded the fact of her travelling 3,500 miles to see the Queen. Mrs. Ricks was one of thirteen thildren.She and all her brothers were sold into slavery, and she never saw any of her family again.

Rev. R. B. Richardson, M. A., D. D., President of Ricks' Institute, and Editor of a monthly paper, was born in Liberia in 1851. He was led to the Saviour by his father, the late Rev. John T. Richardson, who was born in the United States and emigrated to the Republic of Liberia. Dr. Richardson entered the ministry in 1878, and became Principal of the Normal department of Liberia College, 1881. In 1891 he was appointed Commissioner of Education, which office he held until he was further commissioned by President Cheesman, one of the Associate judges in the supreme court. Now he is one of the most influential men in the Republic.

In November, 1891, we returned to good old England, the land of freedom, sailing from Montreal by the S. S. "Labrador," of the Dominion Line, in company with Rev. R. L. Stewart. Tickets were taken for Mrs. Johnson and our little Ruth, but these had to be cancelled as medical advice prohibited Mrs. Johnson from taking the journey, and the doctor only gave her three years to live.

Britain's Shore Once More - Joys and Sorrows

We had a very pleasant voyage; first of all down the River St. Lawrence for 900 miles, and then across to Liverpool, where I was welcomed very heartily by Mrs. Stroud Smith and her daughter, Miss Nellie, at Shalom House. This last voyage made the ninth time of my crossing the Atlantic.

Mr. Stewart and I went up to London to see Rev. H. Grattan Guinness, to ask permission for Mr. Stewart to attend the lectures in his College. He at once very kindly granted this request, and gave this new pupil great assistance in view of his work in Africa.

I had great times and was much helped during my stay at Shalom House, at the Bible Readings and the Gospel Services conducted by Mrs. Stroud Smith and her daughter.

In February, 1892, I attended the funeral of the late Rev. C. H. Spurgeon in company with the vast gatherings of Christian workers. At the funeral I shook hands with a gentleman, and said, "God never makes a mistake." Alas, I knew not how soon that truth was to be tested in my own experience.

The funeral being over, I returned to Liverpool. The next morning as I sat at the breakfast table, the servant came in with a letter for me. "Oh," said I, "good news from home." Turning to Mrs. Smith, I asked to be excused while I read my letter. The first lines were: "Dear Brother Tom, you will be sorry to know that your dear little Ruth is in her grave." This letter was from Mrs. Johnson's sister. I closed the letter and left the table. I had often consoled others with the assurance that God never makes a mistake; now it was for me to accept and realise the blessing of that assurance.

This truth had given my soul comfort some days before when I received a letter to say she was quite well. She was six years and six months old. A short time before she was taken she went to Mrs. Johnson and said: "I do want to go to heaven to see what Jesus looks like; will you go with me?" On the Monday she was taken with malignant fever, and on the following Thursday she went to see what Jesus looked like--"God never makes a mistake."--Romans viii. 28. The following verse came to me:

God never makes a mistake
When He takes health or home,

Our parents or our children--
He only takes His own.--JOB i. 21.

In March, 1892, the Y. M. C. A. "Monthly Bulletin," Belfast, contained a notice of my latest visit to the North of Ireland. But after visiting Ireland and many other places in the United Kingdom my health again began to fail. When April came--the month appointed for sailing--I was unable to leave England. Mr. Stewart and Miss Virginia Jones, who were going out as missionaries with me to Africa, were greatly disappointed. I gave Mr. Stewart all the correspondence for the brethren in Liberia. Through the kind liberality of friends I was able to get these two Missionaries off on April 30th, 1892, when their hearts were made glad by many kind friends, especially Mrs. A. Hansen, of Southport, whose valuable gifts of books made glad their hearts.

Mr. Stewart wrote a letter to the "Baptist Standard," Hannibal, Missouri, while he was in mid-Atlantic, giving his impressions and experiences of England. He also mentioned twelve in America who were anxious to go as missionaries to Africa.

It was a relief to have the two missionaries on their way, for I had then a little time to rest. It was an anxious time when I was getting their outfit together, for I had to look after this and every other detail, and then my final breakdown came when all engagements arranged by my kind friend, Rev. Charles Welton, of Morley, Leeds, had to be cancelled.

A long and interesting letter from Rev. R. De Baptiste appeared in the "Baptist Standard," concerning the state of affairs, and appealing for continued and increased aid for the Mission.

After receiving a very hopeful and encouraging account from Mr. Stewart as to the reception of himself and Miss Jones, and as to the bright prospect before them in Mission work, I sent for Mrs. Johnson to come to England again; my intention being that when health would permit to join the missionaries in Liberia, to do so.

Mrs. Johnson ultimately came over to England, and the "Conservator," Chicago, Of July 2nd, 1892, made very kind references to the fact:--"Mrs. Thomas L. Johnson leaves to-morrow to join her husband who is in England labouring for his Mission work in Africa. . . . . Mrs. Johnson is a zealous Christian woman, whose heart is thoroughly in sympathy with Mr. Johnson and his work. . . . . Mrs. Johnson has determined to leave home and go to England as she can then render much service to her husband. . . . . Together they hope to sail for Africa at the close of the rainy season." On July 16th, Mrs. Johnson arrived in Liverpool and received a very warm and hearty welcome at Shalom House by Mrs. Stroud Smith and daughter and members of the Bible Class.

A Home at Sydenham

We soon removed to London, making head-quarters at Sydenham. We called upon Dr. Eccles, of Norwood, who through the blessing of God, cured

Mrs. Johnson of her long-standing and troublesome cough arising from heart affection, and which the medical man in Chicago thought would carry her off in three years.

We were now in touch with the friends in England, and in correspondence with the Committee in America, and with the missionaries on the field. Encouraging reports were now coming in from Mr. Stewart, who had been very successful with a Mission School; much of the success was due to the excellent native lady whom he married, and who was a great helper in his work. He had twenty-five children in his school--all redeemed slaves.

Mr. Stewart founded this School in December, 1892. He would make trips into the interior, and through gifts would redeem girls and boys from the slave traders and bring them back with him and adopt them into his family with the view of helping them spiritually, socially, and mentally, and with the hope and prayer that God would in His own time and way prepare and use them in the opening up of these interior Missions; and success attended his efforts.

As to Miss Jones, she was a very earnest and devoted Missionary; she worked hard, and saved enough money to meet her own expenses to England. Mr. and Mrs. Bibbs and Mr. Washington also met their own expenses.

"Disappointments--His Appointments."

Again in 1893 I made preparations to go to Liberia; yet my health was not much better. However, I hoped to visit the brethren, and effect the co-operation referred to, and with this purpose appealed for books, maps, and other useful articles for the missionaries and natives, with whom I intended to confer.

I attended the meetings of the African Training Institute at Colwyn Bay, North Wales, in the Spring of 1895. There I met the Rev. W. Hughes, F. R. G. S., the founder and manager, preparing to go to Africa to establish training schools along the West Coast. We decided to travel together; June was settled upon as the month in which to sail.

Charley Stewart was one of the group of twenty-five children seen at the Training School. After Mr. Stewart had laboured faithfully over four years on the mission field, he returned to England, thence to America to awaken interest in his Industrial school work, he brought Charlie with him. After his visit to America he took Charlie to the AFRICAN TRAINING INSTITUTE, when the Rev. W. Hughes, Founder and Director, received him as a student. When he finished his course in the Institute he returned to West Africa to enter upon his life work. On the morning he left the Institute, the following lines were found pinned on his tutor's door.

> The day, oh what a day is this,
> My heart with sorrows swell;

I now must leave my comrades all,
And say to them "farewell."

Oh, such a happy time I spent
While roving in this dell;
But ah! the clock of time strikes twelve,
And I must say "farewell."

My comrades here, be peaceful still,
While I away must dwell;
My eyes with tears, ah yes, do fill,
"Farewell," my boys, "farewell."

Soon after Mr. Stewart's return to Monrovia, he made another trip into the interior, from whence he never returned. March, 1901, came the sad tidings from h wife to say that five months previous to her writing he went into the interior, where he died among the natives and was buried. Mr. Stewart not only accomplished a great work in Africa, but succeeded in awakening a deeper interest in AFRICAN Mission Work among our own people during his visit to America. Miss Virginia Jones, who went out with Mr. Stewart, fell a victim to heart trouble a short time after arriving in the country.

The most of my work was amongst the Y. M. C. A., with which I had been identified from the time I first came to England. Mr. Hind Smith would kindly mention my name to the Secretaries of different branches when asked to recommend some one, and in this way I became acquainted with the late and much beloved Mr. Roberts, of the Plymouth Y. M. C. A., who kindly made appointments for me, and introduced me to many friends and Christian workers in Plymouth and vicinity. Mr. Moon, Mr. H. O. Serpell, Mr. John Yeo (Ex-Mayor), of Plymouth, and Miss E. H. Hingston, booked me several times to conduct Missions in old St. Andrew's Hall, Plymouth, where on each occasion we praise God there was much blessing. Much prayer had been made for success before I came, so that had I not gone God would have sent the blessing. At the close of a Mission in this hall a dear little girl three years and six months old said to her father, "I want to kiss the 'black man,' he loves Jesus"; he brought her to the platform, lifted her upon the table, and said, "Mr. Johnson, this little girl wants to kiss you." I kissed her; when she returned home she talked much about the black man who loved Jesus. The next Sabbath, near about the same hour in the evening, He who said "Suffer little children and forbid them not to come unto Me, for of such is the Kingdom of Heaven," took her home to Himself. The bereaved father wrote me a nice letter and sent me little Mary Ann Rendle's photo. I praise God for the continued friendship of Miss Hingston of and her sister to the present day. It was during one of my visits to Plymouth I met Miss Agnes Weston and Miss Wintz, when I was invited to conduct meetings in the Royal Sailors' Rest at Devonport, and after this at Portsmouth, where, praise God, I had the great privilege of preaching the Gospel to sailors of the British Navy, and at different times, the past twenty years. When I remember the kindness of these ladies to me all these years, which is just the same to-day, when health has failed me, as when I was able to meet all the appointments, in this I can see the hand of One who is continually saying to me, "Yet will I not forget thee." Isa. xlix., 15.

CLIPPINGS FROM A LOCAL PAPER

"The Rev. T. L. Johnson, freed slave and coloured evangelist, has been conducting special meetings at the Royal Sailors' Rest during the week, which have been well attended. His touching references to his slavery days have been listened to with great attention and sympathy. He is to speak at the 'Pleasant Hour' from three to four tomorrow afternoon, and again at the evening service. His farewell meeting is to take place on Monday evening. Miss Weston, LL.D., will preside at each meeting."

I was also introduced to H. O. Serpell, Esq., biscuit manufacturer, Plymouth (now of Reading), who invited Mrs. Johnson and myself to spend a few days with them at "South View," Mannamead. They also became practical friends of the work in Africa. They said to us, "We want you to consider 'South View' your English home." And we knew they meant what they said.

of the portrait (used by permission), and the following abridged record appeared in the "Y. M. C. A. Review," Plymouth, October, 1897:-- "Among the warm supporters are to be found many of the prominent merchants of our large cities, who recognise the beneficial influence of this world-wide organisation upon the young manhood of this century. The subject of our sketch this month has been for many years a true friend of the Plymouth Association. He has for many years been an active member of the General Committee at Plymouth, and throws himself heartily into any project for the spiritual, social, intellectual, or physical improvement of young men. His keen insight into Commercial pursuits has given him wide experience and his wise counsel in the business meetings of the Association has been of the greatest possible value.

"In 1881 he initiated work in a much neglected neighbourhood at Egg Buckland, near Plymouth. Many came to hear the truth, and it soon became necessary to provide a Mission Chapel which was built and opened at Estover in 1882. Ever since, Mr. Serpell has persevered with this work, which has been signally blessed by God. The congregation now employ a colporteur from Mr. Spurgeon's Colportage Association to assist in the services and visit the surrounding district. Five years ago the position of organist at Estover became vacant and Miss Catherine Serpell, the eldest daughter of our friend who was then eleven years of age was appointed. With infinite credit to herself and satisfaction to the people she has since filled this position, walking the four miles week by week in all weathers. Mr. Serpell's eldest son, who is also a member of Plymouth Y. M. C. A., renders valuable assistance with his cornet and Mrs. Serpell, who is deservedly popular with the people, occasionally renders a solo, which is highly appreciated."

I cannot tell how many times I have preached in Estover Chapel, Egg Buckland, where I always had a welcome.

It was quite understood that whenever in Plymouth or neighbourhood I should always make my home at "South View." Mr. Serpell made many appointments for me. The greatest attraction for me in the home were the dear children. I was their "Uncle Tom." There were five children then, but now only one; four are on the other side with our blessed Lord, including the eldest son and daughter referred to. Little Ethel, the youngest, was my favourite. Her name was Ethel May, but when she could talk she called herself Ethel May Johnson Serpell. She wrote this in my birthday book, soon after she could write her name. At the age of thirteen the Lord called her home.

After my return from America, Mr. Serpell made many appointments for me in and around Plymouth. Both Mr. and Mrs. Serpell repeatedly impressed upon us that where-ever we went, or whatever happened, "South View" must be looked upon as our home.

We returned to London; my condition became worse. I cannot describe how I suffered. I consulted Dr. W. S. Eccles, of Upper Norwood, S. E., who after examining me, condemned my going to Africa, and advised my entering the hospital at once; we made the matter a subject of prayer. I cancelled all appointments. The matter was published, and many kind friends wrote to me. The following telegram was sent me.

In Hospital

With grateful feelings I acknowledged the good hand of God. The next morning I received a kind letter from Mr. and Mrs. Serpell, saying, "Come home at once," and we went "home"; it was real home to us. The family physician, Dr. Squire, was called in; he advised that I should at once enter the South Devon and East Cornwall Hospital, and I was received in one of the private rooms. I was taken to the Hospital in a carriage accompanied by Mrs. Serpell and my wife. Nurse Parr very kindly received us and gave assurances to my wife that I should be well cared for. After Mrs. Serpell and my wife left me a strange feeling came over me--"In a hospital at last." Evidently the news of the presence of a black man had circulated through the wards, for many of the officials, without apparent business, visited the room to have a look. I had a conversation with the young man in the bed next to mine. I always had thought the hospital was a place where young medical men students practised on those who were unfortunate enough to be located in such places, but my experience now was that great medical skill and kind thoughtful attention were bestowed upon the patients. I had a complication of troubles, liver and kidney and chronic rheumatism, with attacks of sciatic pain we might describe as a kind of toothache about six inches long in the hip.

The day came when I was to undergo the operation, and I had a serious talk with Dr. Squire as to my aversion to chloroform, but he replied that it was all "nonsense to think such a thing." At twelve o'clock that day I went into the room, and first of all gave myself into the hands of my blessed Jesus, and then into the hands of the doctor. After the operation, and when I awoke, I found Nurse Parr watching me. I asked if it were all over. "Yes," she said, "how do you feel?" "Quite comfortable," I said.

The kindness of the matron, Miss Hopkins, and Sister Maristowe, and the entire staff at the Hospital was to me very great. The prayers of God's people were being offered up for me at various meetings and helpful letters were sent to me from dear friends; these I still treasure. The late Mrs. Spurgeon sent me tracts, and Mr. Spurgeon's sermons, which I was permitted to give to the other patients, many of whom came into my room to hear me play on the fairy belts. Mrs. Johnson was allowed to visit me every day after lunch and remain until after tea. Sister Maristow would send her tea from her table.

One day a large company of school children from the country visited the hospital, bringing beautiful flowers. The whole company marched by my bed. Oh it was such a treat to see so many bright eyes looking into mine, and to receive such flowers. Have you, dear reader, ever carried flowers to a hospital? If not, do so, and write a text and tie it to your floral gift. Many friends made special calls upon me during the time I was in hospital, some of them away from Ireland as well as from London and elsewhere, and very nice and nourishing things were sent for my refreshment. I was led to think of God's great love to me, and His promise, "Yet will I not forget thee." My good opinion and admiration of hospitals now became fixed. The patience, care, and kindness were great indeed. The nurses had to put up with some ungrateful patients. Some of them actually swore at the nurses, and refused point blank to take the medicine, but the nurses talked soothingly and treated them kindly and usually succeeded; Many of the patients that came in became serious in view of their apparent end, and one man who believed not in a future existence began to call out, when he was in great pain, "Almighty! Oh, my God." I called to him from my bed, "Put your trust in God; trust Him."

Is there a Medical Nurses' Christian Association? There ought to be. What a grand institution it would be. What an opportunity these nurses have of speaking the suitable word at the needful time to those willing to hear, and anxious to have the message of comfort and salvation!

After three months and sixteen days, on the afternoon of October 16th, I bade good-bye to the Hospital, and made my way to "South View," where Mrs. Johnson was staying, and it was quite a "home-coming" for me. The telephone was attached to Mr. Serpell's study, and often enquiries were made through it as to my condition when in hospital; but the evening after I had left the hospital there was a "ring up" for me, and on answering I was informed that a package was awaiting me at the hospital. Miss Serpell and Mrs. Johnson went for it. It was a basket of fruit from Miss A. L. Wilson, of Tunbridge Wells. This was followed up by a very interesting letter in reply to my letter of thanks and a little bit of information. She informed Mrs. Johnson that she purposed visiting Bournemouth, taking apartments, and requesting both Mrs. Johnson and myself to visit her. She thought this might be according to the Lord's will, and therefore for our good.

First Visit to Bournemouth

This was very kind of our dear friend, and arrangements were at once made for our first visit to Bournemouth. After taking leave of our dear friends at "South View," and a brief visit to some friends in London--Mr. and Mrs. George Freeman--we came to Bournemouth early in November, 1893. We were received with great kindness, and every attention was shown us. I was very weak and had to be taken out in a bath-chair. I was surprised to be saluted by so many who inquired after my health, and who wanted to know where I had been. I found myself drifting into a mere grumbler, simply reciting my experience in hospital for four months, forgetting that for the past fifty-six years of my life I had never been obliged to enter a hospital before as a patient. Then I began to praise God. The first text I preached from after leaving the hospital, and when I was able to take up any public work, was, "ALL THINGS WORK TOGETHER FOR GOOD TO THEM THAT LOVE GOD."

The Secretary of the Y. M. C. A., Plymouth, kindly gave me a letter of introduction to Mr. W. J. Meredith, Secretary of the Y. M. C. A., Bournemouth, who received me very kindly and helped me in many ways. He also invited me to speak on several occasions at the Y. M. C. A., when he kindly introduced me to friends and Christian workers. I cannot refrain from recording here the names of those who were especially kind to me, and called to see me when I first came to Bournemouth: The Rev. George Wainwright, Rev. R. B. Morrison, Rev. W. V. Robinson, Rev. S. A. Selwyn, Rev. C. E. Stanton; each one of these kind friends introduced me to their congregations. The great kindness of these friends and that of many others will ever remain fresh in my memory; little did I know then God's plan respecting my future. In Bournemouth here again I can look back and see God's hand with me. Here at Bournemouth I had a real good rest. From that Monday morning, April 3rd, 1865, when General Grant marched into Richmond, I cannot remember having such a perfect rest of body and mind. Miss Wilson's Bible Readings after breakfast were as refreshing streams to Mrs. Johnson and myself, and I found myself gathering much spiritual provision for after use. Thus up to the end of March in the next year, we recruited both body and soul. Among all the places which we had visited we found that the climate of Bournemouth was the most genial, and to add to all this, very genial letters reached us from warm-hearted Christian friends in England, Ireland, Scotland, Wales, and America.

Soon after coming to Bournemouth, on December 28th, a post card came to us which brought us much sadness of heart, as it told of the "Home going of Mrs. E. E. Stroud Smith." It read as follows: "Douglas, Isle of Man, December

27th, 1893.--An overwhelming sorrow has come to us; my precious mother lies in an African grave, and my sister is coming home alone, due in Liverpool on Monday next. The letter came by German steamer, and reached us on the evening of Christmas Day. Pray for us. We know nothing more, except that she passed away at three o'clock in the morning of December 2nd, at Virginia, in Liberia. Everything was done that could be done. The doctor and British Consul were there from Monrovia, and afterwards took my sister and all the luggage down to the river, to wait for the first English steamer, the 'Niger.'-- F. E. Stroud Smith." We read over this card several times. This was Miss Smith's handwriting. We were greatly troubled by the message, and then came to us the old truth:

> God never makes a mistake
> When He takes health or home,
> Our parents or our children--
> He only takes His own.

We got another postcard, this time from Mr. Ed. Stroud Smith, confirming the sad news, and to say that Miss Nellie was left with friends at New Brighton, as she was too ill to travel. He purposed taking her home with him the following week, after which he would write again.

Mrs. Smith was a faithful friend of Africa, and had been most kind to me in my work. She and Mr. Smith laboured among the coloured people in America, and when, in after years, she and her daughter called upon us at Sydenham, and we talked of our contemplated visit to Liberia, she expressed a desire to go to the West Coast and visit the native churches. It was with great delight she afterwards wrote to say that arrangements had been made for a tour in the Liberian Mission Field, and that she had received a list of the churches and their ministers. Later in the year she and her daughter sailed from Liverpool, October 14th, 1893, arriving in Monrovia on November 3rd. The last letter I received from her before sailing closed with, "God bless you. God be with you till we meet again. Yours for Africa, E. E. S. S." After one month in Africa she entered the Golden City at three o'clock on December 2nd. Thus wrote her sorrowing daughter, who returned without her beloved mother. The last entry in her diary, nine days before her "Home going," was, "We praise God in and for everything." She was a woman of deep piety and a Bible searcher her life was truly a life of praise, a life truly surrendered and yielded up to God, who had used her in Great Britain, and in America, and in Africa. While Mrs. Stroud Smith lived, I could never cease thanking her for her great kindness to myself and love for my poor long oppressed race. I am still praising my blessed Jesus for what he put into her heart to do for me, and for the continued friendship and kindness of dear Mr. E. Stroud Smith and his two daughters. I could here take up several pages, telling not only of Christian work, Sabbath School work and night school work of Mr. and Mrs. Stroud Smith among my own people in America but also of their daughters, when very young, how they helped in the Sabbath School. I cannot forget the deep impressions made upon the heart of an old man in our Mission, when Miss Nellie, then quite small, looked him in the face and pointedly asked if he was saved. This was only one instance of the many.

I shall ever be very grateful to Dr. E. R. H. Cory, of Bournemouth, for his medical attention both to Mrs. Johnson and myself during our first winter in Bournemouth.

At Work Again

After four months in Bournemouth, and thank God much improved in health, we prepared to return to London, when a farewell meeting was given us in Shaftesbury Hall by the late-- Rogers, Esq., and his daughter, Miss Rogers, of "Eaton," Bournemouth, with other friends, when I was requested to tell the Story of my Life. The late Dr. Cory, sen., was in the chair. A collection was made at the close, which amounted to over £10, and was handed to me, for which I was indeed grateful.

Before leaving Bournemouth we received a letter from Mrs. Richardson, of Bessbrook, Ireland, inviting us over to conduct a Mission. So after a short stay with some friends in London, we started for Ireland, arriving in Bessbrook, Saturday, March 31st, 1894. The welcome there was very hearty. On the Sunday we commenced the Mission in Bessbrook Hall, which was crowded. God gave evidence of blessing, especially amongst the young. Both Mrs. Johnson and myself were very unwell, and the doctor was called in. No improvement being made, Mrs. Richardson sent her carriage into Newry for another Doctor, who came, and after examination, injected morphia to give me some respite from the excruciating pain. The news spread that my life was despaired of but through the blessing of God and the remedies applied, I was able to move about again. The great kindness of Mrs. Richardson and her daughters to Mrs. Johnson and myself during this very trying time, deeply affected us both, and we were constrained to thanksgiving unto God. The family seemed quite exhausted by their personal attention to us both, night and day. When sufficiently well for travelling Mrs. Richardson sent us in her carriage to Moyallon House, Gilford, some fourteen Irish miles. Her maid was sent on in advance of us in order to take our luggage and to make some preparation. When we arrived, Robert the steward, who had been with the family for twenty years, undertook the responsibility of looking after our comfort with great thoughtfulness and kindness. He delighted to tell us of his travels with Mr. Richardson and the young gentlemen when abroad with them.

Here we stopped for a week, Miss Richardson, who was visiting her brother nearby, calling daily to see us.

Colwyn Bay Institute

On returning to London we spent a short time at Colwyn Bay on our journey. This was our second visit. Here we had a cordial welcome at the African Training Institute. While in Liverpool in 1892, and making preparations for Liberia, Sir Alfred Jones gave me a copy of "Darkest Africa, and the Way Out," by Rev. W. Hughes, F. R. G. S. I found in this book that the African Training Institute had been established with the view of training in this country the most promising of the African Christian converts, in the hope that many of them will return to their native land as missionaries, schoolmasters, and useful handicraftsmen, such as joiners, blacksmiths, masons, brick-layers, wheelwrights, tailors, printers, etc., and to send out a number of other missionaries on practical and scriptural lines, in order to open up fresh fields and to superintend the work. The importance of returning each of the students to labour ultimately in his native land is never forgotten. This struck me as being the most practical way to help a long neglected people. Now I had heard things which were calculated to prejudice one against the working of the institute, and so I resolved to see for myself. I received an invitation from the Rev. W. Hughes to be present May 7th, 1892, and to give an address at the meetings to be held in connection with the Institute. Mrs. Johnson and I received a very hearty welcome on our arrival the evening before from Mr. and Mrs. Hughes, and the large family of seventeen native Africans. We were gratified and delighted with all the arrangements and purposes of the Institute. The book which I had read, and the course pursued by the Institute agreed in the high aim of blessing the people of Africa spiritually and materially, through her own children trained in the Truth and in necessary trades. Mr. Hughes was enthusiastic in his work, and Mrs. Hughes was a real mother to these children of Africa. The Institute and its work made a great demand upon the time and resources of these two devoted friends of Africa; and they not only gave themselves heartily to the cause, but stirred up interest, and secured the co-operation of those in a position to help. It was very clear concerning "Darkest Africa," that the way taken by Mr. Hughes was the "Way Out," and I advised my brethren in America and Africa to co-operate with Mr. Hughes in his splendid work.

Mr. Hughes visited the West Coast of Africa in June, 1893. He was met by many influential friends, who hailed his project with delight, and sought to help him. The great and reasonable plan of the native evangelising his native land holds good to-day as it did in the past when men and women were raised up by the Lord to give a message to their own people in their own tongue; and the venerable Dr. Moffatt, who spent over fifty years in South Africa, said, "There is no hope of reaching the millions of Tropical Africa by any white labour possible to be sent to that country." And this is borne out by the sad sacrifice in the early stages of foreign Missions as inaugurated and heroically conducted by the brave men and women who leave their own land for the purpose of spreading the Gospel among the heathen. And Dr. Harford Battersby, speaking at a meeting in the Memorial Hall, London, on behalf of the Livingstone College, said, "He was sorry he could not hold out any great hope of West Africa ever becoming a healthy climate, nor did he think it probable that many Europeans would be able to reside there."

I am thoroughly persuaded that when the different branches of the Christian Church now labouring in Equatorial Africa, turn their attention to the training of native Christians for missionaries and teachers, there will be a brighter day for Africa.

The Congo Institute is now known as "The British and African Incorporated Association." The students in the Institution represent many parts of Africa, most of them being from the West, and representing three thousand miles of that coast, and there are students from South Africa and East Africa. Several of the more clever and advanced students are placed in Edinburgh for the study of medicine that they may qualify as medical missionaries. All this forms a great reason for much praise to God. The Bugle Call, of the Soldiers' Home, Winchester, referring to this Institute and its work, said: "It is being felt more and more by those who have had experience in missionary work that if the Dark Continent of Africa is to be won for Christ, it must be through the Africans themselves. Acting on this belief, the above Institution has been established for the purpose of bringing over to this country the most promising of converted African young men, in order to give them a religious and industrial training of from three to five years, so that they may return to their native land, able, not only to preach the glorious Gospel to their own people, but also to support themselves by means of their trades learned here."

The annual report of the African Training Institute for 1906-1907 states that eighty-one students have been received into the Institute since its commencement. There are fifteen over at present, including those in the London University, Liverpool University, and Edinburgh, finishing their education.

After my return from Ireland, finding myself utterly unfit, either to visit Liberia (as referred to) or continue to do active work for the Mission, I reluctantly resigned, which I did in 1894. I cannot refrain from referring again to the kind friends who helped and encouraged me in my efforts to send the Gospel to Africa, especially the indefatigable help of Mr. and Mrs. W. Hind Smith from the commencement of the work until the co-operation of the Mission with the A. B. M. U. was effected.

"THE CHRISTIAN."

April 20th, 1894.

"Mr. Thomas L. Johnson, of the African Mission, finding himself unable to resume active work for the Mission, has been compelled to resign for the present. He hopes however, to do evangelistic work when his health will permit."

When health has permitted, it has been my joy, thank God, to tell the love of Jesus in different parts of the Kingdom.

Mission Work in the British Isles

While in College I was sent out very often to do Deputation work for the Baptist Missionary Sosciety. God was pleased to allow me to know of cases of blessing, as we will see; hence my heart's desire was to win souls for my blessed Jesus, who had graciously answered my prayer, and allowed me to awaken an interest in African Mission work among my own people. I was often requested to conduct a week's Mission. Space will not allow me more than a very brief reference to a few of the Missions conducted, and the interesting experiences I have had.

My first experience in Evangelistic work in England was in Manchester, 1882. The next was in Norwood.

The Norwood Review, of February 10th, 1883, records one of my first attempts in this work:--"Gospel Mission at Gipsy Road Chapel.--During the past week a seven days' Gospel Mission has been conducted in the Gipsy Road Baptist Chapel, by the Rev. T. L. Johnson, who, on account of having been for twenty-eight years a slave, has drawn together nightly a large concourse of people and detailed to them his interesting though trying experiences of slave life. On Sunday special services were held. In the morning a sermon was preached by the Rev. J. W. Harrald (Private Secretary to the Rev. C. H. Spurgeon), in the afternoon there was a service for the young, and in the evening Mr. Johnson preached the sermon. During the meetings Mr. Johnson has been assisted by the Rev. E. H. Ellis (of Stoke Newington), Rev. B. Briggs (of Bermondsey), Rev. C. B. Sawday (of Pentonville), Rev. W. Thomas (Putney), and Rev. J. H. Banfield (of Stratford). The Pastor (Rev. Walter Hobbs) has taken an active part in the proceedings, which have resulted in lasting good."

Thus God was preparing me for a work which at that time I never thought of. Throughout England, Ireland, and Scotland I conducted Missions at the request of Christian workers. At Carrubbers' Close Mission, Edinburgh; Children's services in the Skating Rink, Croydon; for Sir Algernon C. P. Coote. In the Town Hall, Christchurch, for Miss Tighe; at Ilfracombe Baptist Chapel where the services for children were attended by children from various schools; Mrs. Colonel Robertson's Mission Hall, Callander, N.B.; a week's Mission in connection with Exeter Hall Y. M. C. A.; also at the Baptist Tabernacle, Upper Parkstone, Dorset; at the Baptist Chapel, Christchurch, Hampshire, where I also lectured under the sympathetic Presidency of General the Hon. B. M. Ward.

In 1894 I received a very hearty invitation to visit the Soldiers' Home, Winchester, when I met for the first time Miss Perks, her sister, and Mr. C. Edwards, the Manager, and quite a company of workers, who all gave me a hearty welcome; one could see that there was a spirit of prayer. We had grand meetings and, praise God, much blessing, the result of prayer before I came. In course of time I visited the different Missions in connection with the

Home. Shawford Mission Hall, St. Denys Mission Hall, Cannon Street Mission Hall, Twyford Mission Hall, Fulflood Mission Hall. There were also the lodging, houses visited regularly by the staff of workers. A Colporteur was kept constantly at work. In time I visited Bulford Camp (before the Government erected permanent quarters there), when Miss Perks would have several tents in the Camp, when I had the privilege of addressing meetings of the British Army. It was my privilege and joy also to visit the troopships with Miss Perks, when I had an opportunity to witness for Jesus before a company of young soldiers leaving their homes for the first time for India. One of them said to me, "I know you; Miss Sidey, of S.W. London, told me about you"; then he handed me the little leaflet, "God never makes a mistake." The dear saint of God who told him about me, is now with Jesus, whom she loved and longed to see.

January, 1901, I received a letter from Miss Perks, which made my heart glad; on one of her visits to the Troopship "Sicelia," a young soldier embarking for India gave a nice bright testimony, and said he heard me speak at Bulford Camp in the tent, when he gave his heart to God. He requested Miss Perks to ask me to write to him, which I did.

The Bugle Call, the organ of the Soldiers' Mission at Winchester, contained at various times kind references to my visits, and in the first volume there is a portrait and little sketch, from which we may quote the following: "Our beloved brother, T. L. Johnson, is one of the brave standard-bearers of the Cross, holding forth the Word of Life. His history has been a remarkable one. . . . . Numbers of precious souls have been won to Christ through the loving testimony of this faithful worker. . . . . He went into slavery a pagan; he came out a Christian. He went into slavery a piece of property; he came out an American citizen. He went into slavery with the chains clanking about his wrists; he came out with the American ballot in his hand." Volume second records that a letter of sympathy and my little booklet, "God never makes a mistake," had been sent by me to the Duchess of York in her sorrow, and that she accepted the booklet and sent a nice letter of thanks. In volume seventeen the fact is mentioned that when Lord Roberts visited the Soldiers' Home, Winchester, in 1902, I was one of the number present by invitation to meet him. His Lordship spoke very highly of the accommodation at the Mission for the soldiers, and of the good work being done by the Misses Perks.

After an address to the S. S. Soldiers' Home, Winchester, a group of the infant class gathered around "Uncle Tom," and repeated the Twenty-third Psalm. I think I can safely say, without being egotistic, I am very popular among the children.

The following is from the Hampshire Chronicle, Winchester, after a Mission, 1894:

"Soldiers' Home.--Very wonderful and deeply interesting has been the Mission,, announced last week, conducted by the Rev. T. L. Johnson, returned African Missionary. The large lecture hall has been taxed to its utmost to accommodate the crowds nightly pressing in to hear "the Old, Old Story,' told in a marvellous manner by Mr. Johnson, and illustrated by thrilling incidents in his long and bitter life as a slave for nearly twenty-nine years. Rarely has the Gospel been preached in such a forceful way, and impressions must have been made for the eternal good of those privileged to hear this honoured servant of God. The Mission closes tomorrow (Sunday),but all being well Mr. Johnson has kindly promised to come again for a longer visit to this Mission."

I praise God to be able to say that for the past fourteen years I have (with but few exceptions) been present at the Christmas tree with the children, and New Years' Meetings, and often several times during each year.

Other press accounts speak of my visits to various districts, where I have conducted Missions--Kensington Baptist Church, Bristol; Baptist Church, Tewkesbury; Folkestone Baptist Church; Memorial Hall, Brookborough, County Fermanagh; Ireland, for Colonel and Mrs. Doran; Woodvale Hall, Shankhill, Belfast; Fredrick Street Methodist Church, Belfast; Richmond Street Mission Hall, London; Wycliff Baptist Chapel, Reading; St. Paul's Church, Clitheroe, Lancashire; St. Andrew's Church, West Kilburn; Child's Hill Baptist Chapel, London; Greyfriars Church Rooms, Reading; St. Barnabas Church Mission Hall, Queensland Road, Holloway, London. And I not only lectured at these places, but also at the Metropolitan Tabernacle, London; the Christian Union Buildings, Dublin; the Y. M. C. A., Cork; Miss Sand's Soldiers' Home, Cork; the Y. M. C. A., Belfast; the Y. M. C. A., Liverpool; the Y. M. C. A., Manchester; Chatsworth Road Chapel, West Norwood; Collier's Wood Methodist Free Church, Surrey; Hayward's Heath Assembly Rooms; Herne Hill Congregational Church; Lansdowne Baptist Chapel, Bournemouth, and many other places.

Among a great number of letters sent me by converts and Christians, who had received a blessing in Reading, the following lines came in printed form from a young lady, one of the converts.:--

A long time I wandered from Jesu's side,
I heeded not His word.
I travelled through life with the world as my guide,
With no thought for Jesus the Lord.

But a messenger Jesus sent
To tell me the price was paid
I had only to believe and repent,
And Jesus my soul would save.

I took Him at His word and said,
I will, dear Lord, be Thine,
Thine alone, and Thine for ever!
I am His, and He is mine.

'Tis sweet to learn of Jesu's name,

A name to me so dear;
'Tis joy to have Him by my side,
To feel His presence near.

He warns me when I'm doing wrong,
He helps me do the right,
He holds me in His arms so strong,
And makes my burdens light.

He comforts me in days of sorrow,
He turns my tears to joy,
He keeps me safe through every danger,
Saying, "Be not afraid, it is I."

He holds my hand along life's rugged path,
And still will lead me on,
Till I reach that heavenly land,
To be for ever with the Lord.

A land where angels sing,
Where our loved ones are at rest,
Where Jesus reigns as King of kings,
In that home, for ever blest. E. G.

In the course of my itineracy I have been privileged to visit many places, for which I thank God, and I have preached the Gospel in America, Europe, and Africa. In America I visited seventeen States: Virginia, North Carolina, Georgia, Mississippi, Louisiana, Tennessee, Kentucky, Iowa, Maryland, Illinois, Ohio, Indiana, Nebraska, Colorado, Minnesota, Kansas, Wisconsin; in the British Isles I have travelled throughout England, Ireland, Scotland, and Wales, and the Isle of Wight, the Isle of Man, and the Isle of Guernsey being visited.

The Public Press

The newspapers and the religious periodicals generally have been considerate and helpful. Long reports of sermons and of lectures have been given with appreciative comments, and notices of forthcoming meetings or explanations of my Missions have been of the utmost service to me in my work. Sometimes, however, the personal view of the writer has been rather odd and as oddly expressed. I have been run into numerous literary moulds and have come out in a variety of shapes, until one was doubtful of their own personality; and the literary hand has felt me all over--heart, head, hair, and hand; face and figure; and voice and gesture, colour and clothing have all been discussed with kindly reference.

Not only have quite lengthy quotations been given of sermons addresses,, and lectures, and note been made of special and interesting items connected with my life and work, but some of the papers and magazines put in pictures in illustration of my lectures, as in the Y. M. C. A. Magazine, of Belfast, and quotations would also be given from my hymns. The comparison between the American style and the English style of journalism is worth noticing. The American reports are sometimes like the American railways in the city, which seem to hang in mid-air; while the English on the other hand are more on the level and sometimes in the "tube," where you do not feel so giddy and like toppling over. Still there is a correspondence sometimes. Here is a sample of a brief report from the South London Mail: "Lovers of contrasts must have been more than gratified at Herne Hill Congregational Church on Sunday. Here in a new Free Church, with Gothic windows, stone pillars, nave, transept, and chancel, stood up in the pulpit an old-time African slave, shoulders, head, face, and hair just as if he had walked off the walls of one of the Pyramids. He was telling young Herne Hill public schoolboys and girls how he learned to read by betting with the white boys about his owner's estate that they could not spell the words he wished to know. His language was good, yet he said he had not studied an English grammar till he was past forty years of age. The bright young eyes looking up so eagerly will never see a stranger sight than this educated minister holding up the chains with which the slaves were bound when sent to be sold. He showed the whip with which the slaves were lashed like dogs for the slightest offence."

On October 22nd, 1903, dear Mrs. Spurgeon passed to her rest, and by her departure I lost one of my most kind and helpful friends. I attended the funeral at Norwood. In February, 1892, I was present at the funeral of Mr. Spurgeon, at Norwood. There was a similar manifestation of sorrow on this occasion, but also the same triumphant Christian sentiments expressed. I returned home with the Editor of the Baptist, who referred to the fact afterwards, and to the title of my tract in this connection, "God never makes a mistake." Here is a little hymn I composed at that time:--

GONE HOME

IN MEMORY OF OUR MRS. C. H. SPURGEON

"Because I live, ye shall live also."--JOHN XIV. 19.

God's promise of covenant love,
Which links us to the Home above.

Gone home to live with Jesus,
Our Prophet, Priest, and King;
And in His blessed presence,
Redemption's song to sing.

Gone home to live with Jesus,
The ever loving One:
Who left His home in Glory
That sinners might be won.

Gone home to live with Jesus,
To share that Heavenly Rest:
And with her own beloved,
To be for ever blest.

Gone home to be with Jesus,
His glory to behold:
And hear the wondrous story,
Which grace will there unfold.

Gone home to be with Jesus,
To sing redeeming love,
With Jesus and His loved ones
In you bright Home above.

In 1900 I met with an accident while conducting a Mission in Margate for the Rev. J. Dinnick. In kneeling down to pray, my knee came upon a piece of coal. From this I suffered greatly, as I attempted to meet appointments made a long way ahead, and being anxious not to disappoint the friends, I struggled on for many weeks, often in great pain, but with the idea that it was nothing serious. Mrs. Johnson in the meantime went abroad to see her people, to be away six months. Mrs. Gawin Kirkham, of Croydon, and Mrs. J. Johnson, of West Norwood, had each kindly invited me to make my home with them when conducting meetings in London and neighbourhood. One of my appointments was for Miss Perks (Soldiers' Home, Winchester), a week at Bulford Camp, on Salisbury Plain. I managed to meet this appointment.

When I returned home, the injury to the knee had developed into synovitis, when Dr. J. S. Dickie advised me to cancel all appointments at once. While alone the kindness of friends of the different branches of the Church of Christ I shall never forget. The untiring kindness of Mr. and Mrs. Payne--our neighbours--night and day will ever be remembered.

Referring to my Diary of September 18th, 1900, I find the following:--

"Thank God I had a better night and was up at eight o'clock this morning for a while, but suffered much from my knee. But praise God it is all quite right. How all this will end, He whose I am and Whom I serve knows all about it. In His hands I leave myself.

He knows the end from the beginning.
He never changes.

174

He never makes a mistake.

All this is for my good.

"Praise God for Romans viii. 28."

At this time I was again alone, my housekeeper, (owing to previous appointment) had to leave.

September 19th.--"Mrs. de Satur called to see me. Her visit was indeed most helpful; truly God had sent her. (On the day before and to-day much time was spent in prayer.) I explained to Mrs. de Satur how I came to be alone. When she left she said she would call again. Soon she returned and said, 'Mother and I have arranged to have you come and stay at Ravenshoe until Mrs. Johnson returns from America.'"

Praise God. How good He is to His people. Only trust Him. Psalm xxxvii. 3-5. Entered in Diary, Ravenshoe,

September 20th.--"Praise God for the rest of last night. Psalm lvii., 1, "Be merciful unto me, O God, be merciful unto me, for my soul trusteth in Thee; Yea in the shadow of Thy wings will I make my refuge, until these calamities be overpast.' I could not remain in bed long this morning; the thought of leaving for Ravenshoe seemed at times to make me lose my pains for a few minutes. During this forenoon John Yeo, Esq., of Plymouth, who is in Bournemouth, called to see me. I was indeed much helped by his visit. Truly he has been a kind friend to me."

On arriving at Ravenshoe I received a welcome from the late Mrs. Smythe and Mrs. de Satur and her daughters, which I can never forget. If they had been my own kith and kin they could not have made me more welcome or more at home and happy.

For some days I suffered very much. Finally my leg had to be put into splints. I can never forget the kindness and sympathy of the late Mrs. Smythe and Mrs. de Satur at this very painful and trying time. How they came and each prayed for me.

September 26th I find in my diary: "Thank God I had another restless night. I thank God because we prayed about it, and God was pleased to permit the pains to come; hence it was quite right. It might have been so much worse." I shall never forget October 21st, 1900. In the afternoon. Mrs. de Satur and her niece and daughters came into the room and each prayed for me. Oh, it was such a blessed time at the throne of grace. Each pleaded so sympathetically, so earnestly to God for me, and with such evident power.

The jubilee Singers were in Bournemouth. My kind friend, Mr. Robert G. C. C. Gregg told Mr. Louden about my illness. In the evening of this date Mr. and Mrs. Louden and all the singers but two of their company came to see me. Wealthy ladies and gentlemen were making appointments with Mr. Louden to come and sing before them, for which they were remunerated, but it did just seem to me that God sent them to sing to me, "Steal away, steal away to Jesus." This they sang twice. Miss Adell Buffer's kindness to me will never be forgotten. Had I been her own brother she could not have been more kind.

Day after day Mrs. Smythe would come in to see me, always bringing sunshine with her. She was to me a wonderful Bible student. It just looked as though my blessed Jesus had said--as he did to the disciples-- "Come ye apart and rest awhile." And while resting there what a feast of good Gospel teaching I had. I shall never forget these resting, helpful weeks spent at Ravenshoe. I remembered well when in the hospital in Plymouth, 1893, when God spoke to me in His word so plainly (Romans viii. 28), and said, "All things work together for good to them that love God." So on this occasion I knew that God, who knows the end from the beginning, knew all about it, and that it was quite right.

When I met with the accident--

I WAS NOT OUT BREAKING THE SABBATH.
I WAS NOT AT THE THEATRE.
I WAS NOT IN A DANCING HALL.
I WAS NOT IN A GAMBLING ROOM.
I WAS NOT ON THE RACECOURSE BETTING.
I WAS NOT IN ANY QUESTIONABLE PLACE;
BUT IN THE PATH OF DUTY.

So I repeat, it was quite right. God could have prevented this accident; but no, He had some plan ahead to accomplish that I know not of, and I may never know all until I get to heaven and am with my blessed Jesus, "Who loved me and gave Himself for me," Who said to Peter, "What I do thou knowest not now, but thou shalt know hereafter." There are many things down here that we are ignorant of, and since we dare not question INFINITE WISDOM, we are very, very happy in the thought that God knows all about that accident. He notes the fall of a sparrow, He knows the number of hairs in my head. This tells me how minutely God looks into and notices all in connection with myself. Oh, it is so helpful to one's soul; in all things to remember that God hath said, "All things work together for good to them that love God." Yes, God hath said it. When I listen attentively to what God says to me in Psalm cxxxix. and especially in the fourteenth to the eighteenth verses, then I am convinced it is all quite right. God knows all about it. God never makes a mistake.

October 24th, Mrs. Johnson (who had been sent for to return at once) arrived in Southampton. Mrs. Smythe and Mrs. de Satur kindly invited her to come to "Ravenshoe," and remain until all was ready for my return home.

During my illness God laid it upon the hearts of many kind friends to send me help. I was greatly moved and thankful one day to receive from the Pastors' College Aid Fund (Metropolitan Tabernacle), through Mr. Bartlett, their Secretary, a cheque for £5.

Among these kind friends referred to, and many whose names are not mentioned (for space will not permit), but while I live, I shall not, I cannot, cease to thank God for them, neither can I forget their kindness to me. Among them is Dr. James Steel Dickie, of "Windermere," Boscombe Park,

Bournemouth (already referred to), to whom I owe a debt of profound gratitude for his untiring attention from the commencement of my illness. After removing to "Ravenshoe" he came to see me nineteen days in succession, and on several occasions twice in the same day.

For nearly a year my knee was kept in splints, and I was compelled to use crutches. Occasionally I feel the effects of this accident to the present time.

Many of the kind friends will remember THE APPEAL which Miss M. Bluett, of "Ravenscroft," Upper Richmond Road, Putney, sent out in 1901, which is as follows:--

"Appeal on behalf of Rev. Thomas L. Johnson.--Thomas L. Johnson was born in slavery, of African parentage, in Virginia, in 1836, and continued in slavery, till, at the close of the War between North and South, President Lincoln's Proclamation of Emancipation, on January 1st, 1863, finally abolished slavery throughout America. During this period he had, by great perseverance, and in the face of great difficulties, taught himself to read and write, and in 1857, while still a slave, to man, he was savingly converted, and finding Christ as a Saviour, thus obtained his spiritual freedom. He was baptised and joined a Baptist Church. At the conclusion of the War, he went to New York, where he found employment for a time as waiter in a hotel, and in 1866 left for Chicago, where, while employed by the Pullman Car Company, and as head steward at Kinsley's Restaurant, he found some Mission work to do for Christ. In 1869, he took charge of a little church of coloured freedmen in Denver City, and afterwards Providence Baptist Church in Chicago. But the longing of his heart was to go as a Missionary to "the land of his fathers," as he loves to call it, and in 1876 he sailed to England at the invitation of Mr. W. Hind Smith and Mr. Edward Stroud Smith, for the purpose of taking a course of studies preparatory to engaging in work in Africa. After three months' Mission work in Manchester, in connection with the Y. M. C. A., under Mr. Hind Smith, he entered Mr. Spurgeon's Pastors' College, in December, 1876, where he remained till he sailed for Africa in November 1878; but after little more than a year's earnest labour on the Cameroon River, his health quite broke down, and he was compelled to return to England. Since that year Mr. Johnson has been instrumental in arousing interest in the work of African Missions, both in the States and in England, and has also been signally owned and blessed by God in the holding of Evangelistic Missions throughout England and Ireland, by which multitudes of precious souls have been led to decide for Christ as their Saviour. But his Ministry has been carried on amidst much bodily weakness, and now it seems to his many friends that the time has come when some provision should be made for the future, when he will be unable to continue thus to labour for his Master, as it is mainly through the freewill thank-offering of those who attend his Mission Services that he has been able to support himself and his wife. It is proposed to raise a sum of £950 with which to purchase an annuity for him, and thus relieve his mind from anxiety as to the future. But Mr. Johnson's heart is still in his loved work of Evangelisation, and whenever the state of his health permits, he looks forward to entering into many an open door as he may be directed by God the Holy Spirit; so that it is not to be understood from this appeal that he is not open to invitations to undertake such work in the future."

The appeal was supported by Pastor Thomas Spurgeon, of the Metropolitan Tabernacle, who wrote: "I am very glad to hear it is proposed to render our good friend, Thomas L. Johnson, some much needed and well-deserved aid. He is a man of God, with a most lovable spirit. He has suffered much, and wrought hard; moreover he has been greatly owned and much blessed. We hope he will still be able to evangelise, but often he is laid aside, and the time has doubtless come to make some provision for our dear brother. The more substantial and permanent it is, the better; he is worthy for whom we should do this."

Mr. R. C. Morgan wrote: "I have known Mr. T. L. Johnson for years as an exemplary Christian, and as a useful preacher of the Gospel of Christ. I have known him to be in very delicate health for a long time, and am glad to learn that an endeavour is being made to buy for him a moderate annuity. I earnestly hope the effort will be successful."

Mr. W. Hind Smith wrote: "You are doing a most Christ-like service in your endeavour to provide an annuity for our old and valued friend, T. Lewis Johnson, and I sincerely hope you may succeed beyond your present anticipations. I have known the dear man for over twenty-five years, having first met with him when he was doing an excellent Mission work among his own people in Chicago in 1874. I was so charmed by his truly excellent character that I encouraged him to take up Evangelical work in our own country...I believe our brother has been the means, in God's hands, in leading hundreds to the Saviour. I pray God to bless your effort..."

And Mr. H. W. Maynard, Director of the "Union Castle Steamship Company," also supported the published appeal and referred to his long acquaintance with me and to my services at his hall.

Contributions to the Fund were to be sent to Williams, Deacon, and Manchester and Salford Bank, Ltd.; Mrs. Richardson, Moyallon House, Gilford, County Down, Ireland; and Miss Bluett, "Ravenscroft," Upper Richmond Road, Putney, London.

The English Churchman, The Baptist, The Christian, and The Sword and the Trowel took up the appeal, and other papers kindly gave it a notice. The Sword and the Trowel introduced a copy of the appeal by saying: "The happy face of Brother Thomas L. Johnson must be familiar to a large number of our readers, and we expect that many of them are aware that efforts are being made to provide the means of maintenance for himself and his wife now that he is able only occasionally to conduct the Evangelistic Missions in which he has engaged since he was obliged to return from Africa. We are sorry to learn that, thus far, only about one-fourth of the sum aimed at has been secured, so further efforts are, necessary."

The following report, made by Miss Bluett, was subsequently issued: "The total amount that has been received for the Rev. T. L. Johnson's Annuity

Fund, is £286 5s. 10d. As the state of Mr. Johnson's health has recently become very precarious, and as twelve months must elapse after the money has been sunk in the annuity before he could receive the first payment, several of his friends suggest, that instead of sinking the money, it be left in the bank, and a sum of £30 be drawn out, and paid to him annually until exhausted, through Mr. H. B. Macpherson, Treasurer, and that in the event of his death previously, the balance be paid to his widow. It is hoped that under these circumstances this arrangement will meet the approval of all who have so kindly contributed to the fund."

The list of contributors to the fund was added to the report, and to these dear friends I feel most thankful, and for them I pray always, never failing, morning and evening from month to month. If space would allow, I would like to enter the names of every one who has been kind to me, of both rich and poor.

Ravenscroft, as illustrated, is the home of Dr. Bluett-Duncan, and his sister, Miss M. Bluett, both of whom are deeply interested in all Protestant, Evangelical, and Missionary work. Miss Bluett became a friend to the African Mission before the first Missionaries were sent out, and continued until that body effected its co-operation with the A. B. M. U. We can never forget her kindness to Dr. Theo. E. S. Scholes and Rev. John E. Ricketts, sent to the Congo, and to Rev. R. L. Stewart and Miss V. Jones, sent to Liberia.

From this home many boxes of clothing have been made up by Miss Bluett and Miss Mackenzie, and sent out to these missionaries in Africa.

When Mr. Stewart brought Charley over (who has been referred to), and left him in the hands of the Rev. W. Hughes' African Training Institute, Miss Bluett and her brother often entertained him at this home, and when he had graduated and returned to Africa, these kind friends presented him with many useful and valuable articles to add to his outfit. Here in this home I praise God for the hearty welcome I have received the past fifteen years whenever I visit London.

Christian friends and little children prayed for me when I entered the hospital, June, 1893 (as referred to), prayer was offered for me at the Metropolitan Tabernacle, and in homes in different parts of the Kingdom. In the Spring of 1893 I gave an address to Miss A. Martin's Bible Class, Upper Norwood. While in the hospital I was continually remembered by this class, and all these fourteen years, I am still remembered. I cannot tell how often I have met the class since 1893--to-day there are 130 members, 36 of whom are blind; she also has 30 mothers to see after. When I met with the accident in 1900, again I was remembered in prayer by friends in the Kingdom, when this Class would also remember me each week. When conducting a Mission many friends would remember me while at the throne of grace. I praise God for the hearty co-operation of God's people with me in prayer, and for the gracious answers and blessings received.

Prayer of Little Children

I remember when I returned to England from Africa, I met a Christian worker whose eyes filled with tears as he told me how his little boy had kept me fresh in their memory and prayed for me every night.

I met a lady in Reading who told me that little Louie Corpe prayed for me regularly every night. Little Louie has two birthdays. At one of the Christian police meetings in London, I was told of the son of a Christian policemen who regularly remembered me in prayer; his name was Stephen Peirce. It was a long time before I met this lad, when I learned he had another birthday. Mr. W. Hind Smith's little grandson, Norman, when saying his prayers, was heard to say, "Please bless Uncle Tom, and don't let them make him a slave any more." I have only space to mention these few, out of a great number of instances I have heard of.

> I believe God answers prayer,
> I am sure God answers prayer,
> I have proved God answers prayer.

The reader will have noticed instances in which prayer has been answered on many occasions in my life, which has greatly helped me and encouraged me. I could give many more instances, but will only give one more in closing this life story.

A Direct Answer to Prayer

After the first two missionaries were sent out to the Congo, I was requested to travel in the Western and Southern States of America to awaken deeper interest in African Missions, with head-quarters in Chicago. A lock box was secured at the General Post Office for me for letters, and soon I found myself with only ten cents (fivepence), my health bad, no money in the treasury. I owed the widow with whom I boarded ten dollars (two guineas), I knew this faithful Christian woman wanted her money; knowing my condition, no doubt she was also praying. One morning I took my Bible, opened it at John xiv. 13 and 14, then John xv. 4, 5, 7. I knew in my heart with God's help the Abiding Life was my one thought.

Mr. Stanley P. Smith, of the China Inland Mission, had given me "Abide in Christ," by Rev. Andrew Murray, which had helped me greatly. When on my knees I told God of these promises, and then asked Him, "Please to give me ten dollars to-day." I went over to the General Post Office in Clark Street, thinking perhaps someone from home might send me something. But only The Christian, and The Freeman, and I think The Christian World were there. On my return home I stopped in the office of a friend to read the paper, when one of the firm hurriedly came in to ask me if I had ten dollars in my pocket. I said, "No," and out he went, explaining he wanted it a few minutes; something seemed to say, "it's time for me to go." I had not walked but a few minutes when I met a gentleman who spoke to me, asking after my health and success for Africa; then he took a roll of greenbacks out of his pocket, and as he turned one after the other over, he said, "It's laid on my heart to give you something. I heard you lecture six months ago," when he handed me a ten dollar greenback. Then I thanked him and asked for his name, when he started off and said, "My name is known up there," pointing toward heaven. I returned home and paid the dear Christian widow the ten dollars I owed her.

Hitherto and Henceforth

Did space permit, I should be glad to give, the reader a more extensive account of matters affecting my life and work, and of incidents arising therefrom. There are two things, however, which I want to state with emphasis and with gratitude at this point; the first is: HITHERTO hath the Lord helped me; and second: HENCEFORTH the Lord shall be my help.

I will just mention a few cases which may be of interest and of help to the Christian worker; and in these cases God was very near to help and bless. I have received many letters from converts, and others, expressing their gratitude to God for the blessing bestowed upon them in the missions which I had the privilege to conduct. Some incidents I have already mentioned, but there are others of a special character.

When in the London district I went to Loughton once, to preach. I met the gardener employed by the gentleman at whose house I was stopping, and I talked to him about his soul. This conversation resulted in his conversion; and the gentleman and all his family got to know about it.

In a town in Northamptonshire, where I was sent to preach while in College, I found that two of the daughters of the deacon, at whose dwelling it was my pleasure to be staying, were not saved. Both of them were connected with the Sunday School, and I believe one of them was a teacher. When all the others were out one morning, I had a talk with them about my blessed Jesus, and told them how good He had been to them. Soon they were in tears. Then I asked them if they would at once make a decision. We all three knelt down, and I offered prayer on their behalf; and the Lord gave them both the power of decision, and much joy. When I returned from Africa, the home of these happy people was one of the first to which I was invited.

One Sunday morning, when I was in Glasgow, I was out early for a long walk to take a meeting, when I a man came up to me, saying he was penniless, and in other ways distressed. He looked as if he had just come out of some barn or cave from his night's lodging. His clothes were in a very bad condition. As I walked on, I took out two or three pennies and held them in my hand, and commenced to talk to him about his soul. I could see that this did not take so well. He commenced to walk slowly. I shook the pennies in my hand, and I asked him to come on. He did so, and I told him about Jesus, and when and how He found me. At length I gave him the pennies, telling him that it was God's money and not mine. A very long time after this--it may have been ten months or more--I was again in Glasgow, and had an appointment at the Y. M. C. A. at the twelve o'clock meeting. On my way with a gentleman to the meeting, I saw a man who came hurriedly across the street, and beckoning to me, and wishing to have a word. I requested him to be quick, as I looked at my watch and found that it was just on twelve o'clock. He looked respectable and clean, and had on good clothes and wore a bright smile. "I took your advice, sir." "What advice?" I asked. "What you gave me-- don't you remember?" "No," said I. "Well, I am the man you talked to that Sunday morning--don't you know me?" I did remember, and I was surprised to see him so altered. He told me that he had a good situation, and was getting on nicely. He gave me to understand that he was saved and very happy. I have never seen the man or heard of him since. I did not even ask his name, the whole conversation occupying only two or three minutes.

Once when staying in Ireland with some kind friends, when the maid came about I would talk to her about her soul. This resulted, through the blessing of God, in the maid's conversion. Then on my way to the station, I sat in the front seat, near the driver; and looking up into the coachman's face from the corner where I sat, I asked him about his soul; and told him about my former condition of which he had already heard something. Quite a while after this, the lady with whom I had been staying, wrote me to say that both her coachman and her maid had come to decision by the little personal talk with them.

On my way to Saffron Walden, in the autumn of 1894, while in England, a man I sat in front of me in the railway carriage. He looked very sad. Something seemed to say to me,-- "Speak to that man." At last I asked him if he knew Jesus. Oh, he had been brought up in a Christian family, and had attended the Methodist Church nearly all his life-time. "But are you saved?" I enquired. He confessed that he was not; and then he told me about his troubles, entering into home affairs which were very sad. I tried to show him his only path to peace and happiness, which was in complete surrender to our Lord Jesus Christ; and then I explained to him the way of salvation, and urged immediate decision. He desired me to pray for him, and I did; but I told him he must pray for himself. He said he could not do this. I insisted that it was a personal matter, and that he must give himself right up; I could got no further with him. At length he got on his knees, gave himself to Jesus, and commenced to pray also for wife and children and father and mother. He rose from his knees weeping and happy. When we reached a station where he had to change, he begged me to go home with him to his people, and to go on to Saffron Walden on the Sunday morning.

One evening when on the train from Belfast to Island Magee, there sat opposite to me a very unhappy-looking lady. I could not get rid of the thought that I should speak to her. I wanted some excuse whereby to open the conversation. At last I asked her if she had any loved ones in heaven. "Yes," she said, as her face coloured and her eyes filled with tears; "I am on my way to New York to bury my husband, who has just died." She then entered freely into the whole matter, to her own comfort.

One day when in London, I met a young man who spoke very nicely, and he asked me if I were a stranger. I told him I was not, but that I was hunting for lodgings for my wife and myself. He said that he could direct me. Very soon he had me comfortably placed close by him, I soon found that my friend was a Scotchman, and that he knew much about the Bible; but he was not converted. He kept his fine Newfoundland dog, his birds, and his beautiful flowers. When home from business these absorbed his attention. One day when in the garden together, and while he was looking at his flowers, I said to him that each flower was a miracle. "A miracle?" he repeated with a questioning tone. "Yes," I said; "and so is also every blade of grass, and every grain of sand," I added, pointing to the ground. Then we went on to the Miracle of miracles, the plan of salvation. I took ill some short time after this, and suffered very much indeed. This friend-- Mr. McPherson--came in to see me. I asked him to pray for me. He hesitated. Again I said, "Please pray for me." Then he got down on his knees by my bed, and he commenced to pray for me; but this soon changed into a prayer for himself.

I left England in 1887, for America; when I returned he wrote me a nice letter. I was then issuing the sixth edition of my life, and I asked his permission to put some lines of his letter in it. For many years now he has been an active Christian worker, and continues at work to-day. He has charge of a chapel in Tooting. His late dear mother, who lived in Edinburgh, expressed the desire to see the black man who had led her son to Jesus. In July, 1894, Mr. McPherson and his wife and family went for their usual summer trip to Scotland to see his people. On this occasion he invited me to accompany them, he would pay all expenses. His mother wanted to see me. I went with the family, and the welcome I received will never be forgotten.

Here is a message of appreciation which he sent from Tooting: "I think it right to bear my evidence to the high merits of my friend, the Rev. T. L. Johnson, who is still anxiously labouring in the cause of his African countrymen. The influence possessed by this gentleman is very great. It is strange, but it is nevertheless true, that one who, until the close of the American War, was a slave in the Southern States, and was almost wholly without education, should have acquired a position of great usefulness in America, and should have gained a marvellous power for good over many individual souls. It is not for me to speak in praise of that resolution of character and elevation to Christ which have placed him in the first rank of devoted Christians in the present day, nor can I do more than follow with respectful admiration the successive incidents in his life, his self-education, his training at Mr. Spurgeon's Pastors' College, his year of devotion, loss, and illness in Africa, and his appointment to the important office of organiser of the coloured churches in the great African Mission work. But of my personal contact with

Mr. Johnson I feel that I not only may, but must, speak freely. When I first made his acquaintance many years ago, we happened to be residing in the same house. Seeing that I was fond of flowers, he used the imagery of the garden to lead my thoughts to higher things. From the flowers of nature he led me up to the flowers of revelation--to the Bible, to prayer, and to God my Saviour, and I now rejoice in the salvation offered to and accepted by me. My dearly-beloved mother--God bless her--taught me to say, "Our Father, which art in heaven," but like many more I had almost forgotten not only her teaching, but her God of whom she so frequently spoke to me, until this loving-hearted, Christian gentleman came my way, and constrained me to arise and come back to my Father. Mr. Johnson encouraged me from the first to contemplate working in the Master's cause, and almost against my will urged me to speak to others on the things that had now become dear to me. Above all he impressed me with the importance of full reliance on God's guidance in all the turns and changes of life. At a particular crisis he taught me to take my trouble to God. I did so, and what seemed to be gloomy and dark was turned into brightness and light. Prayer answered enabled me to leave a position that was irksome to me, and to commence work in a house of business in which I have been not unsuccessful from a worldly point of view. Furthermore, as if adding honey to the bread, by the grace of God I have been enabled to commence, and for some time to carry on, an Evangelistic work in South London. To his kindly efforts I owe, under God, such zeal on behalf of Christ as I possess. Is it not right that I should say this? I know that he earnestly desires to bring the light of the Gospel to his countrymen in Africa, and if my humble testimony to his character and past work helps ever so little to rouse in others the regard and esteem which I myself have for him, I shall indeed be happy.--H. B. MCPHERSON."

Since Mr. McPherson's conversion God has blessed him with three children, all three saved, the youngest, with his brother has testified for Jesus in public; the daughter has led the singing by taking her place at the harmonium. These children remember Uncle Tom in prayer.

The Jubilee of the Young Men's Christian Association was celebrated in June, 1894, when Mr. George Williams, Founder and President, was Knighted by Queen Victoria the Good. I was honoured with an invitation to the Reception at the Guildhall. After the reception and speeches, there was a gathering in the Great Hall, and here the Swedish Choir sang several pieces before the Lord Mayor and Lady Mayoress and a great company, for the hall was packed. A gentleman came after me as I stood at the back of the hall, just before the singing commenced, and I was ushered to the platform by command of the Lord Mayor and Sir George Williams. There was no time for reflection or expostulation, for the attendant turned and went towards the dais again, and I had to follow.

During the week of the Jubilee I was appointed to conduct the noon meeting in Exeter Hall. When I entered the Hall, as my friends, afterwards informed me, questions were asked as to who or what I was. One gentleman assumed the role of informer, and, with the air of one who knew, told those about him that, "He is one of Dr. Paton's converts from the Cannibal Islands; he was once a cannibal and used to eat men."

I was requested by the Rev. S. A. Selwyn, of St. John's, Boscombe, Hants, to conduct a Mission, and during the Mission I received very enjoyable hospitality at the home of Mrs. de Satur. The meetings were blessed of God, and the Parish Magazine for December, 1894, referring to the Mission said: "God did indeed hear our prayers and there have been very definite results. God help those who accepted His wonderful gift of salvation. We shall not easily forget the last night of the Mission. Every inch of space was occupied; people blocked up the entrance, and many had to leave the premises because they could not get in. The Holy Spirit's power was indeed in our midst, and many held up their hands in token that they were willing to be wholly the Lord's. We shall not forget our brother's earnest, touching words. We earnestly pray that he may be wonderfully used to lead many souls to Christ."

While in Bournemouth, I felt it would be well to make our home in the neighbourhood, and I wrote to Mrs. Johnson, who was in London, to come down, and together we decided to remain in Bournemouth, but all this was subject to the Divine approval.

Since settling in Bournemouth I have had the favour and joy of fellowship with many Christian workers in connection with the Evangelical Churches and the Y. M. C. A., and I must mention the kindness of the Misses Tighe, of Christchurch, at whose various halls I have conducted services and Missions, and when unable to travel in winter, suffering from the cold, they would have me conduct service in one or the other of their halls, and have me conveyed to and fro during these meetings so that I might not be exposed to the inclemency of the weather, for which I praise God, and will ever feel grateful to them.

The kindness of these friends, and of Miss Perks and Miss Weston, and many others, remains the same to this day; and for them, as health permits, I attend and take part in their meetings.

What comfort I have derived from the words, "Thou wilt keep him in perfect peace whose mind is stayed on Thee; because he trusteth in Thee."

In reply to letters and suggestions as to terms and methods in connection with my work, I have been obliged to put them aside, for I found that it was less binding and disappointing to simply leave the matter with the friends upon whose heart a Mission had been laid, and especially with the Lord who had called me into His service. And as to the places where to go, it was not a great concern whether they were great or small, so that the Lord was in it, But often I had much searching of heart, for though I expressed my faith in God, yet there was much anxiety as to temporal necessities. I rebuked myself, however, with such portions as, "The Lord is my Shepherd, I shall not want"; "The Lord will give grace and glory; no good thing will He withhold from them that walk uprightly"; "My God shall supply all your need according to

His riches in glory by Christ Jesus"; and the Lord's message direct, "Prove Me now."

In the midst of these thoughts, came a message from Pastor E. R. Pullen, desiring a Mission at his Church, in Southampton, making it very clear that they were in the midst of a building scheme, and could not do much as a poor church, but that they would pay travelling expenses, give hospitality, and pay a donation of twenty or thirty shillings, and that they would be greatly delighted if it could be mutually arranged to pay a visit; and then the words, "I commend you cordially and prayerfully to God." I left this matter with the Lord, resolving that henceforth I would trust Him more. He was indeed my only hope and help in all things.

My terms were simple, and I informed the good Pastor that, first: I should expect a week's prayer before the Mission; second, that I had no personal means or income, and depended upon the kindness of the Lord through His people, and warned him not to be over-anxious about finance. I went to Shirley for the Mission, but had I not gone there would have been a great Mission in any case, for the people were ready and waiting upon God. I must add here that wherever I have conducted a Mission, where the members manifested their desire for a blessing by meeting for prayer each night for a week or more before the Mission, God has answered prayer.

It is not possible to quote the long reports of this Mission, but in the local magazine, in a closing paragraph, it is stated: "From the very first the deepest interest was taken in the services, and night after night the chapel was crowded, and on some evenings the aisles, platform, porch, pulpit steps, and schoolroom were brought into use. It was a refreshing sight to see the place thus filled, but more refreshing was it to see the arrow of conviction strike home to the hearts of many. Every evening enquirers came seeking the way of salvation, and of those who professed to have received Christ through these services, a goodly number are our own Sunday School scholars." A thanksgiving service followed, and praise was rendered to God. The report stated that £17 10s. 9d. had been collected, mainly in bronze. The friends gave me £12; this was over and above what anyone had anticipated. From my heart came the prayer, "O God, do with me and by me and for me as Thou wilt." From this time I have looked to and trusted God for all my needs, and He has graciously supplied them; and praise His holy name, He ever will, while I trust Him. When entering the above in this life story, I wrote the Rev. E. R. Pullen to ask if he had kept the letter I wrote him; in reply to his request to conduct a Mission, and the following is his reply:--

"Shirley Baptist Church, Southampton.--I well remember the circumstances attending the Rev. T. L. Johnson's coming among us to conduct a Mission in 1896. At the time, whilst feeling that the work was ripe for such an effort, I could not see my way to financial support, as we were in the midst of a building scheme that severely taxed the resources of our people.

"I frankly talked the matter over with Mr. Johnson, telling him that beyond hospitality, travelling expenses, we might not be able to give him more than twenty or thirty shillings. Mr. Johnson cheerfully agreed to come, waiving larger offers he had received elsewhere, and God gave us a season of gracious refreshing; crowded congregations gathered, many souls were won for Christ, and many backsliders restored. The financial problem solved itself, and in the end we were able to hand over to Mr. Johnson, after paying other expenses, the sum of £12. Truly God was with us, and taught us all a lesson of simple trust.

E. R. PULLEN."

"October, 1907.

During the Pastorate of the Rev. George Wainwright, at Crewkerne, he invited me to conduct a Mission, when God was pleased to add His blessing. Mr. and Mrs. Paull kindly entertained me; there were two children in the home, Elsie and Wilfred. As soon as convenient, I wanted to know if they (each) had a second birthday. Elsie was quite sure she had, but had never confessed it to anyone but her mother. However, during these meetings, she went to Mr. Wainwright, and told him when it was that his message from the Lord lodged into her heart, and then she was happy.

Our Lord tells us in Romans x. 9-10, "We must believe in the heart and confess with the mouth." One morning her brother, little Wilfred, came into the room and brought a text he had written, John iii. 16. When I asked him if he believed it, he at once said, "Yes." Then I asked if he had ever definitely given his heart to Jesus, explaining the nature of a gift, and he answered "No," but he wanted to do so. After referring to different passages of God's Word respecting His love and the gift of His love and how Jesus loved him, we knelt down, when I prayed for him, and then I requested him to pray for himself, and there and then gave his heart to Jesus. Soon he was out into the hall and called his mother and told her how he had given his heart to Jesus. Soon his little friend Charlie Fone came in while Wilfred was yet in tears of joy. We told Charlie all about it; then we took the Bible, pointed out to Charlie how Jesus loved him, and wanted him to give Him his heart. The text that laid hold of Charlie's heart was Proverbs viii. 17, "Those that seek me early shall find me." We all three knelt in prayer, when Charlie gave his heart to Jesus. The parents of both these dear boys were Christians, and now their prayers of years were answered.

Mission at Emsworth

Emsworth Free Churchman, November, 1906.
ZION NOTES

"The whole month has been given up to the Mission. The week of prayer preceding the visit of our friends was a wonderful revelation and preparation. The Pastor gave a series of Bible Readings from the 1st Epistle of John, touching upon "The Ideal Life," "The Family of God," and "Family Portraits," etc. As many as forty persons were present at several of the meetings. Much communion was enjoyed with God, and the spirit of prayer was highly prevalent. In this spirit of waiting upon God we were ready for the visit of our two friends. The singing of Miss Davies will never be forgotten. The editor of our local newspaper truly describes her singing when he says, 'The singing of Miss Davies had the effect of converting the simple songs of the Torrey-Alexander hymnal into classical musical appeals to the souls of the people.' Apart from this, Miss Davies carried the hearts of the people by her deep spirit of prayerfulness and clever tact in dealing with those who were under conviction of sin. The result has been that some wonderful conversions have taken place. Even since the special Mission services, men and women have come forward to express their joy for the truths which have savingly come home to their souls. Our brother, Rev. Thos. L. Johnson, carried his hearers into the realms of truth by his earnest, plain, and pointed enunciation. Personal experience and references to his own deep chequered career gave power again and again to his utterances, the congregations never seeming tired of the addresses. The deep spiritual tone of our brother's life backed up his word, and caused 'great searching of hearts.' Believers were, we have every reason to state, greatly quickened, and the many testimonies of blessing and help received are coming to hand. The building has been strained to its utmost capacity during the Mission. It is calculated that quite five hundred persons were present at the Sunday night's service, which had to be held in the schoolroom as well as in the chapel. Our choir, augmented for the occasion by some younger members, has rendered valuable service, and to them there must come a joy in having been able to help in the great and good work so effectively. Organist, Deacons, and Stewards have all had the work laying hard and warm upon their hearts, and night after night have been at their posts. Truly it has been a reaping time all round; to God be all praise. 'The Lord hath done great things for us, whereof we are glad.'"

"THE HANTS AND SUSSEX COUNTY PRESS,"

October 27th, 1906.

"The Mission conducted at the Baptist Church for some ten or eleven days appears to have been a success beyond expectation. The meetings have been crowded night after night, and on Sunday evening there was an overflow meeting in the school room at the back, which in turn was also overflowing, great numbers of people, though in time for the service, had to turn from the building. The addresses of the Rev. Thomas L, Johnson, pointed and heart-searching though they were, had a fascination for the crowds who attended, and the singing of Miss Katie Davies had the effect of converting the simple songs of the Torrey-Alexander hymnal into classic music appeals to the souls of the people. On Wednesday, at noon, there was a baptismal service in the church, conducted by the Pastor, the Rev. W. S. Wyle. In the afternoon the Missioners, Pastor, workers, and other friends assembled in the arena in

188

front of the Church to be photographed in groups for the purpose of mutual supply of souvenirs of the happy time they have spent together at Emsworth.

Two Birthdays

When able to meet appointments, I so often have the joy to meet little boys and girls who have two birthdays, and they are so happy. While stopping with the Rev. D. Ross, in Darlington, his little girl Dora and I became friends. She was converted at five years old; she was a bright little Christian. I do praise God that when the disciples rebuked those who brought the little children to Jesus, He said, "Suffer little children, and forbid them not to come unto Me; for of such is the Kingdom of Heaven."

Jesus says: "Seek first the Kingdom of God and His righteousness"; "Those that seek Me early shall find Me"; "Remember now thy Creator in the days of thy youth."

The Rev. Thomas Spurgeon, in delivering an address at the Conference held in the Jubilee Year of the Pastors' College, April, 1907, said: "Many of us have to thank God that we felt the grip of the Cross upon our tender years. It may be we were less conscious of our grip of it. Would God that all young lives were thus attracted and grappled. They cannot be too young."

John Ploughman was right when he said:--

> "Ere your child has reached to seven,
> Teach him well the way to heaven;
> Better still the work will thrive,
> if he learn before he's five."

I remember standing by the freshly dug grave of a dear little one. The parents were weeping at my side. When I had spoken a few words I was surprised to hear the voice of song. Then did I bless the grace of God that enabled the stricken father and mother to sing across that dark, deep hole:--

> "Jesus loves me: this I know,
> For the Bible tells me so."

Do you wonder that the crowd was moved to tears? On the homeward way the mother whispered in my ear that she had taught her little boy to sing those simple words before he could properly speak them, and just ere the angel said, "Arise, He calleth thee"; the dear lad cried, "Sing to me; sing to me." "What shall we sing?" they asked. "Sing 'Jesus loves me, this I know.'" Thus does the Cross attract and hold the hearts of children.

CHILD CONVERT SETS TO WORK

"I have the great joy of telling you," wrote another friend, "that one of my children, a little fellow eight years of age was converted at your meeting on Monday evening last. Though he did not come to the front, he, on the following morning told his mother that he had given his heart to Jesus. His first thought then was to call at our next door neighbour's and bring them one of your books, "Get right with God," and ask them to read it, and then give it to the gentleman upstairs. I ask your prayers for this little one brought to Jesus, and that God may use him to win precious souls."

I hope soon (D.V.) to publish for my little friends, "Three Birthdays in one year," when I hope to tell them a great many things which I have not space for in this book.

In the Autumn of 1907, when assisting in a mission in Bishop Auckland, I was invited to the home of one of the workers, whom God had blessed with four dear children. We soon became friends. After my return to Bournemouth there was occasionally a letter. Over twelve months later I received a letter to say that little Bertie, aged five years and six months, had passed into the arms of Jesus. One of little Bertie's favourite hymns was:

"Shall we gather at the river
    Where bright angel feet have trod;
With its crystal tide for ever
    Flowing by the throne of God?

Yes, we'll gather at the river,
    The beautiful, the beautiful river;
Gather with the saints at the river
    That flows by the throne of God."

AN INDIAN GIRL'S PRAYER

An Indian baby was dying. It lay in its father's arms, while near by stood another little daughter, a few years older, who was a Christian.

"Father," said the little girl, "little sister is going to heaven to-night. Let us pray."

As she said this she kneeled at her father's knee, and this sweet little prayer fell from her lips: "Father God, little sister is coming to see you to-night. Please open the door softly and let her in. Amen." —*"Bugle Call," September, 1908.*

British Subject

In March, 1900, I was made a British subject, when the following well-known citizens of Boscombe, Bournemouth, testified before a Government official that they had known me for five years, and that they believed me to be worthy to be made a British subject:--

- THE LATE REV. C. STANTON.
- MR. A. HIBBS.
- MR. C. BAKER.
- MR. T. W. RELF.
- MR. A. WRENN.

At the close of my personal story, in the month of October, 1908, and reckoning from the calculation of a poor slave mother, born the 7th of August, this year I am seventy-two years old. When the estate was divided, upon which we were as slaves, I was ten years old, and from that time I kept account as the years passed by. Through all the years of adversity, in slavery, to man, and the devil, the Lord watched over me. And since He gave me freedom of soul and then freedom of body, and led me out into all service; surely goodness and mercy have followed me and will follow me. Hitherto and henceforth the Lord my helper.

The hand of God has been with me down the years. He requires an appropriate return. I charge my soul as an unprofitable servant, reviewing all the opportunities and the advantages afforded me. He has kept my heart beating 70 times per minute, 4,200 per hour, 100,800 per day, 3,681,720 per year, and never losing sight of me, who am but an unit out of the 1,800,000,000 people in the world. O my soul, but for the blood of my blessed Jesus, where wouldst thou stand to-day? I have been to His feet as I have heard His voice saying, "Come unto Me, and I will give you rest." And I have found that sweet rest. And so will all those who come to my blessed Jesus.

I still wait His will in whatever word or way or work He gives to me, and look forward to that time of the glorious Emancipation of the soul, and of the body, too, from the present bondage of this life to the glorious assembly and Church of the Firstborn written in Heaven. To God be everlasting praise. Amen, and Amen.

CPSIA information can be obtained
at www.ICGtesting.com
Printed in the USA
BVHW032304070921
616287BV00005B/52

9 781789 872590